GARDEN OF THE LOST AND ABANDONED

Garden of the Lost and Abandoned

The Extraordinary Story
of One Ordinary Woman and the
Children She Saves

JESSICA YU

Houghton Mifflin Harcourt
BOSTON   NEW YORK
2017

For information about permission to reproduce selections from this book,
write to trade.permissions@hmhco.com or to Permissions, Houghton Mifflin Harcourt
Publishing Company, 3 Park Avenue, 19th Floor, New York, New York 10016.

www.hmhco.com

Library of Congress Cataloging-in-Publication Data is available.
ISBN 978-0-544-61706-3

Book design by Martha Kennedy

Printed in the United States of America
DOC 10 9 8 7 6 5 4 3 2 1

For Ava and Esme

GARDEN OF THE LOST AND ABANDONED

The Thirsty Baby

The bottle of water sat on Officer Harriet's desk, its contents clear, its slightly crumpled label depicting the ice-capped Rwenzori Mountains. In spite of the heat, the policewoman and the reporter looked upon it not with thirst but with suspicion.

It was Monday at Kawempe CPU—Child and Family Protection Unit—and the two women had a sick baby, a missing mother, and a clue.

A nine-month-old boy, naked and feverish, had been brought to a clinic by his mother. She reported his name as Brasio Seguyo. The nurses diagnosed malaria and put the baby on an IV drip. The mother paid a small deposit on the treatment fee, saying she would come back with the rest of the money. Two days later, she had not returned. Only the bottle of water had been delivered, with a note saying it was for the baby. The plastic cap had clearly been twisted open; the seal on its neck was absent.

The baby in question lay draped over Officer Harriet's shoulder, his body as limp as a warm chapati. Lacking boys' clothes, the clinic had sent him to the police in a blue-and-pink-flowered dress, its bottom now damp-dark from a diaper worn overnight. Harriet flipped through a report folder, expertly avoiding the wet spot as she supported the baby with her other arm.

Harriet Nantaba was one of Gladys's favorite officers. It was easy for CPU officers to become overwhelmed by the daily flood of domestic disputes and abuse cases, but Harriet could always be counted on to gather the Who, What, Where, and When that Gladys needed for her newspaper column about lost children. In addition to being efficient, Harriet was always neatly groomed, her olive-green uniform perfectly fitted—a modern vision of a young policewoman. Children in particular seemed to like her, perhaps because Harriet was also pretty, her classic features offset only by a disarming gap-toothed smile.

"Did the nurses give the baby the water?" Gladys asked.

"I don't know. That's how they brought it. They said they feared—"

"—it may contain something."

"Yes," said Harriet. "It could be contaminated. Maybe the mother wanted to have the baby killed or something like that. So this is an exhibit now for police."

"Yes, we are holding it as an exhibit."

"Hmm."

Their eyes locked on the bottled water. They sweated and stared, the heat swelling with the silence. The CPU was always hot.

While Kawempe Police Station was a proper building, with two stories and a parking area for motorbikes in the front, its Child and Family Protection Unit was an eight-by-twenty-foot shipping container donated by a Finnish NGO. Plunked down on a dirt lot next to an ever-smoldering trash pile, the metal box housed two desks, two sets of bookshelves, four wooden benches, half a dozen plastic chairs, and frequently the maximum seating capacity of bodies. Two small windows provided air but no cross breeze, as they were cut into the same side of the wall. Under the steady glare of the Kampala sun, the steel walls that provided the material fortitude for stacking on a cargo ship became an oven.

Gladys noticed that while she and Harriet sweated, the baby did not. His forehead had the dull surface of a stone. "He's very dehydrated," she remarked.

"We tried to give him some juice, but he vomited."

Gladys shook her head. "He looks really, really, bad off."

"He needs the drip treatment. He only got a little bit." Harriet explained that when Brasio's mother had not shown up with the money, the baby had been taken off the IV. "The clinic realized no one is coming to claim for the child, so they stopped treatment."

"He didn't get a full dose."

"No, of course, he couldn't. Because there was no one to pay."

Gladys sighed. "Now, Harriet, I know we need profits for our businesses. But in such cases, can't someone sympathize with a baby like this and complete the dose?"

Harriet demurred. "I'm not very sure . . ."

"O-kay," Gladys said, steering away from the dead end of the rhetorical. She flipped to a clean page. "And what was the name of this clinic?"

"Family Hope Clinic." The irony escaped the room like an unswatted mosquito.

Outside, the sun shone directly on the wilted line of supplicants sitting in front of the shipping container, and grumbling voices rose up to its tiny windows. Gladys frowned down at her notebook, weighing the possible outcomes of including Brasio's story in her column. Would the mother come forward? If she did, could the police analyze the contents of the mysterious bottle of water? What if she was not sane? They could not release the child to a mother who intended to poison him. But perhaps another family member would recognize Brasio and come forward to claim him.

As she readied her camera, Gladys wished they had boy's clothes to put Brasio in, so as to avoid any doubts planted by the flowered dress.

"Hold him up so I can see his face," she directed Harriet.

Harriet lifted Brasio away from her shoulder and turned him toward Gladys. The boy's eyes fluttered open, and the sight of the water bottle on the desk momentarily energized him. He moaned and thrust out an unsteady arm.

"Ah, ah," Harriet soothed.

Gladys snapped photos as the baby pined for the water; she needed a clear look at his face. It felt bad not to reward him with a drink, but there was nothing else to offer. Given their low wages, police did not have money for amenities like bottled water.

"I wish you could remove that bottle from there," Gladys said.

Harriet gingerly relocated the exhibit to a stack of boxes by the wall.

"Good," said Gladys. "I'm worried that someone may feel thirsty and pick it up."

"It is me. It is me who is thirsty." Harriet laughed, showing the friendly gap in her teeth.

Gladys sighed. Everybody was thirsty.

AFTER A FEW phone calls, Gladys enlisted a social worker to help her deliver Brasio to St. Catherine's Clinic. There the infant drifted in and out of consciousness, failing to stir even when the nurse pricked his fingers for a blood sample. Gladys had endured malaria many times, and she knew the crushing, invisible weight the disease placed on the will as well as the body. This body, limp as a doll's, looked spent, and there was little sign of will. Who could say whether the child was still clinging to this life or it was only the hands of others detaining him a few moments longer?

If the doctor knew, his mild expression gave nothing away. Gladys lingered by the examining table as he gently prodded Brasio's swollen belly. "I'm worried about that stomach," she murmured.

The doctor did not think the swelling was due to malaria. "It's probably malnutrition."

"Ah." Gladys nodded, unsure if that was good news.

The doctor moved to the head of the table, and Gladys now saw that Brasio's eyes were half open, revealing only empty white crescents. The sight froze her in place. How could she leave, with the baby looking so much worse than when she had first seen him?

"Thank you for these good works," she managed, by way of farewell. "For my abandoned babies."

The doctor's nod answered her unspoken question. Only time would tell.

AT THE END of the day, Gladys headed into the Old Taxi Park, where the white tops of a thousand *matatus,* or minibus taxis, formed a mosaic of congestion. It seemed that Kampala, already the largest city in the country, could not possibly accommodate more growth.

But every day hundreds of people left their villages or their districts or even their countries for the City of Seven Hills, hoping to pursue, if not the Ugandan Dream, some chance at a better livelihood.

Kampala was a place of modern buildings, bustling markets, government offices, top schools, swank hotels, stately monuments, and thumping nightclubs. It was also a place of traffic, slums, and unemployment. Still, the city beckoned, like one of these *matatu* conductors trying to lure one more passenger into his overpacked minibus.

Gladys boarded a *matatu* for Entebbe, the city where she had lived through shifts of fortune since her childhood. It was close to eleven by the time she reached her small rented room, and after midnight when she went to bed. Sleep, though, would not come. It was not arguing neighbors or barking dogs keeping her awake, but the thought of the baby, Brasio.

How could a mother abandon her child in such a condition? In six years of writing her column, Gladys had seen these situations before. The push and shove of city life produced many casualties. But on this empty night, the thought of this baby stirred the ashes in her gut, sending up red embers. The mother, the nurses at Family Hope Clinic—they had all looked at this sick child and walked away. Everyone in this life carried problems on their back, but surely the load of one infant would not crush all these so-called adults?

And then the fire died out, and Gladys was left with cold dread. Malaria would take the boy, she was certain of it.

When she needed help with a case—a lost toddler without a place to stay for the night, an orphan lacking school fees, a sick child in need of an operation—she had a small circle of friends she could call on, although one could well imagine the flicker of exasperation on their faces when her number popped up on their phones. Tonight she would not bother them; she would never waste their time with something as unsolvable as feelings. Nothing could lift this sense of futility, heavy with the taint of guilt.

Why guilt? said a voice in her head. *There was nothing you could do for that child, Gladys. Don't stress.*

At least she might have saved him from dying alone. She opened her eyes to the dark, her sleepless night now a vigil. If the child did slip away in these quiet hours, there would be someone to think of him, to ensure that his departure did not go unnoticed.

THE VERY NEXT DAY, at St. Catherine's Clinic, Gladys could not believe her eyes.

The social worker, a cheerful girl in her twenties, held a baby in her arms: a smiling, wide-eyed baby, head bobbing about with curiosity. Surely this could not be the same Brasio? He still wore that flowered dress. Someone had twisted his hair into tiny feminine knots around his head, making him look every inch a happy baby girl.

"Eeeehhhh!" Gladys exclaimed with ear-piercing delight, startling Brasio so much that his body wobbled like a stalk of maize in a rainstorm. He began to wail.

"That's good!" said Gladys. "Before, he could not even cry. I am happy to hear you cry, baby!" The social worker laughed.

It was enough excitement for one day. But then Gladys's phone chimed with another surprise. Officer Harriet was calling from Kawempe CPU.

"The mother of the baby is here."

"The mother!" Gladys exclaimed.

"Yes. We are very busy, but I know you want to talk to her—"

"Yes, please! Keep her there." A dozen questions popped into Gladys's head, but she knew her phone was about to give out, from either lack of power or lack of airtime. "I am coming right away."

Every child Gladys met was a story, a story in its middle. Sometimes one could trace the beginning of the story, sometimes not. But it was hard to find resolution, even a temporary one. The story of a child required a parent. It was parents who set events in motion, and it was parents who determined whether the story would return full circle or go spinning out into the world.

HARRIET LET GLADYS use her desk in the office container for the interview while she went out to attend to other duties. Brasio's mother was Christine, a plain woman in an orange dress. She leaned slightly away from Gladys, eyes tired but wary, like a cornered animal looking down from the branch of a tree that was not as high up as she wished it to be.

"My names are Gladys Kalibbala. I work with *New Vision* newspapers."

Christine nodded politely, in the manner of someone possessing familiarity with the paper but not the means to buy it.

"Every week in the Saturday paper I have a column for children, 'Lost and Abandoned.' I get many of these cases from police. So when I get a call saying, 'Please, come to the station, there is this child here,' I come."

The woman considered her interrogator. Gladys was a big woman, middle-aged and smartly outfitted in a long, flowered dress of black, orange, and white. In one hand she held a small notebook and pen, in the other a folded handkerchief which she periodically pressed to her shiny brow. With its wide cheekbones and square jawline, her face was strong, yet rounded at the edges by its fullness. The result was a look both solid and soft, like those oversized armchairs with the padded arms displayed outside furniture stores on Ggaba Road.

"I don't want you to be afraid," Gladys said easily. "I want us to talk and then we can understand each other."

In a half whisper, Christine began to answer her questions: where she lived (Bwaise), how many children she had (three under four years of age), and what employment she had (sporadic work digging in gardens and washing clothes). While her mind seemed clear, she appeared incapable of eye contact, her glance darting toward Gladys, only to retreat whenever the reporter glanced up.

"Okay. Tell me," Gladys said, "when did you bring the child to Family Hope Clinic?"

"Saturday night. They put him on IV drip, but in the morning they refused to continue the treatment because they wanted me to pay the bill." This matched Officer Harriet's report. "The bill was forty-nine thousand shillings, but I only had ten thousand shillings from my grandmother-in-law."

"So you had ten thousand shillings. Why did you not give it to the clinic?"

Christine shook her head. "I tried to give it to them, but they said, 'No, we want all of our money, the whole forty-nine thousand shillings.' I begged them, 'Please, I will pay in bits as you treat the child.' They refused."

It was not an enormous sum of money, 49,000 shillings, but it was enough to buy a carton of powdered milk. Or some shoes, if they were not leather.

"I had to go look for money," Christine continued. "I tried to breastfeed him before I left."

"Did you feed him?"

"He was too sick and he would not wake up. I knew he would be thirsty, so I brought a bottle of water for him."

At last, that bottle of water. "You thought that the nurses would give your child water, when you had not paid them their money?"

Christine gave a weak shrug.

"Why didn't you call for the baby's father?"

"They told me that he refused to come when they called for him."

"Are you and the father married?"

"We stay together," Christine said, "but we don't get along very well. Sometimes he walks. Sometimes if I can't handle it anymore I walk."

Gladys wrote in her notebook: *Father able but neglecting?*

Outside, it began to rain. Inside the container, a sound like gravel being scattered.

"You left that baby on Sunday morning and you did not come back until Monday night," Gladys pressed. "Don't you think that is a very long time to leave a sick child?"

"I did not sleep, I did not eat, I was only thinking about my son."

"But you could not find the money?"

A shake of the head. "On Monday night I used a thousand shillings to take a boda boda back to the clinic. I hoped the nurses might let me breastfeed him a little bit."

"Yes, that's a mother's feeling." Gladys chuckled sympathetically. She looked down at her notes; something did not add up. "Now,

Christine. You say you went back to breastfeed your son. But you say you had not eaten. How could you produce any milk?"

Christine looked down at her hands. "I don't know if I had milk. But it was the only way I could try to help my child."

"Ehhh."

"But when I arrived at the clinic, my child was gone. They said he had cried so much that they left him with the police. So I came here." She swallowed hard, evoking the urgent thirst that accompanied nursing. "I have no milk now. You see the shape I am in." Shame radiated from her like heat.

"You don't look so bad," Gladys soothed. "Look at your skin — you have nice skin. Do you think that you look bad? I see that you look beautiful."

"I used to be big. Now I'm too thin."

"You were big like me, or bigger than me?" The other woman's hesitation produced a wry smile from Gladys. "Why did you get small?"

"You see my situation."

Sunlight whitened the window glass. The rain had gone as quickly as it had come.

"So," Gladys said slowly, watching Christine, "what I have learned is that you didn't abandon that child intentionally. You did not want to leave that child there."

"No." Her words had been treading water, but here they touched ground. "No."

Gladys flipped her notebook shut.

THE GREAT MOMENT had arrived, and now a flowered blouse threatened to ruin it all. All parties had gathered in the police container: baby Brasio; his mother, Christine; his great-grandmother; and the cheerful social worker. Officer Harriet was busy moderating a domestic dispute in which a hurled plastic chair had necessitated a relocation outdoors, leaving Officer Florence in charge of the baby's paperwork.

Officer Florence had a sore foot. Lacking the capacity to wear her police shoes, she had abstained from wearing her entire uniform. Gladys sighed inwardly. She had sympathy regarding the foot . . . but why a *flowered* blouse? Florence looked more kindly auntie than policewoman.

If Gladys's camera could capture the right moment, no readers would notice the lapse in protocol. Through her viewfinder, she watched and snapped as baby was handed back to mother. The reunion was a bit of an anticlimax. No delighted squeals spurted from Brasio at the sight of his mommy; no happy tears burst forth from Christine. Someone had given the baby a cell phone to play with, and the new toy won more of his interest than the mother he had not seen for several days. For her part, Christine handled her son gingerly, almost shyly, as though he belonged to someone else.

Still, the mood in the container was jubilant. Officer Florence and the social worker waved bye-bye to the baby, and laughed when he waved back. The great-grandmother danced and clapped. Gladys snapped away, calling out, "I like that!"

A FEW MINUTES later, after the papers had all been filed and Gladys and the officers had moved on to other cases, mother and child were left to themselves. Christine sat on the cement curb outside the police container, balancing Brasio on her lap as she lifted her T-shirt. The baby eagerly latched on to her breast. "Eee-hee!" Christine laughed, a joyful peal. But after a few seconds of suckling, the baby pulled away.

Christine offered her breast again. And again Brasio nursed for only a moment before turning his head away.

"Ah!" Christine fretted out loud. She had seen the social worker give the baby orange soda. Perhaps he had lost his taste for mother's milk?

As Brasio whined and squirmed, Christine shook her head. A woman sitting beside her looked over, curious.

"My milk is gone," Christine fretted. The woman, who had a toddler balanced on her knee, cocked her head in sympathy.

But then Christine felt a tug. She looked down to see Brasio's small hand grasping her breast, his hungry mouth open. He raised his head and began to suckle fiercely, not with desperation but with focus, like a dog gnawing a bone for the last bit of marrow.

Christine held her breath as her son, his body still with concentration, attempted to conjure up the mother he knew. When she at last exhaled, he was still suckling. She was his mother, and he would not give up. Holding each other tightly, they waited for her milk to come.

New Vision

"LOST AND ABANDONED"

Many children get lost every day, while others are abandoned by their parents. Every Saturday, we bring you stories of those seeking to reunite with their families.

In 2005, when she was in her early forties, Gladys stepped into the newsroom in Kampala for the first time. It was a bright, modern office with clusters of desks and computers sectioned by low dividers. She should have felt cool in that high-ceilinged space. But she was standing at the desk of Catherine Mwesigwa, deputy editor at *New Vision,* one of the largest newspapers in the country. Sweating.

Everywhere around her, she saw reporters who were closer to her children's age than to hers—well-dressed young professionals from middle-class urban families, with university degrees in mass communication. Here she was, a struggling middle-aged mother of two who had not completed secondary school, asking for a job.

Maybe this woman will ask me to produce my degree, Gladys thought, *the degree I do not have.* What choice was there but to come clean?

"I would like to tell you how it is I am here," she began. "You see, I was working in civil service . . ."

She told Catherine Mwesigwa the whole story. How she had been reassigned from one government ministry to another, so that when job cuts were made, she was among the first sent home. How she searched fruitlessly for employment for two years, during which time the father of her children died, leaving her to care for the young ones on her own. How she tried opening a small bookshop, only to be plagued with break-ins. How all seemed bleak until she heard about a new program offered by the subcounty.

The program had been set up to educate college-bound students in media communications. Gladys had no chance of higher education, but the idea of studying journalism appealed to her on two fronts. First, she came from a family of readers. She would rather miss lunch than a newspaper. While working for the Ministry of Agriculture, she had savored big fat novels like those juicy ones by Harold Robbins. Oh, how time would disappear!

Second, she was relentlessly inquisitive, and no matter her job, people would tell her she was in the wrong profession. "You really ask a lot of questions!" her bosses would remark. "You can scare people with all your questions." "What are you, a reporter?"

GLADYS SIGNED UP for the media communications program, although it had already been in session for two months. Walking into the classroom, she felt old and new and awkward. The other students were half her age; she looked more like their mother than their classmate.

As she began to study, though, her discomfort dissipated. In journalism, her natural curiosity was more than a strength, it was a requirement. A reporter needed to pursue the five *W*'s: the Who, What, When, Where, Why. If Gladys was asking the questions, no one would get away without giving her all five.

While her fellow students struggled to come up with even a couple of articles a month, Gladys found material everywhere. One didn't have to interview the prime minister to have an interesting story; one could have a chat with one's elderly neighbor.

Maybe this profession can work for me, Gladys thought.

It was a financial struggle, but after two years she completed the course. As her younger classmates headed off for college, she went looking for a job.

All this she explained to deputy editor Catherine Mwesigwa. "So

I don't know if your paper can employ such a person as me. As I don't have a degree . . ." She trailed off, ending the lengthy recitation not with a bang but a whimper.

There was a beat of silence. Then the other woman laughed. It was not a mocking laugh but a kindly one. Surprised, Gladys began laughing too.

While Cathy looked younger than Gladys, she was much closer to her in age than the twentysomething reporters who populated most of the surrounding desks. With her patient, low-key demeanor, she projected warmth and intelligence.

"I want you to note one thing," Cathy said, pressing down on each word as if she were signing a document. "Journalism is not about a degree."

Emboldened, Gladys reached for the papers she had brought with her. Around the newsroom, one could hear the clicking of keyboards, the whir of copy machines. Gladys had no printer, no computer. The sheets she held out were handwritten in pen, like a student's homework.

"These are some stories I have written," she said. "So you can see my work."

AMONG THE STORIES Gladys offered was one about an old car, a Fiat, that had been running for over forty years. She knew about the Fiat because it was the vehicle that had taken her to primary school in Entebbe. Roads in Uganda, with their dust and ruts and potholes, were infamously cruel to cars. But the trusty white-and-black Fiat was still puttering away. The owner had not even replaced the seat cushions. "Other than its old registration number, you would hardly believe the car was in existence even during the reign of King Freddie Muteesa II," Gladys had written in her broad, loose hand. But she did not focus solely on the car. She wrote about the owner of the "wonder Fiat," a former printing engineer who liked to play music on the weekends and who had been jailed for two months during the government changeover in 1979, after Idi Amin was finally deposed. "For his leisure, Doka reads the Koran," the article concluded. "His favourite food is kisira (cassava flour) and fish."

They published it. A big, two-page feature. Under the headline "Doka in Love with His 40-Year-Old Fiat," there it was: *by Gladys Kalibbala.*

She was a *New Vision* reporter.

GLADYS SOON DEVELOPED a reputation for her human-interest reporting. She covered many subjects—airport construction, Ebola testing, garbage management, a five-legged bull—but it was her writing about ordinary people that attracted attention. Other reporters declared that without even looking at the byline, they could tell which stories were hers. The seventeen-year-old with severe mental retardation who had just learned to feed himself. The funeral of a ninety-four-year-old local council chairman. The orphan who received an artificial leg.

Cathy told her, "You know what? The stories you are producing, these are unique! We can't get such stories from any of those people with degrees from Makarere University."

Another boss who noticed her work was Dr. Charles Wendo, the editor of the paper's new weekend edition, *Saturday Vision.*

Like Gladys, Dr. Wendo had not entered journalism through the front door. He had risen from poor, rural roots, studying veterinary medicine before switching to the newspaper trade. Journalism, he believed, had great potential to improve society. Over the years, though, he had found it difficult to find like-minded colleagues.

In the 1980s, when Dr. Wendo was a student, good schools were spread out over the country. Even with his humble background, he was able to attend a solid secondary school. These days such an opportunity was rare. The good schools had become concentrated in urban areas around Central Uganda. They were expensive facilities in expensive neighborhoods, accessible only to those with means. So the Ugandans with degrees in mass communication had less and less in common with the disadvantaged.

From what Dr. Wendo had witnessed, journalists fell into two categories. The first contained the vast majority of reporters, interested in prestigious stories: those who hunted after the light, comfortable assignment. Profiling the owner of a new hotel, for example, where the reporter would be welcomed at reception, given a soft chair in the lobby, and served a cup of sweet-smelling coffee to enjoy while waiting for the big man. Or breaking news—say, the juicy corruption scandal that would be on everyone's lips by teatime.

The second—and far smaller—category held those reporters who prioritized substance over glamour or comfort, embracing assignments about health issues, human rights, poverty. As a member of this second category, Gladys stood out. It was rare to find journalists with enthusiasm for covering the disadvantaged. Few wanted to venture into slums, past piles of smoking rubbish, to talk with people in depressing situations.

Reporters in the first category might relax at their desks, conducting interviews on their phones. If those were known in the office as "helicopter journalists," Gladys was a foot soldier: out in the field, boots on the ground. She was always running outside to flag down a boda boda. Those motorcycle taxis were the most dangerous means of transportation, especially for women sitting sidesaddle, but also the fastest. No one else in the office would ride a boda boda for hours to reach someone with a rare disease, or spend half the day in the hospital with an indigent accident victim.

For Gladys, there was no other way to cover a story. The only way to get what she needed was to go to the scene. Especially when writing about a child—what could a four-year-old tell her over the phone? Many rural children had never even held a mobile, let alone spoken to a stranger on one.

The observations Gladys made in the field revealed more than any phone interview. Like the state of a home. Did the family have a mattress, or only mats on the ground? Did the children have shoes? If they lacked shoes, did they have jiggers, those terrible parasites that attacked the feet? One look at a child's face could tell Gladys whether he had eaten supper that night. The way a mother held her infant could indicate her level of affection. Even odors provided information: the length of time since a child had been bathed, the sobriety of a parent.

Dr. Wendo noted Gladys's observational skill and dogged focus, which often put her younger colleagues to shame. Every day he received "helicoptered" stories at his desk in neatly packaged paragraphs, but the information contained within was often superficial or incomplete. Anyone could throw statistics into an article: *family planning is available to only 20 percent of married Ugandan women; over one-third of the population lives on less than $2 USD (6000 shillings) a day.* It was quite another matter to profile a family of eleven huddled under a leaky roof.

Granted, Gladys was not the best writer in the pool. Her work took more of his attention to edit. But given the choice between a good packager and a good gatherer, Dr. Wendo would take the latter any day! Only a fool would choose a mansion of cardboard over a hut of brick.

ONE DAY IN 2007, Dr. Wendo called Gladys over to his desk to discuss an assignment.

His brother-in-law was a policeman at Wandegeya, where lost children frequently showed up. Wandegeya was the closest police station to the *New Vision* offices. Gladys had covered similar stories of neglected and abandoned children; what if she were to go to Wandegeya to write about all such cases they had this week?

Gladys needed no coaxing. She waved down a boda boda and went to the station, where she interviewed the children and gathered information from the officers. The resulting piece in *Saturday Vision* included a half-dozen profiles. Next to the children's photos, Gladys summarized the circumstances of their plight, the locations where they had been found, names of known relatives, home villages, and schools, followed by the phone number of the police station.

The next week Gladys checked back with the police to see whether the article had had any impact. Sure enough, three people had come to the station to pick up their children.

"Oh!" Dr. Wendo exclaimed. "That's great, Gladys!"

He sent her back to Wandegeya. Again more children, again more reunions.

Gladys quickly made the assignment her own. The only assistance she required was transport money and the loan of a company camera. She easily got in the good books of the police, and between the officers and the children, she gleaned every bit of relevant information.

Dr. Wendo was delighted. Again he called Gladys to his desk. "I feel that we can create something with this. Weekly."

Gladys's heart beat faster. A weekly column? "Yes, it is a good idea."

"But will you be able to get the stories every week?" he asked. "I don't want to be disappointed one time when I have the space for you and you can't fill it."

"Trust me! It can't fail."

This was less a boast about her reporting skills than a comment on the state of the world. In Uganda, millions of children were growing up without parents. The mass abduction of children by Joseph Kony for his fanatical Lord's Resistance Army in the 1990s and early 2000s had drawn much media attention, but there were other, less sensational reasons for the neglected generation: extreme poverty, the loss of family members to AIDS, the lack of education, and most of all lack of access to family planning. In 2013, the average Ugandan woman gave birth to six children. Gladys had seen many children having children—girls who had never been taught about sex.

Every day hundreds of these children and children of children washed up on the shores of urban centers like Kampala. How many of them could Gladys feature in her column?

Lack of material would never be her problem. Only lack of space.

VERY QUICKLY, "Lost and Abandoned" gained popularity. The format—a photo of the child accompanied by a biographical haiku—was easy to digest. Every column elicited a handful of responses, usually between one and ten. It was not a large number, but the leads were solid. Relatives would call to claim a child; neighbors would offer information; strangers would donate assistance. Some Good Samaritans were well-to-do; many were not.

As Gladys's phone number was often listed in the column, people began to call her directly. Sometimes ordinary citizens reported children they had found; sometimes parents reported children they had lost. Many times police officers or social workers called to request her help with a case. Gladys widened her rounds to include other Kampala police stations—Kawempe, Old Kampala, Jinja Road—babies' homes, and "reception centers" where older kids were housed.

On Thursdays she hopped on and off of boda bodas, conducting interviews, snapping pictures, taking notes, and making phone calls. On Mondays and Tuesdays she compiled her stories; on Tuesday nights she submitted them by email. Editing and layout were completed by Friday, and on Saturday morning the issue would appear at kiosks and on newspaper racks around the country.

It was a challenging schedule, made all the more so by the fact that her earnings from "Lost and Abandoned" were too little to live on. She had to keep producing feature articles, even if, as a freelancer, she was paid only for articles that were published. The time and money she invested in a piece could well be wasted if it did not find a home on the page.

But there were always subjects she wanted to write about. Programs for people with disabilities. Sleeping sickness. Pollution in Lake Victoria. HIV and prostitution. And everywhere there were individuals whose stories she could not ignore. The young woman scarred by an acid attack. The family battling hereditary disease. The boda-boda driver maimed by a truck collision.

Sometimes people simply showed up at the offices of *New Vision*. If, say, a fruit vendor brought in a stray child, Camilla, the sympathetic receptionist, knew that there was only one reporter to call.

"Gladys, I have someone to see you."

"My program is too full already. Can you call someone else? There are many other reporters here."

"Yes," Camilla would answer, her voice bright with confidence. "But this one needs *you!*"

Gladys might laugh or sigh or do both, but she would come. Because she knew it was true.

Trevor

Although Gladys's round-trip commute to the *New Vision* offices in Kampala was about fifty miles, Entebbe's relative calm and serenity were worth the hours of sitting in minibus taxis. Given its proximity to the airport, its gardens and parks and hotels and golf course, not to mention its many beaches rimming Lake Victoria, Entebbe was a popular spot for tourists and urbanites seeking weekend relaxation.

It was not a cheap place to live. Gladys rented a room in a courtyard behind a row of shops along Kampala-Entebbe Road with a roommate, Esther. It was a tiny space with a couple of beds. No kitchen, no closet, no space for table and chairs. But Gladys was hardly ever there: most days she left home before 7 a.m. and did not return until after 11 p.m.

On one rare night Gladys returned home early enough to turn on the 10 p.m. news. The TV provided background for her evening tasks, and she paid it little attention until a report came on about a police raid at a boarding school. The director had been accused of embezzlement, neglect, and nonpayment of rent. The story of corruption held no novelty, even with the footage of police arresting teachers and matrons. What drew her attention was the terrified students caught in the middle of the raid. Some of the children were frozen in fear; others were screaming and crying, running east and west like chickens in a pen overrun by dogs.

She scanned the tear-streaked faces, noting with pity how young some of them were. A girl of no more than eight. A toddler, barely steady on his feet. A boy . . . She froze, a bolt of adrenaline shooting through her body.

That face. She knew that face. It was Trevor.

SHE HAD FIRST encountered Trevor at Kawempe, always one of the most cooperative police stations on her circuit, almost a year before. According to Officer Harriet, he had been dumped by a woman suspected of being his mother at Katalemwa Cheshire Home, an NGO for children with disabilities. He was small, maybe six or seven years, but he could not confirm his age. He could not confirm anything. When Gladys asked him questions, he would lower his head and mumble at the ground, or he would look off absently and say nothing, as though he had not heard her speak. The only concrete information he could offer was his name: Trevor Masembe.

He was an odd, shambling little figure, with a limp and a lame right hand. His left eyebrow arched slightly higher than his right, lending an air of detachment to his expression that was amusing in one so small. He seemed most comfortable on the periphery of things, a natural bystander. While lingering in doorways or peering through windows, he had a way of lifting his chin and frowning into the distance, as though he were awaiting someone's imminent arrival.

A child so quiet and inscrutable might be easily overlooked were it not for his smile. Trevor possessed a smile of impish charm that bloomed over his whole face; it was a grin of small, perfect teeth, raised brow, and high cheeks. When he smiled, it was as though he were suddenly awakened and delighted by his present company. It took some enticement to draw out that smile — a biscuit, a peek at the view screen of Gladys's camera — but the reward was tantalizing. It was like having the blur of a hummingbird come into still and solid focus on the tip of one's finger. Surely this was a glimpse of the real Trevor, tucked deep within that tight bud of silence.

Fortunately for the children who ended up stranded at Kawempe, the station boasted two recycled shipping containers, one that served as office for the Child and Family Protection Unit, the second as lodging. The metal box contained a wall of sagging shelves and a couple of wooden bed frames, their yellow foam mattresses crumbling like stale bread.

For several months Trevor stayed there. Sometimes he had the company of other boys, sometimes he was alone. At night no police were in attendance, so Officer Harriet would lock the container from the outside. She instructed the boys to urinate in the green bucket in the corner, but most of the time Trevor would wet the mattress.

It was not an ideal situation for anyone. With his lame hand, Trevor could not bathe himself—it took him ten full minutes to button his shirt—so one of the officers had to assist him. During the day there was nothing for him to do except wander around the police motorcycles, groping the handles and growling like an engine until he was chased away.

MASEMBE ABANDONED AT KATALEMWA HOME

The six-year-old, who seems to be paralysed on one side of the body, said he was taken to the home by his mother.

Unfortunately his condition cannot allow him to speak for long. Katalemwa Home handed him over to the Kawempe Police for assistance.

Trevor's profile in "Lost and Abandoned" received no response. Gladys ran it a second time. Still nothing. She submitted it a third time.

"You are running this one again?"

"Yes, this one really needs to locate his family."

Dr. Wendo had moved on from running *Saturday Vision* and been replaced by Hilary Bainemigisha, an editor who also wrote a popular advice column under the moniker "Dr. Love." No muscled Lothario, Dr. Love sported glasses, a slight paunch, and a colorful literary style. He was known for his metaphors ("Marriage is like government. As soon as you capture state power, you have to deploy heavily to protect it from hyenas and vultures") as well as his earthy candor ("You can tell a relationship's stage of development by the ease with which partners fart in each other's presence . . . Eventually, some married people relax and start letting the chemical bombs drop").

Behind his cheeky Dr. Love persona and his first-name-basis familiarity, Hilary operated with a steady professionalism. While he fully supported Gladys's work, he could not ignore the fact that the newspaper's contents needed to stay current and fresh. No one wanted to read the same thing week after week, even if it was for a good cause.

Hilary acquiesced to Trevor's repeated appearances in "Lost and Abandoned," but Gladys knew she was running out of time. Eventually the police would turn the boy over to Probation, and Probation would turn him over to Naguru Reception Centre.

GLADYS DID EVERYTHING she could to keep a child out of Naguru. The facility, which had been built in the 1960s for fifty children, now housed as many as three hundred. It served more as penitentiary than as home, as evidenced by the high walls studded with glass shards and the frequency of escape attempts. In such an overcrowded place, a child could not expect an adequate education or attention to special needs. Children worked at washing clothes, bathing the younger ones, and preparing food. There were reports of frightful conditions in the barracks.

Worst of all for Gladys, Naguru was virtually inaccessible, especially to members of the media. Although it was in Kampala proper, only a couple of miles away from *New Vision*, it could feel as remote as an island. She could not call or visit or even get confirmation that a particular child was held there. Once a child went to Naguru, the thread was snipped.

On one occasion when Gladys had been allowed to enter the gates of the reception center, word of her visit had obviously preceded her arrival. The yard was deserted. A matron told her that the children were all in class. This was hard to believe, as the one classroom on the grounds stood vacant in front of them.

It would be absurd for a journalist to leave the facility without meeting any of its hundreds of children, and after some polite insistence, Gladys persuaded the staff to bring one to her to interview. A girl of about fourteen emerged from a side yard, where she had been doing laundry. Gladys greeted her brightly, but the girl only smiled in confusion and shook her head. Within a few moments, it became evident that the child could neither hear nor speak. It was Naguru's idea of a joke: *send the reporter a deaf-mute.*

WITH THE SPECTER of Naguru on the horizon, Gladys was relieved when she raised enough funds for Trevor to board at a place called Good Samaritan. The school was new to her, and she informed the director of her intention to deliver Trevor to school personally to settle him in. No need, the man assured her. He would send her photographs of Trevor's progress.

No photographs came. Not even a phone call. When she finally reached the director, he apologized for being so busy. The boy was doing fine. Of course she could visit soon. Just not right now.

Something was not right, and she resolved to find out what it was. At one point she dropped by the school at a time when she knew the director would be absent, only to find that the students were not around either.

She did not trust this man. But before she could continue her investigation, Trevor's stricken face popped up on her television screen. Gladys wanted to jump into a taxi that very night and rescue him. But when fleeing the police, the school director had dragged the students along, eventually abandoning them in Rakai, a district over a hundred miles west of Kampala. To find the money for the long trip, Gladys needed a couple of days.

She also needed official permission to take Trevor. The authorities couldn't just hand over a child to anyone. After the police raid, most children were retrieved by their parents. The few who remained, like Trevor, fell under the custody of the Probation Department. Through her contacts at Kawempe Police, Gladys tracked down the local probation officer assigned to the stranded students. She called to introduce herself, but the officer rudely cut her off. A journalist had no business stepping into this situation.

In Gladys's experience, probation officers generally looked upon the media with suspicion. In a country in which half the population was under fifteen, there were many problems concerning children but precious few government resources. The probation officers knew that their bosses at the Ministry of Gender, Labour, and Social Development did not appreciate having any light shed on this disparity.

Gladys explained to the probation office that her involvement with Trevor was more than journalistic—that she had been assisting him for nearly a year, that the child had no known family, that he had a suspected disability—but this officer would not listen. She refused to understand.

There was a difference between the inability to understand and the refusal to understand. If Gladys were to spend a month's salary on airtime minutes talking to this woman, the effort would garner no more response than an impatient sigh. Meanwhile Trevor was somewhere out there, distraught and bewildered and unable to communicate.

What else could she do?

She had to go and get him.

TRAFFIC AND BAD ROADS slowed the taxi's progress; by nightfall it still had not reached Rakai. Gladys was forced to pay for a hotel night along the route, an expense she could sorely afford.

In the morning she reached the probation officer to plead her case again. The reporter's tenacity served only to irritate the officer, who refused to make any decision on the matter. Instead she directed Gladys to go to a church building where Trevor and the other stranded children were being held. "Wait for me there," she ordered.

It was a woeful group that Gladys discovered when she walked through the church door: a dozen children and a couple of matrons, all of them exhausted and hungry. They had not eaten supper the night before or breakfast that morning, and they looked hopefully at their visitor. The only thing Gladys could afford to buy them was bananas.

One of the matrons roused Trevor from sleep. Gladys was shocked at his appearance. His face was grimy and tear-streaked, his T-shirt stained, his feet bare. There were holes everywhere in his clothing. And how he smelled! Worse than a wet boy-goat! The matron said that he had slept in those filthy clothes for over a week, soiling himself every night.

Gladys tried to comfort the boy, hoping that the probation officer would soon arrive. But hours went by and the woman did not show up. It became noon, then two o'clock, then four o'clock. The kids became hungrier and hungrier, and Trevor cried and cried. Still Gladys's calls went unanswered.

Eh! With a stubborn officer such as this, what chance did Gladys and Trevor stand of receiving official permission to leave? What if the woman insisted on detaining Trevor? How would Gladys be able to trace him?

Then the thought came into Gladys's head, with the satisfying decisiveness of a cleaver chop: *Whether the officer likes it or not, I'm taking Trevor with me.*

"Help me get him cleaned up," she asked a matron. If she had known the officer would make her wait all day, she would have washed Trevor's clothes upon her arrival. As it was late in the afternoon and she did not want to be traveling after dark, there was no time to allow the shirt and shorts to dry. They were little more than wet rags when the boy put them back on.

As they left, she felt a twinge of guilt at leaving the roomful of sad, famished kids. One of them was a boy of no more than two years. What would happen to them if their families were not located? For now, it was taking all she had just to help Trevor.

NO TAXIS WERE available, so Gladys had to flag down a boda boda. With Trevor braced between her and the driver, the motor-cycle bounced over dirt roads and veered around potholes. The wind snapped Gladys's dress against her knees, the hard buzz of the motor as unwaning as her resolve. Had the probation officer arrived to find them gone? Was she in a car now, racing to catch them? Gladys did not care. They were going.

They rode for more than an hour, the boy whimpering in his

damp clothes. The boda fare was high, as the route was a long deviation from the driver's territory. Adding in the cost of a simple meal for Trevor and lodging for the night, Gladys would be lucky if she arrived home with a single shilling in her purse.

At least, with his belly full at last, the boy slept.

In the morning they were able to board a *matatu* headed for Kampala. It had not gone far when the probation officer finally called, demanding that Gladys return with the child. "You only have a few hours to bring back the boy," she warned, "or I will have you arrested for kidnapping!"

Now the officer was doing all the talking, and it was getting on Gladys's nerves. Should she attempt to explain that she was not the type to be threatened, that nothing short of an armed convoy could force her to return the boy, that taking care of the other abandoned students would be a far better use of the officer's time? No doubt the woman would refuse to understand.

"Turn around right now! Or I'll—"

Gladys switched her phone off. As the taxi approached Kampala, Gladys turned her phone back on, only to receive another call from the probation officer.

"Why aren't you responding to me? Aren't you going to say anything?" The woman was infuriated by her inability to provoke the reporter into a shouting match. Finally she vowed to make good on her threat: she was reporting Gladys to the Kawempe police. "Deliver yourself to the police, or you will be in big trouble."

Preemptively, Gladys contacted Kawempe. Of course all the officers there, including the bosses, knew her. They also knew Trevor; the boy had lived in their shipping container for a month. When she explained the situation, they suggested she draft a letter for their files to smooth bureaucratic hackles. Then they all shared a hearty laugh over the image of Gladys behind bars. What time would she like them to bring her her tea?

TREVOR WAS NOT a child who could express gratitude. Gladys could not expect a thank-you for the rescue that had drained her account, for the week's worth of missed work and sleepless nights, or for the impassioned lobbying that won him charitable admission into Entebbe Early Learning School, a good school near her home. Gladys's satisfaction lay in the fact of his safety. And the return of that smile.

At his new school, Trevor found his joy in the form of a football. It was an old white thing, a million kicks having erased the colored pentagons from its dusty surface, giving it the look of a ball of chapati dough. Just the sight of it could lift his eyebrows and stretch his mouth into a wide triangle, a grin that was somehow both mischievous and innocent. And then he would be off, his wake of dust masking the drag of his leg.

Gladys hoped that the Trevor behind that smile might gradually emerge now that he was in a stable place. And there were encouraging signs. When the boy had nowhere to stay over the holidays, the school cook welcomed him into her home. Her children enjoyed Trevor's company, and the days passed in harmony. One night after supper, the boy even knelt at the cook's feet and thanked her for the meal.

The cook's report thrilled Gladys. Back in school, however, the news was mixed. Trevor had trouble sitting in class. When he got too restless, he would simply stand up and leave the classroom. While his classmates hunched over their desks, they could hear the *thup thup shuffle shuffle* of Trevor kicking his football around the courtyard.

In a typical school, such behavior would warrant a caning. But Agnes Biryahwaho, the director of Early Learning, did not believe in corporal punishment. "Such children have been through a lot, and we must show them patience," she would say. "Trevor will adjust in his own time."

Gladys couldn't help feeling that the boy needed more than time. She had rescued him not only to keep him safe but to give him a chance at a life. A chance to learn and explore and discover what he could be. Most of the time, though, Trevor observed the world from a distance.

He could speak, but he rarely uttered more than two words. He seemed to understand what was said around him, but he often chose to ignore it. He could laugh and play with his classmates, but he might cry in class when told to hold a pen. And then there was the limp. The lame hand. Was he born with these infirmities? Or had he been abused?

What was his story?

AN AVERAGE ISSUE of a *New Vision* newspaper sold 30,000 copies. Each copy was read by around 10 people. The children Gladys profiled had a chance to be recognized by 300,000 people.

How many people had read Trevor's story by now? Four hundred thousand? Half a million? Someone out there had to know his mother, his father, a relative, even a neighbor. Someone had seen this little one tottering through the village, maybe in pursuit of a football fashioned out of balled-up *kavera*, the plastic bags harvested from trash piles. Someone had lived next to the family of the quiet boy with the smile and the limp. Someone out there had to be able to tell Gladys about Trevor's people and why they had given him up.

And so, risking Dr. Love's disapproval, Gladys inserted Trevor's photo into her column again.

WHERE ARE MASEMBE'S PARENTS?
Trevor Masembe, 6, has been missing from his parents since March 2013. He was abandoned at Katalemwa Cheshire Home, where a Good Samaritan picked him up and handed him over to Kawempe Police . . .

And again.

MASEMBE SETTLES
Over a year ago, Trevor Masembe, 7, was abandoned at Katalemwa Cheshire Children's Home, in Wakiso District. He was taken to Kawempe Police Station, where officers searched for his relatives in vain . . .

And again.

MASEMBE ABANDONED AT CHILDREN'S HOME
A year ago, Trevor Masembe, 7, was abandoned at Katalemwa Cheshire Children's Home, Wakiso District, by an unknown person . . .

A Tale of Two Georges

G etting to a place was always half the battle. Anywhere in Uganda could be tricky to reach, and usually was. Given Gladys's
travel needs, taxi and boda-boda fares could easily eat up half her
earnings. Traffic was terrible. And there were only so many hours
in the day; usually she spent four or five of them just getting from
Entebbe to Kampala and back.

She had learned to be efficient when she reached a place, whether interviewing a group of orphans or reporting on a medical center
or visiting a police contact en route to a story. It was easy to cut to
the chase; it was hard to get to the starting line. How much more
she could get done if she could just get to wherever she needed to be.
But such was life.

The hundreds of children she had assisted over the years had
floated off everywhere like the tufted seeds of the desert rose. It
was impossible to keep track of them all, but there were those who
had taken root in her heart and in the hearts of her readers. When
too many months passed without seeing such children, Gladys felt
a tickling mix of obligation and curiosity. What was happening in
their lives? What were they doing right now, at this moment? She
needed to see them, and for them to see her.

Her readers also deserved such updates, but unfortunately the
paper did not provide for the expenses of such reporting. As a freelancer, Gladys could not even expect an allowance for airtime for her
cell phone.

Occasionally Good Samaritans would offer help with transportation costs, with offers to drive or to pay for a car hire. When Gladys had access to a vehicle, as she did this week, she took full advantage. She called the hired driver, Michael Wawuyo, to find out what kind of vehicle he owned. "Where we will be going, you will need a very strong car," she explained.

Mike informed her that he had a Volvo station wagon, which, though old, was sturdy and well made.

"See if you can get a bigger vehicle," she urged. "I don't think you will want to drive your own car on those roads."

If Mike's instinct had been to defend the robustness of his Volvo, something in Gladys's comment made him reconsider. On the morning of the journey, he pulled up in front of the *New Vision* offices in a white Toyota van with a chrome bush grille over its nose.

Mike got out of the car to greet her, his lanky figure unfolding to nearly six and a half feet. He was an actor who also worked as an art director and a fixer for visiting film crews, among the many jobs he had held over his fifty-odd years. He was the kind of person one valued in a place like Uganda. Fluent in over a dozen African languages, he had met everyone, been everywhere, and done everything. He could charm a bureaucrat and stare down a thug. His severe breed of handsomeness, which suited the police and military characters he often portrayed, belied a congenial personality and an easy sense of humor. Such factors became especially important when spending a fourteen-hour day in the car together.

Gladys informed Mike that in making two stops, they would be visiting eight children. "We will be checking on my quadruplets," she said.

"Quadruplets!"

"Two sets," she added, grinning in anticipation of his double-take.

"Two sets!" Mike repeated. "Not from the same woman, surely."

"No," she said. "Different mothers. But both fathers are named George."

• • •

FIRST THEY WOULD make the long journey to the Kakuru family in rural Kiboga, about sixty miles northwest of Kampala.

Gladys had first met Mary and George Kakuru five years before. The couple already had five young children when, at thirty-three, Mary gave birth to the quadruplets. The family was penniless, the four babies sickly, their mother ill and unable to produce sufficient milk. When Gladys took on their case, her readers responded generously, with donations of hospital fees, transportation, clothes, milk, and food.

But Gladys could not stop there. It worried her to send those babies back home. The family of eleven was crammed into an old thatched hut where swarms of flies buzzed in the urine stench. When it rained, the ragged roof provided no more shelter than the fronds of a palm tree. After Mary's youngest girl got pneumonia, Gladys discovered that the blanket she had given them was being used by the whole family as a kind of damp tent. It simply would not do.

The notion of building a home for the Kakuru family, a true brick-and-mortar structure, sprouted in Gladys's mind. It took over two years of campaigning and coordinating and hard work, but she did it.

"Nobody in my family has ever lived in an iron-sheet roofed house," Mary had declared for one of Gladys's follow-up articles. "I believed the quadruplets were a blessing from God and had a feeling they could even be a turning point for my family! Thanks be to God, for he listened to my prayers."

While Gladys basked in the glow of the Kakurus' delight, not everyone admired her efforts. "What is there to boast of, building a house for those quadruplets?" one of Gladys's friends had sniffed, seeing pictures of Mary's new home. "You yourself are still living in a rented place."

Gladys and her friend were baffled by each other's behavior. It was like discovering that one could perceive colors and the other could not.

Why has Gladys wasted all this effort to help a stranger with too many children? thought Gladys's friend.

Why can't my friend see the happiness in providing a house for a needy family? thought Gladys.

Perhaps it was simply how one was created, Gladys surmised. One saw the colors or one did not.

There were others who saw what she saw. Good Samaritans like the Shalitas, the Indian couple who had helped provide supplies for the family, or Anita, the lovely young woman who had elicited support from the Toyota dealership where she worked. Gladys's first article about Mary and the quadruplets had broken Anita's heart. Perhaps it had something to do with the fact that she had just given birth to her third child.

"I have everything, you know?" Anita explained. "And I feel like I should do more."

On this latter point, Mary felt the same way. She had no shortage of ideas for how others might help her. Even now, on the way to the Kakurus' home, Gladys's phone chimed repeatedly with calls from Mary. Gladys sighed, knowing that it was futile to try to pick up.

In recent weeks the woman had been "beeping" Gladys — calling and hanging up immediately, so her number would appear on Gladys's cell without using up any of her own airtime — about a "very urgent matter."

"The house is falling down," she declared when Gladys called her back. "The rains have started, and we are worried that the wall will collapse on us!"

The house had stood for three years now, but it seemed that the work would never end.

SINCE THE BEGINNING, Gladys's roommate, Esther, had assisted with the Kakuru family. Such urgent cases appealed to her charitable nature.

Gladys and Esther had become friends after Gladys reported on some renovations at Entebbe Airport, where Esther worked as an electrician. It made sense for them to save money on rent together: Esther was supporting a young son through boarding school, and Gladys had her many obligations. They held similar values — hard work, self-reliance, charity—but there were complementary differences as well.

Most striking was the contrast in volume. There was Gladys, large and loud. Her size was due not to lack of discipline (in fact she did not overeat, although her meals were usually fried and starchy and hastily consumed) but to a naturally fortified physical structure. Her bones, her frame, even her cheeks—everything was built for heavy cargo. Bolstered by this foundation, her voice emerged a formidable instrument, capable of foghorn blasts, shrill toots, and everything in between. Her belly laugh could shake the walls.

Then there was Esther, a rowboat to Gladys's steamship. Petite and reticent, she talked far more slowly than her older friend—when she could get a word in. Her abstemious diet—vegetarian, spiceless, teetotal—fed a mild and patient temperament. When accompanying Gladys out in the field, she preferred to sit back and observe. When Gladys's emotions spurted from her in yelps and bursts, Esther favored the verbal styptic. A ten-minute rant about a parent's negligence might muster from her a dry "That one is not good."

If Gladys wore her heart on her sleeve, Esther kept hers tucked in her pocket.

Esther had arranged to take the day off from the airport, not wanting to miss the chance to visit the Kakuru family. She and Gladys made a quick stop at a trading center. Even when her purse was thin, as it frequently was these days, Gladys made an effort to take small gifts when visiting the family. If she arrived empty-handed, everyone would be annoyed.

"Don't buy her beans this time," Esther suggested. "Mary doesn't cultivate."

Gladys agreed, purchasing a kilo of sugar, a few bars of soap, and a loaf of bread. Not that sugar and soap would satisfy Mary, she knew. The woman beeped her constantly with demands, large and small. *The kids need shoes. Someone stole our furniture. Why do you not bring us maize, beans, and soybeans every month as you used to?*

Anita of the Toyota dealership also felt harassed by Mary's demands. "It is her house, not ours," she stressed to Gladys. "She needs to own it."

Agreeing heartily, Gladys had recently attempted to advance the tough-love agenda. "Mary, I think I have done all I can do."

"You are tired of me," the woman replied, pouting.

"No. But this is something I want to put in your head. Now that you have this home, it's high time you own it. *You* own it. It is your concern and your husband's."

Mary seemed momentarily chastened. George was another story. He would answer the phone, which Gladys had bought for Mary, but he could never supply the answers to even the simplest of Gladys's questions.

"Where are the kids?" she would ask him. "Do they have their school uniforms?"

Silence. Perhaps a mumble. It was like talking to a sleeping cat.

En route to Kiboga, the car passed the wall of a school with the painted message POVERTY IS A LION. IF YOU DON'T STRUG-GLE IT WILL EAT YOU.

"That's right," Gladys said, thinking out loud. "You must struggle to overpower it!"

Maybe *struggle* was the wrong word. If you were poor, of course you struggled to keep your head above water. But it wasn't enough just to wiggle your arms and legs. At some point you needed to swim to shore.

THE RAINS HAD indeed come, and the land at Mary and George's place was muckier than usual. Mike had to park the white van on the road, as the path to the house was a patchwork of grassy spots and brown puddles of indeterminate depth. Maize grew tall on one side of the path; on the other side, longhorn cattle grazed on thick grass. Neither the maize nor the cattle belonged to Mary, who stood in the middle wearing a smile stretched thin by impatience. Like Gladys, she was a large woman, but with a lower center of gravity. It settled below her waist and filled out the folds of her kingfisher-blue dress, giving her the immobile bearing of a concrete road divider.

After boisterous greetings, Gladys and Esther followed Mary toward the house. The visitors lagged behind their barefoot hostess as they tried not to muddy their shoes. Long ruts stretched irregularly across the path, leading to the inevitable wet steps and yelps of dismay.

Mary seemed not to notice her visitors' awkward dance as she launched into her speech. "The house is coming apart," she warned. "People who see it agree that the whole wall needs to be demolished and rebuilt. The local workers don't want to repair it. They say you have to replace it."

As the litany of faults grew longer, it was impossible not to imagine the worst: a house with bread-crust walls, beams poised to crush children's heads if one of them should emit a loud sneeze. Gladys was used to Mary's complaints, but clearly something was wrong. What if the house did need to be rebuilt? What would she tell all the Good Samaritans who had placed their goodwill—and money —in her hands?

"The house is really scaring us," Mary claimed as they reached the concrete structure with three large rooms and a bathroom. Yes, there were fissures snaking up the corners of the doorframe and the windows, but nothing so severe as to indicate imminent collapse. Gladys and Esther ran tentative hands over the cracks. No cement crumbled under their fingertips.

"See?" Mary accused, perhaps sensing her presentation's lack of climax. "The doors don't close. The whole house is slanting."

Mike walked in and out of the house, peering up and down, tapping the walls and the cracks like a woodpecker searching for grub tunnels. On one wall of the sitting room, a cheerful chalked message from three years before now took on a sarcastic bent: YOUR WELCOME TO THIS HOUSE.

"The ground is wet and soft here," Esther explained. "The foundation shifts."

"But still, something can be done," said Gladys. "What about iron bars to support the cracks?"

"They need to make holes to put a ceiling beam in," Mike called out from the sitting room. "And then cross some supporting beams inside. An *L*-shaped beam. That's it: the house will be held in position."

Mary dismissed their suggestions. "The whole wall should be brought down."

"That will cost a lot of money," Gladys countered. "How much money do you have?"

"I don't have money!"

"What about the solar business?" Applying her expertise, Esther had installed some wiring to place a solar panel on the roof, providing Mary with a small phone-charging enterprise.

"The battery for the solar stopped working. I already called to tell you," Mary scolded. "There's so much I tell you about, I don't know why you don't listen."

This made the women laugh. "You are being abusive now!"

"What about planting?" Gladys continued. "What are you cultivating now?"

"A little cassava. I did some beans. But most of them were killed by the rain." She peered into the bags that the visitors had brought her, taking measure of the offerings: sugar, soap, bread. She glanced up. "Why didn't you bring me beans this time?"

"I can't bring you beans all the way from Kampala. It doesn't make sense. You have to plant your own beans."

Mary shook her head, a smile twisting her mouth.

"Mary," Gladys chided. "Why do you always ask me to bring you beans?"

"It's your fault. You've gotten me used to getting beans from you. I can't stop asking, because you've gotten me used to asking."

"But the beans cost two thousand shillings. And you can grow your own."

"Then bring me more beans so I can plant some!"

The women giggled together, Gladys's laugh trailing off into an "Ahh..." Gladys infused her sigh with as much reproachful dismay as one syllable could carry.

Mary took no notice, let alone offense. "See that crack in the ceiling?" she said, one hand gesturing up, the other fisted on a hip. "It's because water seeps into the house. You need to fix it before the roof falls in."

"Can we go by and see the children?" Gladys asked, desperate to change the subject.

"No, they are still in school."

"Can we see them on their return?"

"No, they are still in school," Mary said stubbornly.

Gladys peeked in the bedrooms, which were scattered with donated clothes and drooping laundry and soiled sheets. The sting of urine tinged the air. The beds were unmade, the mattresses still wrapped in the plastic that had covered them when Gladys had purchased them. The headboards were of good quality, their gold cloth upholstery as incongruous as a watch on a panhandler's wrist. Some foreigner, a *mzungu,* had donated the beds and some chairs.

"What happened to the chairs?"

"Someone stole the chairs," Mary said. "And the white lady didn't replace them."

Esther glanced at the floor space where the chairs had formerly resided. "At least you can make some mats to sit on."

"Me? I can't make a mat," Mary retorted. "I've never made a mat in my life."

"This one . . ." Gladys's aside was in English, so she did not lower her voice. "She expects me to buy mats and bring them to her."

"Gladys wants me to stop asking for things," Mary went on, as though she had understood. "But she had better start looking out for my children for Christmas!"

All three women burst into laughter. They rocked back and forth on their heels as though sharing an unsteady boat.

"She'll not stop asking!"

"Better get shoes for our children!"

"Better stop complaining!"

AFTER MORE DISPUTE over the house's condition, the group wandered out onto the small veranda to take some much-needed air. For a moment the only sound was the gaudy song exchanged by a couple of birds, a territorial squabble or a love duet.

A slight, delicate-featured man in an eggplant-colored shirt lingered nearby. He looked both uninterested and sulky, like a man dragged to a party he could not leave.

"Is this the husband?" Mike asked.

"This is the husband, George," said Esther. "Who first ran away after Mary gave birth to the quadruplets."

She spoke to George in Luganda, the widely spoken Bantu language. "Isn't that true, you ran away?"

"Yeah, I did," George answered plainly. "I took off."

"But when the house went up, you came back."

George had disappeared for a year and a half, leaving Mary and the nine kids dependent on Gladys. Upon his return, Gladys had asked him to explain his desertion.

George had replied, "I left to find work."

"So where is the money?"

"Well, I failed to find work."

Mike looked out at the pasture, where distant cows' horns spiked the green like white thorns. George and Mary were Bahima, traditionally a nomadic cattle-herding tribe. "How many cows do they have?" he asked.

"None. He collects others' cows from the village and looks after them," answered Gladys.

"So he is paid in milk."

"Yes. Then he sells it to make some money. But the problem is, he sells it and drinks. There were times when he'd come back in the morning fully drunk. One time he didn't close the paddocks fully and the cows broke out and ate people's food. He had to work for three months that brought no pay. I was *annoyed!*" Gladys looked at George, nearly succeeding at keeping her expression neutral. "Now he says, 'Gladys, I am saved. I no longer drink.' I don't know whether that is true."

"Gladys, you see the clothes I'm wearing?" Mary jumped in. "When you come to visit, you should bring me new clothes to wear."

Everyone laughed, the joke still ripening.

"I don't fear Gladys," Mary boasted. "I'll always tell her what I need to tell her. When she comes, she should bring me clothes."

• • •

EVENTUALLY MARY AGREED to take Gladys and Esther to see the quadruplets at their school. In this she mined a new vein of complaint, criticizing Gladys for her failure to visit the school of the other five children as well. But Gladys did not rise to the bait, as she still had another set of quadruplets and another George to visit that day.

When they walked back toward the van, they found Mary's George sitting on the ground, staff in hand, his back to the path and his eyes on the cows. He could remain in this posture for hours, lost in the green vista and its dots of brown, unaware of everything else: his wife's complaints, his children's belly growls, the ruts deepening in his road, the cracks growing up his walls like thorny vines.

George seemed to pine for another time, the era of his grandfathers and great-grandfathers, when a man's role was to count his cattle and his children. George was poor in cattle but rich in children. He had been able to depend on the birth of a new child every year or two to add to his family stock. But now it appeared that that well of pride had run dry as well.

When George returned home after his eighteen-month disappearance, Mary worried that she might get pregnant again. With the quads getting healthy and their house under construction, the family was afloat. But their load was still heavy, and a tenth child could sink them. Enlisting Gladys's assistance, Mary visited a clinic to get fitted with an IUD.

All was well for about a year, until it dawned on George that his wife was not getting pregnant. Why was she failing to give him more children? He threatened to throw Mary out of the house.

It was unimaginable! With nine children and no steady work, he was going to punish his wife for not producing more babies? Gladys stormed, vowing to take the little man to court if he dared to chase his wife away from the house that her supporters had built. George quickly deflated. While he might have suspected that Gladys's presence had something to do with his wife's sudden infertility, he lacked both the leverage and the energy to fight.

For her part, Gladys tamped down her indignation. It did not help the children for her to become an enemy of their father. To be effective in such cases, she had to be a friend to the family—the whole family. Even George.

At least the man seemed sober this morning. Perhaps he really had stopped drinking; he looked miserable. The question was, did he look more miserable than usual?

"Let us get a picture with you and George," Gladys said to Mary.

"My husband is right there." Mary shrugged. "You can take his picture."

"Take a picture with your wife," Mike said to George.

"No, I am sitting here."

After more coaxing, Gladys prevailed, and George grudgingly rose to his feet. Standing six inches shorter than his much heavier wife, he looked more sullen child than husband.

"Mary is so fat," George grumbled. "Huge."

"Gladys always takes pictures," Mary grumbled. "But she never gives us copies."

"Gladys is not a photographer!" Gladys retorted. "And you have no email."

George then insisted that Gladys join the picture. "You are so fat," he said to her as he stood sandwiched between the two women. "You are bigger than my wife now."

"That is a classic faux pas." Mike shook his head, incredulous. True, Bahima people appreciated large women, but this was the twenty-first century. "Don't call a woman fat, ever!"

George walked with the group the rest of the way to the van, observing Gladys's attempts to navigate the puddles and mud traps. Tiptoe, tiptoe, stretch . . .

"How do you like my road?" he asked her pointedly.

. . . tiptoe, step to the side, tiptoe . . .

"Can you make for me a road?"

He expects me now to make him a road? Gladys fumed inwardly. *As if I am the head of the home. Or the head of the state!*

She did not answer George. She had come to a point in the path where she had a choice between traversing low, wide puddles where her shoes would surely get soaked and crossing a potentially unstable

mound of earth and grass. Taking a deep breath, she stepped carefully on the slick mound. Her heel sank in a bit, but the ground held.
She placed her other foot down, shifting her weight onto the slope,
and—

"Ma ma ma! Aaahhhh!" Gladys slipped, losing a shoe and falling
to one knee in the mud. "Ma mamamama ma! Whoo-oo-oo-oo!"

"There is not safe," Esther commented, somewhat unnecessarily.

Mike sprinted over to help Gladys, who was attempting to mini-
mize the mud on her hands as she pushed herself upright. One foot
and its wayward shoe were planted squarely in the mud, and there
were brown streaks on her knee and on the hem of her dress. George,
who had drifted a few feet away to the edge of the cow pasture, made
no move to assist.

"I'm used to our flooding," Mary commented mildly, walking
past Gladys to the van. "This mud is no problem for me."

THE SCHOOL WAS two tiny brick buildings and one rickety classroom made of mud and branches, all of which emptied of children
on the arrival of the big white van. A crowd of eighty students created a flowerbed of color: the girls in bright pink jumpers, the boys
in yellow shirts, with other bright shades mixed in from those not in
uniform.

Gladys greeted the children as they surrounded her. "How are
you today? Can you say 'good morning'?"

"Good morning!"

Once she had extricated herself from the sea of curious faces,
Gladys was able to lead the quadruplets to the shade, where she
could take a good look at them.

"*Banange!* Goodness! Don't they look cute?"

But no, they were more than that. At five years old, they were
beautiful. The two boys were an identical pair, as were the two girls.
All four had slender oval faces with gentle eyes that shone bronze in
the sunlight. Their skin was light brown. How Gladys had laughed
when, upon seeing pictures of the four babies, some of her *New Vision* colleagues had asked, "Are they Indians?"

The girls smiled sweetly at Gladys as she asked them about school and quizzed them on their English. The boys stood by, waiting their turn. Their father's placid expression, so infuriating on an unresponsive adult, was winsome on their smooth faces.

Mary watched from a nearby bench, chin in hand, petulant as a vendor watching a shopper squeeze her produce.

The children seemed healthy, Gladys concluded, waving goodbye. As she recalled their precarious beginnings, each as fragile as a petal and as tiny as a piglet, a swell of pride lifted her heart.

Too soon, though, her bubble of pleasure was pierced by Mary's needling.

"Why don't you at least get some bags of cement?" Mary persisted as they dropped her back home. "That way it will be ready for when you come back to fix my house."

AS THEY DROVE away from Kiboga, Gladys brushed at the dried mud on her skirt. "I am not worried about that house," she remarked. "That is not a place that is falling down anytime soon, like she was telling us."

Esther and Mike agreed. The house needed repair, but it was no lost cause.

"By the way, do you know how she has been complaining? 'The wall will be falling on us at any time!' When I didn't have money and could not even reach the village. What am I supposed to do? And she kept on beeping. 'When are you coming to check on it?' I got so annoyed, I told her, 'Okay, if the house is falling, let it bury you, and tell the neighbors to call me when you are dead.'"

Gladys was venting now, and she did not care. "Mary is running me mad, surely, with her demands. My God. You know those people who always ask for more? They are just beep-beep-beeping until you can't stand it and you call them. Then they tell you their stupid stories and ask for money."

"'The beans are finished,'" Esther piped up, imitating Mary's petulant drone. "'You need to drive from Kampala with more beans.'"

Gladys, laughing, also channeled Mary: "'I have no sugar, the children refuse to eat porridge because it doesn't have sugar.' Eh!"

"'What about Christmas? We will be looking for our presents!'"

The mention of Christmas dampened Gladys's mood a bit. She knew it wasn't her responsibility to provide the family with presents, but she recalled the kids' delight in the clothes and shoes of Christmases past. At the moment she lacked the money to buy anything for herself, let alone for a family of eleven. And she could not ask her friends for help, now that the quadruplets were big and healthy and no longer teetering on the brink of survival. No dose of logic would reduce the fever of Mary's demands, though, and Gladys could only brace herself for the barrage of beeps.

Am I not doing enough? Gladys lamented.

Mary's answer would be *No! Where are my beans?*

Gladys let loose a chuckle. "Some of these people are so annoying!" she announced to the car. "They make me annoyed and make me laugh at the same time. If I didn't laugh, I could not continue helping."

"You can't stay annoyed, because that's the way they are," Esther said. "You just have to choose how you are going to help them."

Gladys nodded at this wisdom. "My urgent issue is to see those kids go to school. I keep telling Mary, 'I'm looking at the education of your children, not your feeding.' I need to encourage them to plan for the future. Surely I have struggled with the Kakuru family. Surely I have struggled. Oh my *Gooooddd* . . ." Gladys's sigh was half shudder. "People ask, 'How much money did you get out of it?' I get none out, I only put in! Then people ask, 'Are you related to them?' Can you imagine! They don't understand."

"To be honest," Mike said, "I don't understand."

The comment was not made lightly, and Gladys thought for a moment before answering. "I can only tell you, when I find such people in a fix, this feeling automatically comes to me. Though I complain at times, I can't just ignore them. It is the way I was made.

"These four babies, they looked so bad. I just felt sympathy, and

I decided to follow them. And after seeing their home, there was no way I could abandon them. Because if I had run away, I don't know whether those children would have survived." She beamed. "Don't you think they look nice now?"

THE ROAD AHEAD of the white van was empty save for a solitary boda boda wobbling oddly in the middle of the lane. As Mike cautiously passed the motorcycle, the head of one of its two passengers lolled to the side.

Esther glanced back. "Eh, they are waving." The boda had stopped, its driver signaling frantically with one arm as he tried to keep his motorcycle vertical. His two female passengers appeared on the verge of falling off.

A few minutes later there were two more women in the van. One of them was ill, and the other was trying to get her to hospital. The sick woman was so weak she had lacked the strength to sit up on the boda seat. The nervous driver had entreated Mike to take the two off his hands.

Gladys knew the way to the hospital well. It was Bukomero Health Centre, the same place she had taken both Mary and her kids to on the many occasions when they had fallen ill. There was the time when the youngest daughter had stayed in the hospital for two weeks. The time when Mary had started bleeding. The time when one child had been bitten by a snake. And so many other crises.

"The woman is shivering," Esther reported. She was always level-headed in situations like this. "She has a cough. Probably malaria."

They pulled up in front of the hospital. Mike, Esther, and the sick woman's companion assisted her from the van. As lifeless as the woman appeared, with her closed eyes and listless limbs, odds were she would recover fully now that she had reached a clinic.

Again, getting to a place was half the battle. The women had been lucky to catch the attention of Mike's van. Transportation was limited out here in the villages. In an emergency, a chance encounter with a passing stranger could mean the difference between life and death.

As Gladys watched the sick woman disappear through the door of the clinic, she remembered how Mary had appeared when she had first seen her. Having lost an alarming amount of weight after the quadruplets' birth, she looked as feeble as her scrawny babies. It was her desperate condition that had cemented Gladys's determination to help.

So too a chance encounter had made all the difference for Mary. Just look at her now, so big and noisy. Gladys cocked her head up toward the roof of the van. Was it possible for a person to be *too* healthy?

George the Second

As the van turned north again, in the direction of Kyankwanzi, Gladys's thoughts turned to the day's second set of quadruplets.

A week after giving birth, the mother of these quads had died of a suspected pulmonary embolism. George Rwakabishe and his wife had been married only a year. Now he was alone with four newborn babies.

Some neighbors had read Gladys's articles about Mary Kakuru's quadruplets, and they urged George Rwakabishe to make contact with the reporter. Gladys wrote about the young widower's situation and appealed to her readers for help. Having learned from her experience with Mary and the first George, what she aimed to get these quadruplets was not a house but a livelihood for their father. Like the first George, this second George was Bahima, and a herder. He hoped to start a cattle business.

Donations came in totaling 800,000 shillings, enough to purchase two cows. A Bukedde TV story showed George Rwakabishe receiving the funds at the *New Vision* offices.

Camilla, the *New Vision* receptionist, marveled: "Gladys, you are a very lucky person. Every time you write something about a needy person, someone will come up to assist. You know, not every story brings assistance. That's why other reporters are complaining. They don't want to write such stories, because they write them and people don't turn up."

Gladys knew it was a matter less of luck than of persistence. Sometimes you needed to run the story multiple times. And if people responded, you had to follow up and show the results. That was part of the reason she kept following these cases, even when they were in far-flung places.

George Rwakabishi and his quadruplets lived in Kyankwanzi, eighty miles west of Kampala. The distance from Bukomero was not so great, but the journey took time, as the family lived in an outlying area. Gladys and her companions would arrive late, but how late, one could not say. Working in the field meant that Gladys frequently ran behind — operating on what everyone wryly called "Uganda time." With a destination like this one, an appointment time was a mere daydream.

The Toyota van lost steam as it transitioned from tarmac to macadam, from macadam to dirt, and from dirt to scrub. Finally the van rumbled into an area that seemed to have no road at all, only bush. Mike slowed to a crawl as Gladys peered about, getting her bearings.

"Okay," she said finally. "I think we go here."

Mike looked through the windshield, dubious. The van idled hesitantly in front of a wall of green.

"What is this place called?" he asked, perhaps wanting reassurance that the place had a name.

"Rwebitoomi." Meaning "muddy place." Tourism evidently was not the area's mainstay.

"So where do we pass through?" Mike asked.

"We are passing through this," Gladys answered, pointing ahead.

"We go straight through here?" Mike nosed the van through the brush, which was as tall as he was, expecting it to lead to the mouth of a road on the other side. But there was no other side. There was only more brush. "Whaaat?"

Mike rolled ahead, moving toward a flatter area where there were indentations in the foliage, like hair that had been parted after yesterday's bath. "This one?" he asked.

"No, branch there, on that road."

"What road?"

"Your road."

"*What?*"

"This is a place where the car makes the road."

Mike gamely plunged forward, charging through bushes and branches and bouncing over rocks and in and out of holes.

"Oh!"

"Eh!"

"Seriously!"

A maize field provided a temporary edge for Mike to trace, followed by a series of footpaths to straddle. But soon they were again floundering in a sea of overgrowth mined with boulders.

"Br-branch here!" Gladys called out as the car tossed them back and forth like beans in a skillet.

"How are you sure to branch there?" Mike shouted back.

"I have been here before."

"What? You have been to this place before, and now you are back?"

Gladys giggled. "I have been to this place several times."

"I am sorry to tell you, Gladys, but you need your head examined."

She refrained from mentioning that she had made the last trip with malarial fever.

Suddenly a huge crater appeared before them, flanked on all sides by bush, like some kind of big game trap. "Whaaat?" Mike protested again, his voice rising siren-high.

He steered hard to the right, drove a few feet straight into the bush, then angled back toward the road, crushing his way back to the other side of the crater. Toyota van as bulldozer.

"Y-you see now, Mi-ike, why I insisted y-you should get a stronger vehicle," Gladys called as they lurched back onto solid ground, her voice cutting in and out like a poor mobile-phone connection.

"If I had taken my own car, it would have fallen apart. Right now I would be standing in the road with only a steering wheel in my hands."

Their laughter mixed with the *thwack thwack smack* of reeds and branches whipping the windshield.

"I'm starting to fear you, Gladys. You've come here before, and you continue coming here? I didn't know you were such a mad person!"

"I run through *jungles* to get to my cases!"

THEY JOSTLED THROUGH the bush, jaws clacking, for the better part of an hour. Or in Mike's view, the worse part of an hour. He seriously doubted that Gladys knew where to go, especially when one section of foliage appeared as indistinct and impenetrable as the other. Some holes in the ground were so deep and close to each other that he had to stop the van and get out to determine how to navigate around them. He'd be damned if he'd get his tires stuck out here in the middle of nowhere Muddy Place.

Occasionally they would emerge at a clearing where paths led to huts, and Mike would wait for Gladys to shout, "We are here!" But again and again Gladys pointed instead to a break in a maize field or a flattened section of grass, insisting, "The road is there!"

"There is no road," Mike would protest.

"If you need a road, you make the road!"

Besides the huts, the only reassurance of civilization was the occasional villager, face frozen in surprise at the sight of a vehicle. It was probably like seeing a long-horned steer among the *matatus* in Old Taxi Park. Not unthinkable, but a little absurd.

"There he is!" Gladys pointed. They were approaching an intersection of sorts, where two makeshift paths crossed. There was a teenager standing next to a bicycle, and a bald man in his late twenties wearing a light-blue polo shirt. The bald man waved. "That is George Number Two," Gladys said. "He will lead us the rest of the way."

Like the first George, the second George carried a thin staff. He greeted Gladys with a small wave and a look of mild concern.

This George possessed a deliberate, serious manner. He insisted on riding in the van's cargo space rather than taking a proper seat.

Perhaps he was conscious of his body odor, which faintly scented the van's interior. While Mike and Gladys and Esther had laughed and shouted and yelped on the trek through Rwebitoomi, now they fell silent in order to hear George's quiet directions.

Overhead, gray clouds had started to form, and the sky turned the color of wet newspaper. "It is going to rain soon," Mike warned. "We need to head back as soon as possible." If darkness fell on them out here, they could be stuck for the night.

After fifteen minutes of obeying George's soft commands to "turn here," "go left," and "straight this way," they crashed through a stretch of weeds that culminated in a thicket of grass ten feet high.

"Here is the gate," Gladys announced.

"What gate?" Mike asked.

"The gate. The gate is here."

"Here? Where? There is no gate here!" Mike swiveled around in exasperation. George climbed out of the back of the van and disappeared into the green.

"George will show you the gate."

It started to rain, the drops sparse but ominously heavy, hitting the windshield like warning shots. Foliage shrouded the car on all four sides. The afternoon felt like midnight with a full moon. "Gladys, I do not see how the vehicle can pass through this place."

"George will open the gate — he just needs to get another person to help him."

"I'm sorry, I am not going to drive the car any further."

"But the house is just there, through the gate!"

"There is no gate!"

They argued the point like priests of opposing religions until Gladys surrendered. Gate or no gate, Mike was right: Muddy Place was about to get muddier. They needed to get back on the main road before it started to pour. Gladys and Esther would dash through the bush to the house, see the quadruplets, and run back. Mike would stay with the van.

When Gladys and Esther popped through the weeds, they found

George and a neighbor starting to lift the long branches that made up the "gate" behind the massive wall of grass.

"Don't bother," they told George. "The car is not coming."

AFTER A FEW minutes of walking through the bush, the group reached George Rwakabishe's homestead, a collection of several mud huts on an island of open space. The grounds outside the huts were immaculately swept and circumscribed by a tidy fence of branches. Even the sky brightened a bit above this clearing, the clouds withholding their showers.

An older woman came out of one hut to greet them. Once George's sister-in-law, she had now taken the role of his wife. Usually stepmothers aroused Gladys's suspicion, as they rarely cared for children who were not their own. But this aunt was the only mother the quadruplets had ever known, and she appeared to dote on them.

Unlike the leaky, smelly hut of the first George, the huts in this compound were well thatched and spotless inside, with clean mats in lieu of beds. The family had fewer possessions than George and Mary, but what they had was neatly kept.

The stepmother beckoned to the children. The three girls and their brother appeared wearing a vivid assortment of clothing, unlike the matching outfits sported by Mary's quads. On their feet they wore identical sandals, but in different colors.

They were small for four and a half years. Some Bahima fed their babies only cow's milk for the first few years, and as toddlers the quadruplets had weighed only half what doctors said they should weigh. It took some time to convince the family that their diet could lead to health problems, especially in such vulnerable infants.

Gladys cooed over the children and handed each a sweet, which was hesitantly accepted. They were less responsive than the other quads, having inherited their father's solemnity. Three of the four noses were runny, she noted. But they had come a long way. For a full year now they hadn't fallen seriously ill.

As raindrops began to spot the ground, Gladys quickly snapped some pictures and followed George and Esther back to the van. After hours of driving and battling the brush, they had visited the family for about six minutes.

Gladys knew it seemed mad to make such a trek for so short a visit. "Why don't you just call them?" friends and coworkers had asked her. But she needed to see everything with her own eyes. She couldn't trust what was reported to her over the phone. How would she know that a child's clothes were clean? That a stepmother was being kind? That a house was not falling down?

MIKE HAD MISSED the good part, so anxious was he to return to civilization. The "road" he had made on the way to the quadruplets' homestead had largely disappeared, but George again crouched in the back of the vehicle to help guide them through the thickest part of the bush.

George hopped out just as the clouds began to break open. He thanked Gladys for her visit. In the rearview mirror, they could see him standing there, watching the van drive away until the curtains of rain and reeds erased him completely.

"What happened to George's cattle business?" Mike asked, then clarified, "This George, George the Second."

Gladys explained. "With many of those multiple births, if one gets sick, the others will follow. And the fees for medicine are a problem. You must buy it yourself. Mary and George the First would never get the medication for their kids. George the Second did, and it used up his funds. I kept calling him and asking, 'How is the business?' And he would say, 'I haven't started yet—the children are in the hospital again.' So the business didn't have a chance. Can you imagine taking those four children to the hospital every month from that remote place? They would all go on two boda bodas."

As he was presently attempting his escape from the morass of Rwebitoomi, Mike could only nod with respect.

Gladys had taken out a loan to send George the Second money for a third time, but only for his children's expenses. "I want to empower this George so he can build his own house someday. I think he can do it."

"You did not see it," Esther told Mike. "But George the Second made a second homestead, three huts on the compound, to accommodate his mother."

"The good thing is, this George is willing to work, not like George the First," Gladys added. "George the First is hopeless! He wants everything to be done for him."

The mention of the other George set Mike's head wagging. "George the First has no ambition. You can't change his mind."

"For George the First, looking after people's cows is okay," Gladys said. "He's seen his grandparents do that, maybe his father did that."

"But now those pastoralists have changed," Mike said. "They have fences. They don't need a guy hiding behind the cows like that George the First."

"Yeah. Put your cows inside the fence, and you do other work!"

"George the First is just lazy. He is sitting down there, empty. Just empties his mind as the cows graze."

"By the way," Gladys began. She had heaps of kindling to add to this fire. "When I started on the foundation for Mary and George the First's house, I thought the builder could hire George as a porter. George refused. 'Auntie Gladys, I can't lift cement. It's too heavy for me.' Do you know what he said? 'If you want somebody, go hire a boy in the neighborhood.' Can you imagine! You are telling me to pay for someone when you are sitting there with no money to buy soap? What I was trying to do was to make sure he could get some daily income. Working on his own house! And he says he can't carry sand!" Gladys's nose twisted up as though smelling spoiled milk. "George the First is so *annoying*."

The car rocked with laughter, Mike's deep bellow filling out the lower registers and Gladys's cackle hitting several octaves above.

"George the First is a waste of space," Mike said, snorting. "He needs to stay with the cows — they are his colleagues. They don't ask too much of him."

Rain pounded the roof like applause. "George the Second is a man of purpose. He has a compass. A direction. With George the

First, the direction is . . ." Mike cupped a hand to his mouth, hollering, "'George! Just run to the lake and keep going! Don't stop!'"

AS WITH SO many journeys, the way back seemed shorter than the way there. After miles of rock-studded terrain, the tires of the van suddenly rolled over tarmac. It felt like floating.

"Here we will get back to the main road," Gladys announced. "And Mike will call it a day!"

"Yes, now that Gladys has taken us to the end of the world," he complained.

The rain continued to fall. Mike didn't mind. Once they reached Kampala, a downpour would clear the streets of pedestrians, peddlers, panhandlers, and boda bodas. For those in a car, it would be smooth sailing down the wet streets, presidentially nicknamed "the River Museveni."

Gladys giggled. Mike glanced in the rearview mirror inquiringly.

"You know . . . the gate?" she asked. "Back at George the Second's place?"

"The gate that was no gate?"

"It's like that story with that king who says he has expensive clothes but he looks naked. Everyone says, 'Yes, we see your new clothes.' And do you remember there is only one who is not seeing the new clothes, who is saying, 'But where are these clothes?'"

"'But where is the gate?'" Mike threw up his hands, exaggerating his earlier confusion.

The women howled.

"The gate is the bush!"

"The bush is not a gate!"

"If you say it is a gate, it becomes a gate!"

AND IT WAS that way with so many things in life. Something became something when you declared it would be so.

"This is a place where the car makes the road," Gladys had informed Mike as they had crashed through Muddy Place. Wasn't the whole world just an extension of that tangled expanse? There was no clear and easy path. "If you need a road, you make a road!"

Gladys had made so many of her own roads. Some had proved dead ends, or reached impassable junctures — the bookshop that was twice ransacked, the fish business that mysteriously burned down. Those failures hurt, of course, but she had not sat down to cry or pound her fists. You needed to be creative, to find another way forward. Eventually you would get somewhere. In her case, all those setbacks had led her to this, her vocation.

She thought back to the morning, to the comment George the First had made as he watched Gladys stumble over puddles on the path from his house. "Can you make for me a road?" It had shocked her. Did he really expect someone else to pave a road to the house others had already built for him?

You needed to make your own road. Gladys firmly believed that. But she was not so naive as to believe that everyone could. Just as there were George the Seconds, who endured tragedy and rose to the challenge, there would be the George the Firsts, who would make no effort. It was for that reason, as much as any other, that Gladys could not abandon the Kakuru quadruplets. George the First would never make his own road. But his children had a chance to try.

It had stopped raining by the time they reached the taxi park; bodas and pedestrians began to crowd the streets. The exit from Kampala and on southward to Entebbe would be slow.

But she had seen these eight of her children, and they looked fine. Perhaps on the long ride home she would sleep.

The Children of Strangers

It was not a fact that she broadcast to her colleagues, but Gladys was descended from a distinguished lineage. Her great-grandfather, Michael Kawalya-Kagwa, was the first prime minister of the Buganda Kingdom, still the largest of the country's traditional kingdoms. He was credited with bringing electricity to the country in the 1950s. In Uganda, though, pedigree is no protection against misfortune.

In the half century since the lights came on, the country had witnessed turbulent times: the violent power struggles surrounding Milton Obote, Idi Amin ("the Butcher of Uganda"), Obote again, President Yoweri Museveni's National Resistance Army, and Kony's Lord's Resistance Army. Survival was a precarious business for everyone, from the grand to the humble.

In the early 1960s, when Gladys was born, her branch of the family tree was educated but not well-to-do. Her father was a government clerk; he was also an alcoholic with many children by many women. Six of those children were born to Gladys's mother, a primary school teacher who struggled to run her household. With little salary and no spousal support, she sent four-year-old Gladys and her two-year-old brother Godfrey to live with their grandparents.

Thus began the storybook chapter of Gladys's life. As an Anglican minister, her grandfather, Obadiah Kaweesa, lived on church grounds. Everything the family needed was right there: the house, the garden, the playing field, and the church, which seemed to young Gladys the biggest and most beautiful in the world.

With fourteen children of the Kaweesa clan running around, it was a bustling compound, but a tidy one. Each child had a role: sweeping the yard, fetching the water, washing the bedsheets, feeding the dogs, who were always named Simba. After their chores and prayers and homework, they would play. Gladys was young, chubby, and the only girl, but she jumped right in with the boys. The scar on her left knee was a testament to her enthusiasm for netball, if not to her skill.

Her grandfather, who had once been a teacher, believed deeply in education as the key to a full and independent life. With studies given high priority, the children, including Gladys, performed at the top of their classes.

In her grandparents' home they had sugar in the porridge, flowers on the table, and paraffin after dark. Early on Sundays the children were allowed to beat the two big drums announcing morning services. What joy, to pound out that noise, to feel the sting and thrum under one's fingertips!

People were always coming into the home—parishioners in need of counsel or assistance or a place to stay for a while. While Reverend Kaweesa encouraged resourcefulness, he was generous to those who struggled. Gladys regarded him as a real man of God, not like so many of the fake preachers she saw these days, selling religion like lottery tickets.

When Gladys was seventeen and still in school, her grandfather died. The blow knocked the nest out of the tree. All at once the family lost its champion, its sense of security, and its haven at the church compound. Gladys and her brother were sent back home. Back to a house now filled with kids, an overwhelmed mother, and a father who brought little through the door but strife and drink.

And then things got worse. While the rest of the family attended the traditional funeral rites, the women singing for three days over the reverend's body, Gladys's father went back to her mother's house and sold off everything, even the house itself. And then he took off with another woman. How Gladys hated him then! Leaving his grieving family with no home, with nothing. The seven of them were forced to move into two small rooms with only a bare floor to sleep on. Complaining of headaches, Gladys's mother stopped working. The family hit bottom.

No more suppers at the big table. No more netball games. The beat of the Sunday drums faded to silence. But Gladys had never been one for sitting and crying. As the firstborn, it was up to her to care for her siblings. She dropped out of school and began to look for work. Her first job was at the Ministry of Agriculture, performing clerical duties.

"You are so young!" grownups would remark. "Can you really manage?"

She had no choice. Her uncles pitched in, but since they had their own families, there was only so much they could do. It was Gladys who provided meals, scrounged up school fees, tended to illness, and provided comfort. For all intents and purposes, she became her siblings' mother and father.

On the rocky uphill climb of those years, Gladys lightened the family burden by discarding her own aspirations. Other girls her age were preparing for university and buying new dresses, nice shoes. Gladys knew that if she were to buy shoes, Godfrey would not have tuition, Alex would not have a school uniform, Veronica would not have books. Indeed, she mourned the loss not of the shoes but of the education. The love of learning her grandfather had instilled in her was a luxury she could no longer afford.

Still, the achievements of her siblings brought her happiness, particularly those of her brightest brother, Godfrey. As his star rose, through college and the start of a career in law, so did Gladys's hopes.

GLADYS HAD REACHED middle age, but three of her siblings were long deceased. Veronica and Juliet both succumbed to illnesses in their twenties. Her other brothers now worked in skilled professions, but Godfrey was struck down by an aneurysm shortly after making plans to support Gladys through college. The wound from his loss ached to this day.

Gladys never got the chance to attend university, but she was determined to see that her own son and daughter did. Her mother and uncles helped with the kids while she worked six days a week. Now in his midtwenties, Timothy ran a web-hosting firm. Sarah was finishing her teaching degree.

During the bad years, Gladys and her siblings did not see their father. The man never checked on his children, not even one time, to see if they were sick or hungry or homeless. He had fled the scene like a hit-and-run driver.

What a shock it was then, when, more than three decades after he disappeared, he resurfaced, sick and destitute. His other woman no longer wanted to deal with him and his drunkenness. Gladys could not feel anything as potent as hate for him, only a kind of curious pity. Her father had ignored his abandoned children; he had ended up an abandoned old man.

Gladys and an aunt helped him through urgently needed surgery, but he resumed drinking before he even left the hospital. Pity curdled into irritation. Could one really say that she and her siblings had not been better off without such a man?

One never knew what life would bring. Greater opportunity was no guarantee of good fortune. And bad luck could mean an escape from something worse. While Gladys was not rich, she found her work gratifying. Without all her struggles, would she ever have jumped at the chance to join a journalism class for secondary school students?

Perhaps that was part of what drew her to intervene in the lives of others. A person's story might head in a dark direction, but that did not mean it was destined to end as a tragedy. There was always the chance for dramatic reversal. Maybe not dramatic as in those Harold Robbins novels—ordinary fates did not hinge on Hollywood producers and race cars—but even minor incidents could make a difference. One small push could alter a person's trajectory a few degrees, just enough to skirt the precipice.

Gladys did not have much. Indeed, on most days she was just scraping by. But it did not take so much to give a little push, especially to a child.

Many people did not seem to understand this impulse. Instead, Gladys's support of so many kids struck them as a kind of compulsion. Why did this woman care so much about the children of strangers? Children who were not her relatives. Children not from her village.

As is the way in Uganda, the questioners wielded their curiosity with a blunt edge. "Why do you want to look after so many children? Is it because you don't have any of your own?"

Gladys would demur, explaining that she had grown children.

Ah, they are grown, her questioners' knowing nods would say.

Maybe she was making money. Maybe she was cultivating religious converts. There had to be a practical reason for all that effort and expenditure.

Upon hearing that Gladys had sent yet another child to school, one of her work colleagues once remarked, "I think it's you people who will go to heaven." The "compliment" bothered her for days. Did he think he could not possibly extend such assistance himself? She was not holy!

Yes, Gladys helped many children, but not to feather her nest in the afterlife. It was just that sometimes a thought would sprout in her mind: *Maybe I can help this one.* Sometimes it meant buying a plate of food. Sometimes that plate of food led to an article in the paper or some phone calls or transport back home or school fees. But she did not leave her home in the morning thinking, *Things have been too calm around here. I really hope today I will find another needy child or two to support on my meager pay.*

And still—it happened.

LATE ONE AFTERNOON Gladys returned to *New Vision* after a long day in the field. Her climb up the stairs was a bit slow, as she had gone without breakfast and lunch. Out of the corner of her eye she saw a figure seated in the waiting area. At once she sensed something amiss, the way one knows a dog is dead, not sleeping, when one passes it on the street.

Turning to look, she felt her skin prickle from head to toe. Someone was sitting in there. Not an adult. A teenager. One half of his face was swollen to twice its normal size.

Gladys moved to the reception desk. Camilla, who questioned everyone entering the waiting area, reported that the boy had come for Bukedde TV. Like *New Vision* newspaper, Bukedde was owned by the multimedia conglomerate Vision Group, and its offices were next door. Desperate people often came to the building hoping to attract attention through the station, which broadcast in Luganda.

In the field and in her daily life, Gladys had seen countless physical disabilities, but none exactly like this one. It was more localized and extreme than the swellings she had seen on cancer wards. But could it be cancer?

Gladys waved to the boy. "Hello," she called. "Come over here."

He approached, a slight figure clad in a flowered T-shirt, shorts, and slippers. Up close, the distension on his face was painfully taut, as if a melon had been thrust under the skin. The right side of his head was so inflated that he had no nose, and the right eye had been pushed an inch higher than the left.

"What's your name?"

The boy turned his head to look at the big woman. Hers was a generous, open face. Her cheeks were plump and high enough to crowd her eyes when she smiled, as she was doing now.

She introduced herself in a calm, warm voice. She was a journalist at the paper, and she was curious about his situation. Unlike the few other strangers who had spoken directly to him, she did not pretend that nothing was wrong.

She asked, "Were you born like this, or is it a disease?"

It was an unusual encounter, surely, but then it became extraordinary. Because the woman, this Gladys Kalibbala, reached out and touched his face.

FOR EZRA, THE TROUBLE had started after he turned three. That was when the right side of his face began to swell. That was when his mother abandoned him.

The boy went to stay with his father, who was alarmed by his son's strange metamorphosis. With several wives and more than ten children, he had many obligations, but he did what he could to find a cure.

Visits to witch doctors and herbalists had no effect on the condition, however, and by the time Ezra turned seven, his features were so contorted that no classmate would share a desk with him. He dropped out of school.

Eventually his father took him to a hospital, where they told him an operation should be attempted before the swelling became too acute.

Ezra's father tried. He sold off everything he could find in the home. But the cost of the operation was too steep. One day he told his son, "As you can see, we are so poor here. I did the best I could, but it is beyond us now. You must try to stay alive."

When Ezra was twelve, it was his father who died, leaving the boy to the mercy of a stepmother. This woman, who had her own children to care for, proved unsympathetic to the boy's plight. His ugliness repulsed her. Ezra could feel her disgust, as palpable as heat. Resentful of his presence in her home, she sent him out to do heavy labor and endless chores. From morning till night, Ezra was expected to toil like a machine. No matter how hard he worked, he could not please her.

Ezra's condition gave him excruciating headaches, and the stress only increased their frequency. Sometimes the pain physically incapacitated him, provoking his stepmother's ire. "You useless thing," she would spit. "You're good for nothing. That's why God made you this way. Your own mother ran away from you and left you behind, and now you are just wasting my space."

As his illness and his stepmother's abuse intensified, so did Ezra's sense of urgency. By the time he entered his teen years, the headaches were constant, the vision in his right eye had degenerated, and the strain on his mouth and nose constricted his breathing.

His father had told him to stay alive. Ezra was determined to try. At sixteen he came up with a plan to go to Kampala, find work, and save up for his surgery. To raise transport money, he started taking on extra work, digging in people's gardens and making bricks to sell in the village.

On the day he left his village in Kibuku, none of his relatives —not his siblings, not his aunts and uncles, and certainly not his stepmother—expressed concern. Perhaps they were relieved to see Ezra leave, as he carried with him the source of their family's embarrassment.

The big city was farther away than he thought it was. When his money ran out, the taxi dumped him somewhere halfway. He decided to travel on foot, but the going was hard. In his own village, he was used to neighbors snickering behind his back. Here among strangers, the abuse was thrown right in his face. "Monster!" people taunted. Kids pelted him with rocks. One man took one look at him and burst into jeering laughter. Something in the man's gleefulness nearly broke Ezra. He could not stop crying, but he did not stop walking.

Fortunately, he encountered a sympathetic traffic officer who started flagging down cars and asking drivers to take pity on a wretched boy. Through a combination of short rides and long walks, Ezra finally made it to Kampala.

"DOES IT GIVE you very much pain?" The woman's fingers moved over the stretch of his cheek, feeling the drumhead tightness of his skin.

It was the first time anyone had touched his face in over ten years. Well, there was the doctor who had examined him when his father was alive, but that did not count. This woman not only touched him, she listened to him. In her look was something more nuanced than pity, more probing than sympathy. It was interest.

"You are here alone? Why is no one with you?"

Communication was bumpy, as she did not understand his local language, Lugwere, while Ezra spoke rudimentary Luganda and no English at all. Plus his mouth was compressed in such a way that he had difficulty forming some words. Despite the obstacles, it was easy to open up to this lady, who absorbed every detail of his story, from his childhood to his arrival at Kampala. She seemed in no hurry to ascend the stairs and get on with her day.

When he revealed that he had slept overnight at a bus station, the woman's tone grew stern. "You must never, ever sleep on the street again! Whatever happens. Ask someone to show you the nearest police station. Do you understand?"

"I understand."

She took his photo and asked for his contact information, but Ezra had no phone, and he had no numbers for anyone in his family.

"Ah," the woman sighed. "I really would like to help you. But even if I put your story in the paper, there is no way for anyone to contact you."

Wishing him luck with his plans, she started toward the steps.

On impulse, he called out to her. "Auntie, can you write your number on a piece of paper? Maybe if I come across a line I can call you."

The reporter seemed a bit dubious that he would be able to obtain a phone. But she wrote down her name and number.

"If you go to any police station, I will be able to trace you." She gave him a 1,000-shilling note, with directions for where he could buy a chapati. "Today that is all the money I can offer. But if you find you still need help and you call me, maybe I will be able to see the way forward."

TWO DAYS LATER, Gladys got a call from Central Police Station.

When the boy's visit to the TV station had failed to yield any funds, he sought help in finding the nearest police, just as Gladys had advised. Upon seeing his condition, though, the CPS officers wanted to return him to Kibuku.

Ezra refused. He would not go back home. He had come to Kampala to work, and he intended to work so that he could get care for his face. He was sixteen — old enough to know there was no future in turning back.

Gladys had assisted all kinds of children, but she reserved a special place in her heart for those who were truly bold. Not the reckless ones who disregarded consequences, or the brash ones who were confident and outspoken, but the vulnerable ones who knew what they were risking when they planted their feet and refused to move. There was a difference between fearless and brave.

Ezra was young, ill, alone, and penniless. But here he was, telling these police that they could not make him go home. How could she not help such a one?

"Gladys!" an officer exclaimed. "Do you know this one?"

"Yes," she said. "I know him."

Ezra watched in awe as Gladys pushed and cajoled and reasoned and admonished the police to let him take refuge at the station. He had never had someone fight for him before.

At last the officer in charge relented. The boy could remain at the station, but only for a little while.

"I will find a solution," Gladys said reassuringly. "Just give me some few days."

With the boy off the streets, she set to work, making phone calls to Uganda Cancer Institute and writing an article about Ezra's predicament and the necessity for a CT scan. If it was cancer, Gladys knew it must be quickly diagnosed. Among the many pictures she had taken of the boy, she chose a close-up portrait to submit with the piece.

To Gladys's dismay, the photo was rejected by the editors. The image was too upsetting, she was told. Readers might complain. No one wanted to sit down with the paper on Saturday morning and spit up their tea.

Gladys was angry, but she was also hurt. The anger was because the decision rendered the article useless. How could they expect anyone to step forward to help a boy whose deformity no one could see? The hurt was for the boy. She had moved through town with him. She had seen the world through his eyes. How people gaped and pointed. How taxi passengers recoiled and changed seats. It made you feel small. Like you were not as good as other people. Like you were too ugly to have your picture in the paper.

Such censorship seemed hypocritical, given the sensational leanings of the Ugandan media. For a decade every outlet in the country had tracked the antics of Godfrey Baguma, who won the national

"Ugliest Man" contest. Known as Sebabi ("the ugliest of them all"), this former cobbler carried a dramatically misshapen head atop a small body. Articles, TV stories, and even a music video gleefully celebrated his marriage to a pretty young wife, his defense of his "ugliest" title, and the birth of his eighth child. And Gladys was supposed to worry that Ezra's medical condition might make readers cringe?

The article ran without a photo. It received no response at all.

AFTER A MONTH and a half at CPS, Ezra was no longer allowed to stay. It was not proper for the police to house a child, and they had done so for so long only because Gladys had forced them to. Given no alternative, she took the boy into her own small home, where he would remain for over three months.

Again Gladys submitted her column with Ezra's story, telling her editors, "Run the boy's photo with the profile or don't run it at all."

This time Ezra's photo dominated the page, the distended side of his face appearing to pop out in three dimensions. *Look at this!* it seemed to shout. *Let's get this terrible thing off this boy's face before it explodes!*

The response was immediate. Some readers gave donations; one offered to take Ezra into her home before the operation. Kampala Hospital gave Ezra a CT scan that ruled out cancer. Doctors made a diagnosis of fibrous dysplasia of the maxilla, a genetic bone growth disorder. If left untreated, the disease could cause Ezra to lose the function of his right eye, and his brain might suffer increased pressure. But there was good news: CoRSU Rehabilitation Hospital agreed to perform the surgery without charge.

As he was not yet an adult, Ezra had to return home to get a letter from his village's local chairman, certifying permission for the operation. He announced to his family that CoRSU had scheduled the date for his surgery. But none of his relatives seemed to take him seriously. How could anyone fix a face like that? *Don't waste our time,* he was told. Once again he went to Kampala by himself.

Gladys was dismayed by his family's lack of support. While there was no cost for the surgery, the hospital did not cover accommodation, food, or transport. She knew the family was poor, but it was not only a matter of money. Ezra would need special care after the operation, including full-time attention for the first ten days. There was no way that Gladys could tend to him and retain her job.

Perhaps the boy did not fully explain to his relatives. "Let's call them," she suggested.

Gladys could not speak Lugwere, so when they managed to get the stepmother by phone, it was Ezra who did the talking.

"If you want to go through with it, fine," responded the stepmother. "But we don't have time to help."

They contacted an aunt. Although she lived in Kampala, she claimed she was too busy even to visit.

They reached out to a brother. Gladys could not follow the conversation, but she could hear the begging tone in Ezra's voice, and she could see his tears. The brother refused to come, claiming he had two cows that needed grazing. Gladys boiled. How she wished she could speak the language. She would have harassed this brother thoroughly for valuing livestock over his own flesh and blood.

A few days later they tried the stepmother again. The number no longer worked. She had shut the phone off.

Gladys persisted in her fundraising efforts, making appeals to friends, colleagues, her church. She put all her own money toward Ezra's care, leaving nothing to help her own son with his university fees. Timothy was having a hard time making ends meet, but he was a young man now, and she knew he would not starve. This sickly boy had no one.

AS EZRA LAY down on the gurney, Gladys snapped more photos, documenting the boy's swollen face for the last time.

"Thank you so much," he kept saying, effusive in his excitement. The surgeons would be hard-pressed to find anyone more eager to face a scalpel. "Thank you so, so much for what you have done for me."

Gladys smiled down at him, but her heart was racing. She had just been doused in a cold new fear. As she was preparing to deliver

Ezra to the hospital, a friend had warned her not to go. "You are not from his tribe, the Bagwere. It's too risky. Do you know about the Bagwere?"

The friend, a police commissioner, was a Musoga. "We Musoga know the Bagwere well. For you, you are staying here in the Central Region. You do not know them! The Bagwere are witches! If they just look at you in a bad way, you may drop dead! That thing on the boy's face is a very delicate matter. If you take him in for the operation, there is a chance that he could die. Although his people have refused to come to the assistance of the boy, they will hold you responsible for him."

Gladys felt the blood drain from her head like sand in an hourglass.

"His tribe is very fierce. If the boy dies from the operation, they will hunt you down," was the friend's dark prediction. "They will kill you and your entire family."

Gladys had not been raised to believe in witchcraft, but mob justice was an undeniable plague. The papers frequently published stories of crowds attacking suspected thieves, beating or burning them to death on the spot. If a person could be killed for stealing a phone or a goat, what mercy would be shown to someone purported to have harmed a child?

"We've seen you struggling to help this boy, and to help other children. But as a friend, I am telling you, let this one be." Any remaining kernel of calm was crushed by the commissioner's final statement. "However much we would want to protect you as police, if the Bagwere come after you, we will not be able to help you."

What if the man's words were true? If the boy died, she would die too, and it would all have been for nothing. But how could she back out? How could she tell Ezra, "I'm sorry, but your tribe is so fierce that I'm scared for my life—goodbye"?

In the end she said nothing to Ezra as he headed happily into surgery. There was no way she could abandon him now. The Bagwere were right. She was responsible for him.

Gladys sat on a bench with only her fear for company. She could not eat, she could not rest. She could only stare across the walkway at the double doors under the sign OPERATING THEATRE.

Hours passed in a hell of waiting. Every time a gurney ferrying a green-sheeted body emerged, she jumped up to look. But none was her boy.

Why is he not coming out? Something must have gone wrong. Surely nothing that went well could take so long.

Gladys prayed. She prayed harder than she had ever prayed before. *God, have mercy on the boy. Have mercy on me. Let this operation succeed, so that this boy survives and so his people don't come to kill me or my family.*

Why? came the skeptics' refrain. *Why do you care so much about the children of strangers?*

Because she could help them.

Because she couldn't help it.

Because those doors might open at any moment, and when that boy came through, there should be at least one person to greet him.

AT LAST, AFTER an agony of waiting, Ezra's gurney rolled out of the operating theater and into the recovery ward, where Gladys settled in for more waiting.

It would take some time for the boy to regain consciousness, but at least now she could look at him. He was wrapped in a sheet and a blanket, the right side of his face covered by a bulky red bandage patterned with ladybugs. His face was puffy from the trauma, but she could tell that the mass had been removed.

Finally the boy stirred. He was awake, but he could not open his eyes.

"Where is my mother?" he croaked.

After all he has been through, Gladys thought sadly, *he still calls for the mother he has not seen for all these years.*

"My mother," Ezra persisted. "Where is my mother, who takes my photos?"

"Eeeee!" Gladys rushed to Ezra's bedside. If he could not see through the swelling and the bandages, he would certainly recognize her warm, weighty hug.

"Mommy, you're here!" he cried. And then he fell back to sleep.

WHEN THE BANDAGES came off and Ezra first looked at himself in the mirror, he felt a jolt of shock, followed by overwhelming joy. No longer was his cheek inflated like the throat of a tree frog. The curse was gone.

"It was like I was carrying a very big load," he told Gladys, who was just as delighted. "Now all at once it has disappeared."

As he healed, he watched his face settle into its new shape. It was not perfect. A long scar bordered the newly flattened ridge slanting down his right cheek. And no surgery could erase the seismic effect of the bone growth, which had permanently raised his right eye higher than the left. But these residual flaws could not compare to what he had regained. The ability to breathe freely. To speak without slurring. To enjoy a day free from headaches and cruel comments. To blink his eyes! He had not been able to grin so freely since he was three years old.

Sometimes when Ezra stared at length at his reflection, he thought he glimpsed his father's son—the boy he was meant to be, before the disease hijacked his identity.

Curiously, over the months and years after the surgery, this sense of discovery did not dissipate. Every day he looked in the mirror and saw a difference from the day before. Maybe it was because he was also growing up, but he felt that his true face was gradually being revealed, like a leaf rising to the surface of a murky pond.

All of Gladys's agonizing over the family's reaction to the surgery had been for naught. No mob materialized on her doorstep, demanding proof that the boy had not been harmed. In fact, not a single one of Ezra's relatives even called. Were they not even curious about how the boy was doing? He was still a member of the family, and he had been gone for half a year.

Gladys could not understand it. The boy was respectful, gracious, and hard-working. And so tidy! Perhaps it was overcompensation for his past deformity, but few other boys his age kept their things so clean or took such care with their personal habits. Who could fail to care for such a humble young man? Everybody in her own family who had met him—her grandmother, her uncles, her aunts, her siblings, her son—took to him immediately.

His own family's indifference did not distress Ezra, however. When his face was healed, he came to Gladys with a wish: "Mommy, I want to go home for a visit."

Her expectations for the reunion were not high, but she began to look for the funds for his travel. The boy was bold. If his family would not come to him, he would go to them.

WHEN EZRA WALKED into his village, everyone stared at his face. But this time they stared for a new reason. It was a miracle! His relatives, the neighbors, the children—they came from all directions. All those people who had treated him poorly were now crowding around, asking him questions as if he was someone. And he was. He was the boy who had set out to cure himself, the boy who had returned with a new face.

When Ezra saw his stepmother, she pulled him aside. She said she was sorry for what he had gone through—for what she had put him through. Her words stunned him. Ezra could hardly accept that his stepmother was acknowledging the past, let alone apologizing for it. The improbability brought tears to his eyes. Through all those years of rage and cruelty, he had never imagined a moment of such unambiguous redemption.

He forgave his stepmother. He forgave everybody. It was not that he had forgotten the pain they had inflicted. But now that he was at peace with himself, he did not want to be at war with anyone else.

IN THIS SPIRIT of harmony, Ezra longed for his two families to meet: his relatives in the village and his new mother. Gladys was curious to meet these people who had been able to twist her insides into knots from so far away. As soon as she could arrange transportation, she and Ezra went.

In the village, Gladys greeted everyone graciously, but she could not resist prodding Ezra's brother about his decision to attend to his cows rather than his brother's surgery. Her spear was blunt, though, and everyone laughed.

The stepmother thanked Gladys for looking after Ezra, admitting surprise that a stranger would care about him. She said, "I thought that people like you existed only in stories."

Gladys could not retain any anger toward the woman. She had treated Ezra harshly, but many stepmothers brutalized stepchildren or threw them out of the home. This one seemed genuinely happy at Ezra's good fortune.

Still, it was hard to digest the collective cheer without a sprinkle of salt. The surgery had not altered Ezra's character. He had always been a fine boy. But it was only after the surgery that his people could see it. *Now that he has a brighter future,* the cynical might conclude, *everyone wants to cozy up to him. They did not help plant the maize, they did not help shoo away the birds, but they want a share of the harvest.*

The more charitable view might be, *Life is not easy in a poor village such as this one. Why begrudge anyone a small taste of someone else's feast?*

When it was time to go, their departure illustrated how radically Ezra's status had changed. The family gave him a chicken, and the entire village escorted him down the road as if he were a prince leaving the palace! Gladys giggled at the sight of Ezra flashing his new smile in the middle of the dusty entourage, his stepmother at his side, kids darting up to the front. Even the babies on their sisters' backs craned their chubby necks to catch sight of the prodigal son.

When he had first left the village for Kampala, nobody had even bothered to wave. Now everyone clamored to touch his hem.

"Eh! This is our boy!"

FIFTEEN MINUTES. That was about the length of their first conversation at *New Vision,* when she had spotted Ezra in the waiting area.

Fifteen minutes had turned into six months. Then Ezra was in the hospital and she was the one in the waiting area, praying for both of their lives.

Six months had turned into six years. Now Ezra was a young

man, working to complete his primary education. For six years Gladys had supported him at boarding school, fretted over his marks, and welcomed him for holidays.

Six years would turn into what? Three decades? Four?

She had not planned such a long journey. But this was the manner in which she became involved in many of her children's lives. One small push led to another. Then the child was moving forward, and it was natural to assist with the next step, and the next one after that. Before she knew it, the two of them were running side by side. At that point she might turn around. Not to measure the distance by which she had overstepped her professional boundaries, but to appreciate how far they had come.

Even these days she would occasionally caress the side of Ezra's face, just as she had done that very first time at the reception area of *New Vision*. Now, though, the touch would set off a peal of laughter, as though she still couldn't believe the two of them had pulled it off.

"Eeeee! Eh-eh-eh-eh! Look at my boy now!"

Mommy Gladys

When one had to hide from children, it was time for a change. Over the past few years, Gladys had placed not only Trevor and Ezra but seven other needy kids at Entebbe Early Learning School. It was a primary school of modest size, with students ranging in age from six to the early teens, in grades from Primary 1 to Primary 7. Most pupils attended by day, but there were two crowded dormitories in which a few dozen children boarded. Although the school was intended to operate as a business, with tuition-paying students, its director, Agnes Biryahwaho, was a tender soul who found it tough to close the door on hard-luck cases. For several of Gladys's charges, Agnes was the Good Samaritan mentioned in the "Lost and Abandoned" follow-ups.

Gladys's kids had no one to pay their fees or for their books, their bedding, their clothing and personal needs — except her. The income of a freelance journalist barely covered her own expenses, so when Gladys visited the school to deliver supplies, she often hid from them — not an easy task for someone of such visible stature entering an open courtyard.

Her favored strategy was to use Ezra, the oldest and most responsible of her charges, as the go-between. A quick handoff and she could slip away. Or if she needed to talk to Agnes, she might call to say, "Wait for me in your office. I will jump off the boda boda and run inside." But many times she did not even make it to the gate before hearing the cries of "Mommy! Auntie! Mommy!"

It was always Deborah who spotted her first. The child was pre-ternaturally sharp-eyed, and even with her humpback quick on her feet. The others would come swarming behind her, from the class-rooms and dormitory and playground, as telepathically coordinated in their movement as a murmuration of starlings. *Surely this time,* the pounding footsteps seemed to say, *Mommy Gladys has brought something for me!*

"Mommy!"

"Auntie Gladys!"

"Auntie!"

"Mommy, Mommy!"

Today the crowd swirled around her like bodas in a traffic circle. There was Ezra, of course, who had missed nine years of education; limping Trevor, whom she had rescued after the raid on his corrupt school; Deborah, born with a spinal deformity; Douglas, who had walked barefoot to Kampala to escape a cruel stepmother; Evelyn, whose relatives had tried to kill her; Katamba, the boy whose drunk-en father had cut him with a panga; tiny Rose, shy Jeremiah, Faith . . . Her children had really suffered. The sight of their eager faces filled her with delight.

And dread.

"I don't have books, Mommy."

"Did you bring me a handkerchief this time?"

"Our pencils are all finished!"

The children enveloped her in a cloud of pungent affection. It was not hard to guess their next request.

"We have no soap!"

THIS MORNING GLADYS came with Esther and Mike, carrying only a bag of sweets between them. With these children, even a small treat could make the day sing.

"Take only one, okay? That way there will be enough for every-one." The upturned palms circled Gladys like the petals of a sun-flower. "Did you get one? How about Ezra back there?"

Ezra, ever unassuming, accepted his candy with his sloping smile and a nod of the head. "Thank you."

"Am I hearing thank-yous?" Gladys chided the others.

"Thank you! Thank you!"

As the cluster tightened around its candy-bearing nucleus, the odor of unwashed child grew increasingly sharp. Well, school would break in a few days. And as Agnes would say, *They will not die from being dirty.*

"What are your plans for the holidays?" Gladys asked.

"I'm going to celebrate my birthday here," Faith piped up.

"And when is your birthday?"

"It is the twenty-fourth of December, Auntie."

Gladys sighed. Why did she ask? Now that she knew the child's birthday, the girl would not let her forget it. She would need to come up with something.

"December third is my birthday," added a boy.

"My birthday was last Sunday," Rose said.

Gladys cocked her head at this teacup of a girl. "Rose, do you know your date of birth really? Are you lying to me?"

Rose hooked a finger in her mouth and pulled her head from side to side.

"Okay, how was it?" Gladys grinned, playing along. "Did you cut a cake? Did you even keep a piece for me?"

"But you did not come!"

"Did you invite me?" Gladys pouted.

The delicate chin lifted to a queenly angle. "I will make another birthday!"

"Hee hee hee!" Gladys turned to the others. "Do you know your birthdays?"

Headshakes and stares, a few slow nods.

"Ezra doesn't know his," Gladys assured them. "When is your birthday, Ezra?"

"January first," the older boy answered promptly.

"January first. Eeeh!" Gladys squealed with amusement. "He just came up with it!"

Ezra looked quite pleased with himself. And why shouldn't he simply claim a date? His mother had not left him with one. Consider Trevor, standing off to the side, worrying the remaining button on his faded shirt. His profile had run in "Lost and Abandoned" half a dozen times, with not even one response. What chance was there that anyone on earth knew Trevor's actual birthday?

One of the girls raised a hand. "My birthday was in September. But I did not have anything."

"Nothing. Oh my God," Gladys murmured, as though to herself. Was it worse not ever having a birthday celebration because one's birthday was unknown or to know one's birthday but feel its unmarked passage every year?

And then it popped out of her mouth: "I think what someone can do is maybe to pick one day and everybody celebrates on that very day."

Gladys chuckled, and Mike and Esther joined in. But as the laughter dried up, the idea crystallized.

"Just combine it!" Gladys said. "You just gather all of them, get one cake, each one of them holds the knife, they cut! Everyone can blow out the candles together. Although it is for different ages . . ." She frowned, assessing the logistics on the fly. "People blow out their candles according to ages, is it right? What do you do when it is different ages? Okay, you put the candles there, ask Deborah to blow some, ask Rose to blow some . . ." How would a child blow a few candles without blowing out the others? And how many candles could one cake hold? Nine children—that could be a hundred candles. The cake would look like a miniature forest fire.

She erased the image with a shake of her head and glanced around. All the children were staring at her, eyes as shiny as roasted coffee beans.

"At the moment I can't promise," Gladys mumbled, although it came out exactly like a promise. How did she talk herself into these things? Her list of obligations was full, and here she was, scribbling in the margins. "It means that I have to find some money first. We will work out something, don't worry."

The kids did not look worried at all. *Mommy Gladys is going to make a birthday party!*

• • •

IT WAS WITH some relief that Gladys turned toward the sound of Director Agnes's car pulling into the driveway. The kids dispersed en masse, the air flowing on the office veranda as suddenly as if a window had been opened.

"Oh, he is really running!" Gladys and Esther watched Trevor scamper ahead, his limp undetectable in his dusty scramble toward the car. "He will say, 'Auntie Agnes, I need a bread. Auntie Agnes, I need a chapati.' She must have some coins somewhere!"

Agnes emerged from her car dressed in a loose dress as red as a macaw. In fact there was a design of parrots splashed across the skirt. Evidently she had come from the restaurant and guest house on Lake Victoria that she ran with her husband. A woman of multiple occupations, she was also a trained dentist, a trade that came in handy for estimating the age of some of the orphans Gladys brought to her doorstep.

The children flanked her on all sides, skipping and jumping like flying fish racing a boat. Deborah darted ahead, announcing, "I was number one. Number one, I was number one!" On her heels, Rose waved something in her hand like a trophy.

"And that is Auntie Agnes's purse? You've run away with her purse!" Gladys exclaimed. She could barely catch her breath for laughing. "Oh my God . . ."

The school director and the journalist held a glance that vibrated with the rueful recognition that they had only themselves to blame for getting into this boat, taking on too many passengers, and giving away their oars.

Gladys was grateful for such an ally. Out in the field she visited many schools and homes. Hearing of her children's cases, the administrators at such places might cluck in sympathy, but only Agnes would burst into sobs, crying, "Bring the child here!"

And Agnes cried often, as evidenced by the number of Gladys's charges she had accepted into her school. Their trampled-flower stories conjured Agnes's tears no matter how many times they were recounted. Her willingness to absorb the pains of others had permanently creased her expression into one of bruised sympathy. Even in laughter—and she and Gladys found many occasions for mirth

—her contracted brow and contorted mouth could, at a distance, be mistaken for grief.

The two women had met when Gladys was assigned an article about primary school leaving-exam results, and Agnes was the only school director in the region less interested in the scores than in the students. Some of her students were like the needy kids Gladys profiled in her column, and she felt that God had sent the journalist her way. Gladys felt similarly, especially when Agnes agreed to let Ezra attend the school as a boarding student. After all the boy had endured, neither woman could bear to let him languish at a rural school where a classroom might be the ground under a tree. Where a twig or a finger might be a pencil. Where one class might contain ninety pupils. Where an overwhelmed teacher might not have the time or the patience to teach a seventeen-year-old how to spell his own name.

At Early Learning there were classrooms, desks, benches, a library, dormitories. Everything. Even proper toilets. To Ezra it was yet another miracle. And it had been made possible because the school director and the journalist had agreed to split the boy's tuition.

They were both middle-aged Christian women with great love for children, but that shared palette was shaded with contrasts. Unlike Agnes, Gladys hardly ever cried. This made her less womanly by some standards. People might assume she bore the emotional calluses of a clinic nurse or prison guard. In reality, Gladys's heart was often touched, but she had never been one to sit and sob in the face of bad news. When had tears ever solved a problem?

Then there were philosophical differences between the two women. Agnes funneled her compassion for her charges into doctrinal molds. Under her care, classroom lessons often had biblical underpinnings and Muslim children were given Christian names. Little Evelyn's original name was Aisha. Ezra's was Muzamiru. Faith's was . . . ? Gladys could not keep track. As if life were not complicated enough already!

After some time at Early Learning, Ezra had begun to talk about wanting to preach the word of God. Gladys inwardly grimaced. She would rather he talked about wanting to be a teacher or an engineer.

But she held her tongue, as it was not her future to decide. What was the point in giving children opportunities if you did not give them freedom?

When Ezra asked her to take him to get baptized, though, she drew the line. Some might expect that as a Christian, she would be eager to see a Muslim boy be born again. But she had no desire to tamper with anyone's religion. If Ezra wanted to get baptized, fine. But he would have to do it without her.

It was not Gladys's place to challenge Agnes in the running of her school. But in Gladys's opinion, the assistance offered to the students should not be clouded by anyone's personal beliefs. For many lost and abandoned children, their names and their culture were the only inheritance they could keep from their families. It was not right to pry that away from them, however gently. Such young saplings did not require pruning, only water.

THE SCHOOL DIRECTOR took Gladys, Esther, and Mike for a stroll around the new vegetable garden. Early Learning had recently moved to this location, and the grounds were still being developed. As usual on these visits, Gladys and Agnes discussed all the news concerning the children. Ezra's stalled progress in his classes. Douglas's impressive performance in his. The HIV status of one of the girls. Trevor's persistent and unsettling use of rude language. Gladys had hoped that after nine months at the school, the child might have settled into his studies; instead the acclimation had let loose an aggressive side.

"Your boy Trevor, he abuses me a lot," Agnes reported. "He says things like, 'You stupid woman, don't fool around with me. I will beat you with stones!'"

This was disturbing news to Gladys, as Trevor was very attached to his Auntie Agnes. The boy used terrible language around his classmates, but now he was talking this way to adults?

"I think as he was growing up, those are the words the mother used to use," Esther speculated. "As his brain was growing, it was doing the opposite of what the mother wanted. So she would be saying, 'Stupid boy! Stop doing that or I will beat you!'"

"And in fact that is how he talks," Gladys agreed. Trevor barely spoke, but when he did, it was only to declare "I will beat you!" or "I will kick you!" As though those were the only phrases he knew.

The women moved on to the pressing question of the P7 boys, including Douglas, who would soon be graduating from Early Learning. Secondary school would cost a good bit of money, which no one had.

"Don't you think there is some way these older ones can continue their education?" Gladys inquired.

Agnes shook her head emphatically. "I want them to learn life skills." She pointed around the grounds at the school's new water cistern, drainage system, and sturdy chicken coop. "You see, the ones working here, they are very clever," she explained. "The plumbers, the electricians, none of them ever went to university. University students go and collect all the knowledge here for four years"—she tapped her temple firmly enough to hurt—"but all that knowledge does not come out."

Gladys gave a noncommittal nod. True, higher education was no guarantee of success, but it seemed premature to trim a fifteen-year-old's future prospects. It had been over three decades since she had had to drop out of school, and the loss still stung.

Douglas was clever with machines; Agnes reported that the boy could fix all kinds of phones and radios. And he had walked many miles—Gladys recalled how his poor legs were swollen like the fruit of the sausage tree—looking for a better life. Surely he deserved a chance to aim high.

But such a chance required means. Gladys had none.

"What we learn has to be applied," Agnes was saying. Deborah, ever attentive, stood at her side. The director circled the girl's rounded shoulders with an arm. "Deborah. When you came to school, you knew nothing. What did you get here?"

"I got knowledge," the girl answered.

"And after knowledge?" Agnes prompted. "What did you get?"

"Understanding."

"And after understanding, then what?"

"Wisdom."

"And what is wisdom?"

"Wisdom is the application of what you have learned to do."

The testimony stretched on, Agnes leading her young witness with a lawyer's precision.

"And the Bible says that wisdom is much more than gold," Deborah stated.

"If you do not apply your knowledge, do you need to be in school?"

"No."

"No. If you do not apply it, you do not need to be in school. You should go home to the village and sit down and do nothing."

"If you don't apply it, you are . . ."

Agnes nodded her head encouragingly. "You are what?"

"You are foolish," said Deborah.

"You are nothing," said Agnes.

"You are George the First," said Mike.

"Oh my God!" Gladys chortled. "You are George the First!"

"George the First!" Esther repeated, giggling.

"Eeeeeee!" Gladys doubled over, almost losing her balance on the bumpy path. The school director and the children looked on, bemused, as the band of laughter played.

Mike: "Hah-hah-hah-hah-hah!"

Gladys: "Whoo-woo-woo!"

Esther: "Eh-eh-eh-eh!"

After a full minute, Gladys straightened up, wiping a hand across her streaming eyes. "Oh my God. George the First. Made my day!"

AS THE VISIT came to a close, Mike surprised one of the children with a gift. Though the tall man exuded severity, he had a soft spot for the quiet ones, the ones easily overlooked. The boy he singled out was an orphan who spoke so rarely that the adults had little occasion to use his name, even to remember it. Jeremiah.

"Boy!" Mike called, pointing him out with a raise of his chin.

Jeremiah made his hesitant way up to the front of the crowd, his eyes fixed squarely on Mike's belt buckle.

A curtain dropped into his view. It was a shirt. Not the typical used shirt that made its rumpled way from child to child before disintegrating into thready cobwebs. This was a man's shirt of thick, fine cloth, with long sleeves, buttons down the front, and a handsome pattern of traditional designs accented in egg-yolk yellow.

For a brief moment the boy seemed unsure whether Mike was giving him the shirt or just showing it to him. But then Mike shook it open for the boy to try on.

The shirt hung on him like a lab coat, but Jeremiah's smile was huge, undimmable.

"Ah-*hahhh* . . ." Gladys cheered. "It looks niiiiice."

"I just remembered it was in the boot of my car." Mike beamed. "That shirt cost forty thousand shillings. I have not even worn it yet."

Jeremiah's narrow shoulders lifted as though a row of medals had been pinned to his chest. An inconspicuous child like this one, Gladys knew, could feel the brief warmth of a spotlight forever.

"Thanks so much, Mike, thanks so much," she said.

The other children looked on, not so much in envy as in wonder. The shirt was so fine.

Gladys patted Deborah's hand. "Next time it will be your turn. And Rose, and Evelyn. And Faith. We will try to get something. Okay?"

A delegation of girls, led by Deborah, accompanied the visitors to the car. Behind them, his happiness temporarily eclipsing his shyness, Jeremiah followed, hands clutching his lapels to keep the miraculous shirt from flying away. As Mike bent his angular figure into the driver's seat, looking much like a praying mantis retreating into a knothole, the boy's eyes fixed on him with something between awe and love.

Deborah used Gladys's window frame to pull herself up on tiptoe. "Mommy Gladys," she whispered, "we need pads."

"Ehh! You don't have?"

The girls shook their heads, and Gladys shook her head along with them, clucking in dismay. How could these girls attend school with no sanitary pads?

Pads were forever lacking. So were books, shoes, clothes, sheets, medicine, and soap! And secondary school tuition and, *oh my dear,* birthday parties. Oh, Gladys was in problems! The persistence of these needs was overwhelming, like raindrops that could bring down a hillside.

"I will try to get something," she pledged.

The girls blinked expectantly. The tall man had magically produced that fine shirt; might Mommy Gladys also possess secret reserves?

But then the Volvo was pulling away.

"So, Mike, you see why I must escape."

"I am driving the getaway car." He laughed.

Gladys's chuckle faded, the rattle of the last beans shaken out of a sack. "We may joke about things, but it's bigger than I can handle. I don't know. There are times when I just don't know what to do."

Three Acres of Shade

After every visit to Early Learning School, Gladys walked away with an empty purse and a full mind. Good Samaritans might help with a child's initial resettlement costs, but long-term responsibility was another matter. How long could Gladys keep juggling her kids' needs? Paying for this one's medical expenses and deferring that one's tuition and begging patience and seeking support and worrying about her own expenses . . . Sometimes it felt like she was in an endless drought, trying to water a garden with a leaky bucket. If she ran fast enough, she could splash each plant with a few drops of water, but it was not enough for any of them to thrive.

The persistence of her needs wearied those around her as well. At the *New Vision* offices, she occasionally let her colleagues know when a case required immediate assistance, when a matter could not wait for the next issue's publication. "This girl has no money for transport," she might plead. Or, "This boy must have medicine right away."

Usually her coworkers responded. One might donate 2,000. One might dig deeper in a pocket for 5,000. Another might grumble, "Ah, you with your children. I only have money for lunch. Just take this 1,000." No matter the size of the contribution, Gladys would accept it with a smile. People gave what they felt they could give.

Recently, though, she had encountered a disturbing exception. The urgent case had involved a toddler with hydrocephalus named Mukisa. In Uganda, it seemed, a child was not named "lucky" for his or her circumstances but for having survived them. The baby's condition was severe, his swollen head taut and balloonlike atop his spindly body.

Gladys had made contact with CURE, a children's hospital in Mbale, close to the Kenyan border, that treated hydrocephalus cases. In order for CURE to help Mukisa, Gladys needed to find 25,000 shillings to deliver mother and child to the hospital. When she made the rounds with the story at the office, one particular woman, an editor, grilled her: "You want transport money to give to a needy mother? Where is she?"

Gladys said, "If you go downstairs, you will see there's a woman seated in reception there. With a boy with a big head."

The editor seemed unfamiliar with hydrocephalus, so Gladys explained the condition, the family's situation, and how the boy needed to go to Mbale to see if the doctors could perform the operation to stem the accumulation of fluid in his brain.

Others in the newsroom had contributed generously to Mukisa's cause, with several friends giving 5,000 each. The editor looked at Gladys, then at the bouquet of bills in her hand.

"But how sure are we that you are taking all that money to this woman?" she said.

Gladys was so shocked she could not move. It was as if the editor had thrown ice water and hot tea in her face at the same time. Did this person really see her as a charlatan? As someone who would use a poor woman and a sick baby to raise money for herself?

No one who knew her could accuse Gladys of self-indulgence, let alone corruption. Gladys didn't even go to the canteen in the newsroom. A lunch of 6,000 shillings was an extravagance she could not afford.

In the sting of the moment, Gladys almost walked away from the woman's desk. But she knew she must think before acting. *This is one of the editors to whom I have to submit stories,* she reminded herself. *So. Let me just ignore it.*

Gladys smiled patiently. "As I said, the mother is at reception. If you like, you can escort me down there when I hand the money over to her."

The woman gave her a prolonged, narrowed-eyed stare, followed by a single 1,000-shilling note.

Gladys reached for the bill, humiliation flooding her face. This from a coworker. A born-again woman, a "savedee."

In the end Gladys succeeded in raising the sum needed for Mukisa's transport, and some weeks later the operation saved the child's life. It frustrated her that the encounter with the editor burned as strongly in her memory as the boy's successful recovery. She could not forget how the woman had looked at her: like she was one of those beggar women holding up a baby in traffic, tapping on a car window with her hand out.

While she could not excuse such uncharitable behavior, she could not deny that in this country, people had grounds to be suspicious of do-gooders. There were so many con artists and fortune-seekers scattered about, from witch doctors to evangelists, bureaucrats to charity operators, land sellers to street hustlers, each with a convincing story to tell.

It was a matter not of defending her honor but of changing the situation so that she did not have to answer to anyone except herself. As the burden of her obligations to her children had increased, so had her dependence on others. It discomfited her. She had always been the self-sufficient one, the one who labored the longest hours and slept the least; the one who went out to work, raised her siblings and eventually her own kids; the one who took on whatever responsibility needed taking on.

Was Gladys the Capable becoming Gladys the Needy? A few years past the half-century mark, she was still sharing a small rented room, still owned nothing upon which to build a future for her growing brood of dependents or herself. She was no longer young, of course, but now she felt it in her bones. She had always plowed through her long days with an indefatigable energy, but her bimonthly bouts of malaria were harder and harder to push past. Her legs hurt all the time. People said she needed to lose weight. They scolded, "You must control your eating, or you will burst!" Gladys laughed off the suggestion. She had always been fat; she had not always been poor. She needed to control her finances.

"But Gladys," one of her less diplomatic friends had once re-marked, "you will always be poor because you work with the poor."

Her thoughts had been circling this problem for some time when she took on the assignment of profiling a woman farmer for the paper. Jane Bbale had begun farming after being driven from her marital home by her husband. Left with no income, she started bit by bit to cultivate. Over time she had amassed four cows, five goats, twenty pigs, a banana plantation, and a garden of fruits and veg-etables—all on a plot of one acre. "I had children and did not know how to cater for their school fees," Bbale told Gladys. "Ever since I started farming, life has changed for the better."

Gladys was impressed to learn that a pig could produce profit-able litters and then bring six to eight times its price at market. The woman's cows also provided a steady income stream through their milk production. And then there were Bbale's gardens. Vegetables alone brought in at least 20,000 a day. The profits of her enterprise, the farmer asserted, had put her children through both primary and secondary education.

This could be the solution Gladys had been seeking. Farming. Gardens. Land. It all sounded so solid. Productive. Fundamental.

There were, she acknowledged, a few hitches in this plan. One: she didn't know anything about starting a farm. Two: she didn't know anything about buying land. Three: she had no money to buy land.

New experiences excited Gladys more than they intimidated her, and this idea seemed very exciting indeed. Raising livestock, sell-ing produce, hiring workers—these were all activities regular people performed every day. She was a city woman, but as a child she had worked in her grandparents' garden. If she applied her full effort, there was no reason why she should not be able to acquire the neces-sary skills to start her own.

ON TUESDAYS, *New Vision* ran a section on farming called "Har-vest Money." Gladys began to scan those pages regularly, studying articles like "I Started Farming on One Acre but Earn Millions," "Cucumber Has Changed My Fortunes," "An Acre Can Grow

20,000 Cabbages," and "I Am Enjoying a Juicy Purse, Thanks to My Mango Trees."

It appeared she wouldn't need very much land. Just an acre or two nearby. She'd sell her produce to pay for her kids' school fees and expenses. As the gardens flourished, she'd be able to raise some livestock. It would make her very happy to start a piggery. Eventually she could build a house on the land, with a couple of rooms for kids to stay in. No more running from place to place every time she got involved in a case, trying to squeeze a child through a crack in some door.

Imagine. Someday she might even be able to build a small children's home on the land. Just for a dozen kids. Twenty at the most. This home of hers would not be crowded. It would not smell of urine. Men would not leer through the windows at the girls. Kids like Ezra and Douglas and Deborah could live there and eat healthy food from the gardens. Trevor would have plenty of room in which to chase his football. It would be a bright, happy place, where she could be sure her young charges were safe.

Of course, she was standing at sea level, imagining the view at the top of a mountain. But the mountain was not so very high, was it? It was not as though she were planning to win the lottery or become president. She only wanted a children's home. It felt like a big ambition because she had so little. And because she knew in her heart that this was her life's dream.

When she discussed her new plan with friends, she skirted the part about the children's home. Many already considered her involvement in the kids' welfare excessive. Gladys focused instead on the potential of the farming enterprise, and the response was encouraging. Cultivation was a wise investment, everyone said. Her boss, Cathy, even advised her to take out a loan from work to secure the land. She could borrow money at a low interest rate and have the payments taken directly out of her wages. Camilla, the *New Vision* receptionist, had put her children through school with help from this loan program.

This news made the plan suddenly feasible. But how much

money would Gladys need? As she lived in Entebbe, she naturally researched land prices nearby. A relative told her that a good price for an acre in Entebbe was 200 million! And prices in Kampala were even more outrageous—up to 850 million an acre there.

How naive she had been. One could not hope to buy farmland by a major urban center like Kampala or Entebbe. One had to go further afield. It was Cathy who gave her the lead on some land for sale in Luwero District, up in the Central Region.

"Luwero!" Gladys exclaimed. "How far away is Luwero from Entebbe?"

Perhaps sixty miles, Cathy replied.

"No," Gladys demurred. "I can't travel that far. I don't have a vehicle."

"So you think that is very far?" Cathy cast a sideways glance at Gladys, knowing well how her colleague commuted for hours every day from Entebbe to Kampala, and how she somehow managed to get herself to the farthest-flung places in pursuit of a story. "Listen. In Luwero, I know a place where you can get a three-acre parcel for ten million. Other places are ten times as much!"

Gladys became convinced, then excited, then discouraged. She borrowed money against her earnings, not realizing that land title and lawyers' fees required an additional chunk of funds. Esther and another friend came to her rescue, loaning her the necessary amount.

Once the three acres were hers, she allowed herself to feel excited again. It was a rectangular stretch of unruly bush, grass, and thorny acacia that would need to be cleared, tilled, planted, watered, fertilized, and harvested. It represented endless work but also endless potential, and if she allowed herself a moment to daydream, she could envision her future compound in the middle of a tidy plot, surrounded by maize and banana trees and vegetable gardens and pigs and goats and playing children.

And then her stomach would suddenly flip, her thoughts turning again to the enormous financial hole she had dug for herself. This was not the first time she had launched an enterprise, but her investments in the bookshop and the fish business had been of a far smaller magnitude. This was certainly her last, biggest risk, the one that would either propel her into stability or sink her into ruin.

How would she ever pay back those loans? What of the capital needed to pay laborers to work the land? How long would it take before she had maize or beans to sell? How many harvests before she started to see any profit? How often could she even make the journey to check on her plot? So many questions. She did not know if she really wanted the answers.

Oh God, she thought. *Have I really taken this on?* She had. She was doing this. And it was about time.

There was an old saying: "Old men sit in the shade because they planted a tree many years ago." That's what she wanted for herself and her children. A little patch of shade. It was a late start, but at least she had planted her tree.

The Enchanted Chapati

For months a dry spell had choked the country. There was no escape from the collective dread. It wafted in the stinging air. It weighted the dust that collected in noses and throats. It shriveled the silk of the young maize.

Then it rained. Gloriously, for days. And when the sun returned, it revealed a world of color as saturated as the *gomesi*, the ladies' dresses, at a wedding party. Red soil, blue sky, and everything else green, green, green. On the side of the road, cows were tethered on fresh patches of grass, grazing contentedly in the afternoon's long shadows. Goats knelt on folded front legs, as though in prayer, to nibble at soft new shoots.

Feeling the cooling breeze whisking through the windows of Mike's car, Gladys glimpsed in every direction figures bent intently over the land. After waiting so long for the rain, people rushed to tend this good damp soil. In bristling rice paddies, scanty bean patches, and endless maize fields, backs might be aching, but the sight of such industriousness cheered the heart. With hard work, what might her own plot of land soon produce?

Gladys recalled the sweaty satisfaction of working in her grandparents' gardens. On Saturdays she and the rest of the children would be digging, each sprout and seedling a tiny investment in the season. There was a mild, steady pleasure, like the breeze of a fan, in the knowledge that what they helped cultivate would someday be served at their own table. Groundnut, cassava, sweet potato, sugarcane, papaya—all was grown not for selling but for eating.

The garden produced fine coffee too. They would dry it, roast it, and grind it. Her grandfather and her grandy would sit at their own small table with individual steaming pots. And the flavor! That one was so good. The coffee people drank today, it was brown water compared to the coffee of Gladys's childhood. And they wondered why she only took tea.

Back then she was not Gladys. Everyone called her by her nickname, Gida. As the only girl among the fourteen children in the home, Gida was assigned to the gardens' only decorative crop: flowers. Every Sunday she would cut fresh blooms for the sitting room: red roses, pink roses, and some buttery yellow ones. One expected visitors at the reverend's house after church, and it was up to Gida to create a bouquet to welcome them as they walked through the door. How she had loved that job!

What happened to that culture? she wondered now. Maybe everyone had gotten too busy. When her gardens started producing, perhaps she would set aside a patch for flowers.

Gladys reeled in her mental kite string to focus on the afternoon's mission. She, Mike, and Esther were running late even by their own loose standards. The morning police station rounds had delayed their departure from Kampala. They were only midway through their three-and-a-half-hour drive northeast to Kaliro District, and already the sun was dropping as fast as a stone in water.

Well, they might end up convening at dusk, like moths. So be it. It was an important meeting, as it concerned a baby.

BEFORE SHE COULD make any plans to help a child, Gladys needed to find out all she could about how that particular child had come to be endangered. Some children were simply lost—those who let go of a mother's hand in a taxi park, for instance. Others were abandoned by overwhelmed relatives. Then there were kids who were mistreated or kidnapped or forced to beg in the streets. In every case, it was crucial not only to locate parents or relatives but to assess whether those family members might be counted on to assist the child.

Whenever possible, Gladys pursued her own investigations in order to make these assessments. Most case reports she received were little more than lists of facts. Sifting out the real story could be like guessing a fruit's flavor from the description of its shape, color, and weight. In the end, one had to climb the tree to taste it for oneself.

Take the report on today's case. It told her that the victim in the matter was a baby named Benjamin, now one year old. Benjamin's father, Ivan Nabwami, was being held in remand for child neglect. According to the report, Benjamin's mother was Ivan's second wife, Sylvia. Five months after giving birth, Sylvia had left the boy with Ivan and his first wife. In their care, Benjamin had suffered severe burns. The first wife claimed that she had intended only to bathe the baby, not to scald him. The police detained her, but as she was heavily pregnant, she was released. The baby had been temporarily placed in Young Hearts Orphanage, a children's home in Jinja.

Gladys planned to check on Benjamin, but first she had questions. As one officer had recently observed, with a mixture of admiration and bemusement, "The police just want to know who, what, where, and when. Gladys wants also to know why!" Of course! What good were four of the *W*'s without the fifth? How could one find proper solutions without the Why?

To get to the Why, Gladys wanted to meet the second wife, this Sylvia who had placed her newborn Benjamin in such a situation. What woman would give up her baby of five months and dump him with the man's first wife? Everyone knew of the problems when a cowife was forced to assume care of another woman's baby. Sylvia might be mentally defective. Or maybe, Gladys surmised, she was young and unable to cope.

Also, Gladys had not seen many fathers put in prison for neglect. Men were almost never arrested in this common situation. The report said that this Ivan had actually been brought to court and locked up. Why this one?

* * *

TO GET TO the heart of the matter, she would trace the story back to the Where: the home of Benjamin's mother, Sylvia, near Kaliro town.

They reached Kaliro in classic Uganda time — so delayed that everyone feared to look at the clock. Gladys got out of the car and looked up and down the street for Collins, the probation officer on the case. But she did not know what he looked like, as they had not met before.

She called his mobile. "We are finally here. Just look for the fattest lady in town."

A pause on the other end, then: "I see you."

A thin middle-aged man in dark trousers and a long-sleeved plaid shirt advanced toward the car, phone in hand. Though he had waited for her for hours, Collins returned Gladys's greeting of "Sorry, sorry!" with a light smile.

"This is Martin Waiswa, the grandfather of Benjamin, the father to Sylvia," Collins said, introducing the solemn-faced man stepping up beside him. Martin had a dusting of white stubble on his scalp and a deep, bird-in-flight crease extending across his forehead.

The family's village was a little over a mile away. Even for the short drive, Gladys could not hold back her questions.

"So, old man, why did your daughter dump her baby of five months?"

"The girl was impregnated when she was still in school," Martin answered.

"So she is young?"

"Yes. Sixteen."

"Ah." Gladys's hunch had been on target. This case involved not just one child but two.

IN THE FEW minutes it took to reach the village, the afternoon began its surrender to evening, the sky shifting from blue to gray. A few crickets started up a mild chorus, chirping at a heartbeat tempo.

Martin's compound was surprisingly large, with one finished brick house and five small huts: three for sleeping, two for kitchen and storage. Gladys and Esther stopped to appreciate the new green maize planted nearby, and a cheerful patch of beans. Soon there would be a nice harvest from this investment.

As family members emerged from the house with a bench, a couple of wooden stools, and a plastic chair, Gladys met Winnie, Martin's wife. The woman had to be close to forty, but the loose blue cloth around her small, impish face gave her the air of a child playing dress-up.

"So where is your daughter, the mother of Benjamin?"

"She is that one," said the mother, pointing. "Sylvia."

Gladys looked over to see a girl in a long red skirt and a pink-sleeved top decorated with a rainbow and the phrase HAPPY SWEET MISS. Sylvia smiled shyly at the ground as she knelt in greeting.

"My God! This sweet one . . . eeeeh!" Gladys's exclamation stretched out as long as a rooster's crow. "She even fears to look at people. Look at me."

The girl lifted her chin, but she still did not meet Gladys's gaze. The roundness of her features was not completely youthful; there were shadowed furrows extending down from the inner corners of her puffy eyes, as though a flow of tears had left permanent tracks.

Gladys placed an arm around Sylvia, cooing like a doting aunt. "How are you? But you look cute. What class are you studying?"

"P Six."

"P Six. Oh my God." This "second wife" was still only in primary school. "Where do you go to school?"

"I am not in school now."

"Eh?"

"I dropped out when I heard my son was burned."

A dozen bystanders, many of them young, had collected in the compound. "Are your brothers and sisters here, Sylvia?" Gladys asked, scanning the group. "Let me get a photo of the family first, before it gets too dark."

Martin and Winnie perched on the two stools as Gladys tried to weed out the onlookers from the offspring. "This one is also your child? Okay, you come here. The little ones should get in the front. Are you Sylvia's brother? No, I am pointing to that one . . ."

In the end the photo contained the couple, Sylvia, and four of Sylvia's siblings. "Are all of the children here?" Gladys asked, sizing them up in her viewfinder.

"Some of the boys are not here," replied Sylvia's mother. "We have nine children." Nine! No wonder they had so many sleeping huts.

Gladys now had the full Who of the story: Martin and Winnie were the parents of nine children, of whom Sylvia was the oldest girl. Sylvia and the arrested Ivan were the parents of baby Benjamin, who had been abused by Ivan and Ivan's first wife.

The camera clicked away. No one smiled, nor did Gladys prompt them to.

"Okay. Let us sit and have a talk."

AS THE NIGHT descended along with the mosquitoes, Gladys parsed out the tale of Sylvia and baby Benjamin, relying on the probation officer, Collins, and Mike, who also spoke the local dialect. Recounted at length, the What of the story was far more repellent than the case report had indicated. If God was in the details, so was the devil.

Ivan Nabwami, a married father of four, was thirty-five when he set his sights on a pretty young girl in the village: Sylvia. When Martin and Winnie tried to chase him away from their home, he charged like a rutting buffalo. Brandishing a machete, Ivan hacked the family's plastic kitchen basins to pieces and threatened to do the same to anyone standing in his way. The man's behavior grew increasingly shocking. The family would find him in front of the house with his trousers down, shouting, "Don't mess with me!" He would even shake his private parts at Sylvia's mother.

Soon Sylvia became pregnant by Ivan. She was fourteen.

Contrary to the police report, Sylvia was hardly a "second wife," and Ivan's interest in her evaporated well before Benjamin was born. Martin went to him to demand money for his grandchild's support:

one million shillings to be paid within five months. While Ivan was not wealthy, he had employment as a brick loader for trucks. Even the magistrate insisted he must pay. But the man refused to produce even one shilling.

Stymied by his defiance, Sylvia's parents went to the police to try to get Ivan arrested for defiling their daughter. But they did not have her birth certificate, and the police said they could not prosecute.

"They could not ascertain her age?" Gladys interjected. The girl was unmistakably a child. "But can't you just look at her and see?"

"You must prove it," Mike said.

Sylvia's father played his last card. He went back to Ivan and insisted that if the man was unwilling to pay for Benjamin's upkeep, Ivan would have to take the child into his own home.

The bluff backfired. Ivan promptly snapped up the child. Now Sylvia's family was left with no money and no baby.

In his father's home, Benjamin was left at the mercy of Ivan's first wife, who had her own four children to take care of. The unwelcome stepchild was abused and neglected to the point where the authorities were alerted, bringing Collins into the case.

"The police could not give the child back to Sylvia's family because what? The matter was still before the court." Collins had a way of turning a statement into a question, which he would immediately answer himself. Fearing that his listeners would lose interest, he rushed in like an actor meeting a perfunctory curtain call. "So what I did was withdraw the child from both parents. Because probation is given the power to remove the child from what? A place of danger."

"Tell us," Gladys pressed, "what was the danger in the home where the baby was? What was really happening?"

"The stepmom would go to do her work, locking the baby in the house. Likewise the father disappears. So Benjamin would be what? Left alone, helpless," Collins explained. "I received reports that they would leave him in the kitchen, where he was defecating on himself."

"What I want to know is, didn't they have some other children in the home?" asked Gladys. "Why was Benjamin being isolated in that kitchen?"

"They always segregated him from the other children," Martin answered. Even when the adults were home, they would sometimes tie the infant's hands or pen him in the chicken house. "When they were taking porridge, they would leave him on the side. If he tried to get food, they would beat him. He would be beaten all the time."

"When we rescued the boy," Collins confirmed, "the child was wanting in feeding."

"Malnourished," said Gladys.

"Malnourished. Bony. And he was burned. The whole of the buttocks, and this part." He leaned forward, gesturing toward his lower back. At this, Sylvia turned her face away.

"And how old was he? By then?"

"About one year."

"Who burned him?"

Sylvia's mother, Winnie, spoke up. "The other children told us that the first wife burned Benjamin because he stole from her. He tried to take some of her food."

"A one-year-old baby? Can he steal food? He's just hungry! How do you accuse a one-year-old child of stealing?" Indignation amplified Gladys's words. She was attacking the messenger, but she could not help it. "That is wrong! Even a child of three years cannot be said to be a thief. If a child takes food, it is only because he's hungry."

"We were told," said Winnie, "that the baby would eat his own feces."

HOW COULD THESE adults starve a baby in their own home, let alone a baby who was the man's son? A man who had employment and a chicken coop and a roof over his family's heads? This was no consequence of poverty. Nor was it the neglect so common with an unwanted child. This was cruelty.

Cruelty required an expenditure of effort. Cruelty was willful. It was not a lightning strike but a struck match.

No matter how many times Gladys encountered such cases, she felt the shock of the offense. The breakdown of culture, the disregard for humanity—each was a crisp, stinging slap. While such behavior was not inconceivable, it was unacceptable. It affronted not her sense of piety but her sense of decency. Every collision with an Ivan sent a shudder through her foundation.

But that foundation always held — cemented, as it was, in the childhood her grandparents had provided during those golden years before everything fell apart. It was through them that she knew how life should be. How life could be.

Even with fourteen children under her grandparents' roof, every mouth was fed. And at dinnertime, others often joined in. The long dining table had simple benches on both sides, so the family could always squeeze. Friends were excited to visit the reverend's house, as they knew they would be invited to stay and eat. And how good it had felt to be able to invite them.

To her grandy, feeding well had been a priority. That did not mean meat every day; it meant variety. Whatever was in season — maize, sweet bananas, pawpaws, mangoes, so many fruits and vegetables! — she would bring to the table. On special occasions she might serve a chicken.

Gladys's grandparents expected the children to heed and respect their elders, but they did not place the needs of the young below those of the old. In many rural homes, children ate last, on leftover scraps that gave them swollen bellies. Gladys hated to see that, especially when those young ones would be sent for water in the morning without food. Growing up, she and her siblings and cousins fetched water, but they always ate breakfast.

Many homes raised poultry only to sell the eggs, but her grandy wanted her family to have that good food too. Whichever child collected the eggs would keep his or her eye out for the ones that the chickens had pecked. The intact eggs Grandfather would take to Kampala, but the imperfect ones Grandy would serve for breakfast. Oh, the grandchildren ate well. Their grandy would not even allow the herdsman to dilute the milk.

For all this apparent abundance, though, her grandparents had not been rich. They did not live a posh life. There was no treasure tucked away. Everything they harvested and earned was folded back into the welfare of those who depended on them, and the children in turn practiced the basic decency of sharing their better fortune. One measured one's wealth not against the negative balance of others but by how far it could be spread. How could one enjoy filling one's belly if a hungry baby sat crying in the kitchen?

SADLY, IT SEEMED these days that Gladys's grandparents, not the Ivans, were the anomalies of the world. What was surprising about the case of baby Benjamin was not the abuse but the arrest.

"What I really wanted to know," Gladys asked Collins, "I rarely hear about fathers being put in prison like this one—what was so special about this case?"

"The father of the child is a bit arrogant, I could say. He doesn't care, even if he is talking to a police officer," the probation officer replied. "He was taken to court first for torturing the child. The court warned, 'We are giving you back your child. But don't repeat this.'" But then Benjamin was burned, and the court did not take kindly to Ivan's disregard. "The magistrate said, 'Oh! You are again back in court. After we warned you.' So that is the reason why he is in what? Prison."

"For not obeying the court's order."

"Yes."

So. The defilement, the harassment, the nonpayment of support, even the abuse of the child—these alone could not send a man like Ivan to remand. It was not enough to prey on the powerless. One had to annoy the powerful.

THE THICKENING SKY was proving moonless, and Gladys strained to see the writing in her notebook. She still had questions, ones which she felt Sylvia could answer more fully in her own tongue. "Collins—sorry to bother you, as we came late, but there's some things I really want to know. Sorry about the time."

The probation officer dipped his head graciously. In his profession, one counted days rather than hours.

"In this case, okay, it was defilement," Gladys began. "But did Sylvia go into this relationship with Ivan willingly? As someone in love? Or was she forced?"

Collins addressed his translation to the girl's mother, Winnie, but Gladys redirected his attention toward the girl.

"Please, I want you to ask her the questions. What promises did that man give? Did he say, 'I will marry you'? Did he say, 'I will be catering for your needs'?"

Collins translated. Sylvia listened, her eyes cast downward. Fireflies circled her head like embers stirred up by a breath.

"Yes," she answered.

"Like what? What did he promise?"

"He said he was going to buy me shoes."

They waited for more, Collins leaning in to catch the girl's soft voice. The crickets' chorus was almost deafening now. *Why are you people still out here?* they seemed to shout. *At least give us small things the night.*

"What else?" Gladys prodded gently.

"He said he was also going to rent for me a place."

"Anything more?"

"That is all. He would buy me shoes and rent for me a room."

"So when he said those things, that's when you accepted to be with him?"

Sylvia shook her head slowly. "I had refused, but he bought me a chapati and put some spells on it. After I ate it, I followed him."

In the pause that followed, the visitors exchanged looks. They could not easily see each other's faces, but Mike's expression was clear: *Are you kidding me?*

People in these rural areas believed in charms and spells and curses and possession. Illness, infidelity, accidents, all could be traced to witchcraft. Even the jiggers infesting their children's feet were sent by spirits. Medical doctors were less trusted than witch doctors. After all, could a physician restore health, enact revenge, or make a person rich?

To Gladys, it made no sense. If a witch doctor could make someone rich, why was he living in a hut? Why did he require money to help people? And why were his children not in school? Still, belief in such magic had deep roots. As the granddaughter of an Anglican reverend, Gladys was raised with different beliefs, but she kept her opinions to herself.

"How did you get to know that the chapati had charms on it?"

The relayed question evoked no audible response. Sylvia's silence spoke to her conviction that the man had cast spells on her food. Like her baby, Benjamin, she had eaten because she was hungry. And like Benjamin, she had gotten burned.

"That Ivan. Did he even buy for you those shoes?" Gladys asked.

The girl did not meet her eyes. "No."

Gladys turned to Collins, addressing him in reporter mode. "What comment do you have about such men who defile young girls? This situation, and what brings it up?"

"In this community we have what? Poverty. Poverty has eaten up the communities. And you find that because of poverty, a girl is interested in someone who can provide, if her father cannot provide certain things. And what happens is even the father might say, 'You go with him, he looks after you.'"

"Eh! So the parents accept."

"Uh-huh. So you will find that they will not report a situation like this. This father might say to the man, 'Okay, bring me one million shillings, and I will leave you alone.' But if the man does not bring the money, that's when they involve the police."

Collins spoke of poverty, but this family was not starving. Sylvia's father was not grasping for a lifeline, he was trying to reap a harvest. A million shillings was a large sum, enough to buy a couple of cows.

"So what you're saying is, if Ivan had given Sylvia's parents that one million, they wouldn't have gone back to court. And we wouldn't have heard of this story."

"Most likely."

Here now was the Why. Gladys had wondered why a mother would dump her baby of five months with a cowife. The decision had rested not with Sylvia but with Sylvia's father. He had gambled with his grandchild and lost.

• • •

IT WAS FULL night now, the sky illuminated sporadically by distant lightning and the blinking trails of fireflies. She knew that Collins should be headed home, that all the kids should be preparing for sleep, and that she should escape the mosquitoes attacking her arms and legs with carnivorous abandon. But she could not leave without giving a few minutes to Sylvia's mother, who was not well.

Out of earshot of the group, Winnie had confided that she had been having complications after surgery—a hysterectomy had not properly healed. Having written often about women's health issues, Gladys thought she might be able to offer some advice.

"When your uterus comes out, it can be from too many births," she commented, hearing that the difficulties had started during Winnie's pregnancies. "You have nine children. Why did you keep on producing when you were already having these problems?"

"The trouble is, when I was delivering these children, my husband was not pleased. Because we were producing mostly boys. He doesn't like boys."

"Your husband wanted girls."

"Yes, so I kept trying to produce girls. I had three boys, then I finally got this girl here. Now I have six boys and three girls."

The picture was becoming clear. Most men wanted boys, to continue the family and leave a legacy. But this father wanted girls. Why? For dowry. In marriage, girls could bring a price; boys had to pay that price. In an effort to balance profits and expenditures, this woman had pushed out baby after baby until her insides collapsed.

"When this man showed up for Sylvia, I really cried," Winnie said, her eyes shining in the dark. "We tried to get her away from him, but she couldn't listen. It was because of those charms on the chapati. When the man came to the house, the girl would follow him, because of those charms."

Gladys, keeping both hands firmly on the lid of her incredulity, asked softly, "Is your daughter safe? When Ivan gets out, can he come for her again?"

"I don't know."

"You are the mother. What is your plan?" Gladys continued, more sternly now. If she did not say these things to this woman, perhaps no one else would. "That this girl will just be here to produce more children? Instead of studying?"

"I would try to encourage her to study," Winnie offered meekly. "But she is just sitting here now. She just sits."

"As her parent, can't you at least take her to some people who can talk to her about family planning? Even if she gets another boyfriend, she does not have to get pregnant. She must control it."

"She doesn't want a man. She says she hates men."

It was not a real answer, and they both knew it. The girl was only sixteen. Why pretend that she would never want a man? What other route of escape did Sylvia have?

The crickets were in full force, their trill urgent and metallic, the ticking of an overwound clock. Gladys encouraged another visit to the doctor and slipped what little money she had into Winnie's hand. The woman thanked her effusively but quietly, so as not to draw attention to the exchange.

Martin approached, offering his hand in farewell. Behind him, his daughter sat on a stool, just as her mother had described. Wilted and inert.

Gladys pressed: "Tell me, why is your daughter still not back in school?"

"Right now she is not really understanding much of her education," Martin said with a shrug. "She does not feel very clever. She can't pick studies."

"Maybe she can learn some tailoring, or how to plait hair," Gladys suggested. "It's very, very wrong to keep her sitting here." Sooner or later baby Benjamin would need to be resettled with family. How could his teenage mother provide for him, with her limited schooling and no skills?

It seemed that Mike had had the same thought. He stood over the girl, counseling her with the intensity of a coach sending a player into a crucial match.

"If you think you can't do well in the classroom, learn to do stuff with your hands," Mike urged. "Learn to fix cars. Learn to be a carpenter. There is no job that is not meant for girls. You can do anything a boy can do."

Esther the electrician nodded approvingly. For her part, Sylvia seemed startled by this attention from an adult male — attention that was neither authoritarian nor seductive. She ducked out of its path as if it were intended for someone else.

"If you can learn to make sweaters," Gladys jumped in, picking up the thread, "you can make sweaters for different schools here, and before you realize it, you will have changed your life! So you mustn't just sit here and think that there's nothing you can do." She circled the girl with an arm. "I don't like hearing that you don't want to go back to school. Is this what you want? To stay in the village and have these men make babies in you all the time?"

"Maybe I will go back next year," Sylvia mumbled unconvincingly.

"Next year? And miss two terms?"

No answer came. The girl's eyes were opaque in the full dark. The night had left no light to reflect in them.

"WHY DON'T THESE men like Ivan want to use contraception?" It was a short drive to get Collins back to town, and Gladys would not waste her remaining minutes with the veteran probation officer.

Collins spread his hands. "They say that God told them to do — what?"

"'I'm sending you into the world to produce so that your number grows,'" Gladys paraphrased.

"Yes!" Collins uttered, startled that one of his questions had actually been answered.

"So they quote the Bible."

"Yes. And they say that family planning is put there by the *mzungus* to keep the numbers of Africans down."

"Ah, so they think the Europeans want to make Africans reduce their number." Gladys had heard this theory before. "But do they see the *mzungus* producing like this?"

Collins's laugh was good-natured. He stepped out of the car and into the late night, waving away Gladys's thanks and apologies. The man had the patience of a tortoise crossing the Kalahari.

The main road was clogged with swaying sugarcane trucks, their cargo piled precariously high above the walls of their beds. As the car grudgingly trailed the overloaded caravan, Gladys mulled over the evening's revelations. What could she form out of this story, now that she had her Who, What, Where, When, and Why?

She found her thoughts drifting past baby Benjamin to his teen-age mother. Sylvia was a child too. She lived under her parents' roof. She appeared healthy. Yet she still seemed somehow "lost and abandoned."

"I didn't like how Sylvia thinks she can't learn," Gladys mused out loud. "It's good that Mike has tried to talk some sense into her. Just because she has produced a child doesn't mean she can't go back to school or go in for something!"

"The father is putting that idea in her head: *You can't pick studies,*" Mike responded, bristling. "So they are agreed on that — they confirm each other's low opinion of her abilities."

"That's very, very wrong!" Gladys said. "You can't tell a girl of that age that she can't do anything. No. She's too young to give in like that."

"The problem is, they don't have anybody around who is an example," said Esther.

"Yes. An auntie who is a nurse or policewoman . . ."

"The only example she has is marriage."

But for Sylvia, even that path had become obstructed, Mike reminded them. A girl who had been sampled and burdened with another man's child was damaged goods. She would not fetch a high dowry.

A man might normally demand two cows for a daughter, Mike estimated. "Then maybe three or four goats. And two chickens."

"People in this area cannot afford such a dowry," Esther countered. "You might find in some cases that it is just one goat."

"In this century!" Gladys smacked her lips in disapproval.

"It is what is happening in many villages," Esther observed in her impassive way, as though she were talking about the traffic or the weather or the corruption of politicians.

"But how do we change it?" Gladys scolded, glaring out at the oil-black countryside. "It must change, surely!"

It made no sense to treat a wife like a breeding sow and daughters as livestock. Why not just raise cattle or goats in the first place? Or plant more crops. Or educate your child to enable her to contribute to the family upkeep. Surely that was the best investment the family could make. It was the only form of wealth that could not be taken away.

"And the price of a chapati?" Mike prompted.

"Five hundred," the women answered in unison.

"So this man Ivan, he gets himself sex, he takes everything from this girl, for five hundred shillings." The price of one minute of airtime. "Can you imagine?"

"'But he promised me chapati and shoes.'" Gladys imitated Sylvia's soft voice, then gave a yelp of physical pain. "*Eee!* Oh my God. All your future, you surrender. For a chapati. And shoes that do not come."

It wasn't only girls in rural families. In his latest column, Dr. Love had chastised parents for pressing their daughters to find husbands immediately after college. He urged them to give their graduate "say, ten years, so she will have time to see the world, discover herself, and make money." It was a tough sell. At every level of society, a girl was a hanging piece of fruit, prized only as long as she was ripe for picking.

EVERY DAY THAT Gladys had lived with her grandparents, she had known her value. She learned as the boys learned, she played as they played, and she worked as they worked. In Grandfather Obadiah's eyes, however, she was not the boys' equal. She was something more. When he went into town to sell eggs and gather provisions and make visits, his Gida was the one he chose to accompany him. Sitting at his side, how could she fail to feel important?

Gida was the only kid who was never caned. Oh, the canings were funny to remember now. Her grandfather thought it wrong to break off a stiff branch to use on a child, so he would use the soft banana leaves used for wrapping food. Although it was like being beaten by a feather duster, the naughty boys would cry and put on a show. But Grandfather could never punish his beloved Gida. He could not even pretend to punish her. She was special.

Ah, but that life was good! And even when life became bad, after her grandfather's death, her father's abandonment, and so many other reversals, she never forgot that she was special. Perhaps it was this knowledge that had carried her through everything that came to pass. *If the ones who raise you give you love,* she thought, *there is a way you feel that your life is worth living.*

And here, this Sylvia. This was a beautiful young girl. But everyone, including the girl herself, had written her off as a loss. Her value was less than that of a goat.

No wonder she had succumbed to the charms of that chapati. It wasn't magic. It wasn't witchcraft. It was only that the chapati made her believe that she was special.

Zam

Life was tough for the very poor. More so for very poor women; most of all for very poor young mothers. But the bleak truth was, no matter how difficult their lot, it was up to these girls to build something out of their lives. No one would be there to do it for them.

In her work Gladys paid special attention to struggling mothers, stressing to them that their lives had not ended. "You are young," she would urge. "You can still be creative. What do you feel you can do? What help do you need to do it?"

Sometimes they needed a bit of shaking up. There were some, like Sylvia, whose belief in their own dependency had made them vulnerable in the first place. But given half a chance, a girl could show surprising resourcefulness.

A year ago, when Gladys was researching a story on the problems of teen pregnancy, she met two young women at a resource center for teens: Banura, seventeen, and her cousin, Zam, twenty-two. Gladys was drawn to the plight of Banura, who had been raped by an uncle when she was thirteen. Now HIV-positive and the mother of a three-year-old daughter and an infant son, the girl was so dispirited she hardly seemed to notice her children. Zam, who was acting as a "peer mother" to her younger cousin, was pregnant herself.

As Banura mumbled and sighed out her answers to the reporter's questions, she absently nursed her baby at her breast. Gladys said nothing at the time, but this risk of HIV transmission worried her for days. Even if she scrounged up 40,000 shillings to buy Banura infant formula, what would happen when the tin went empty? The girl needed some means to support herself and her children.

Some poking and prodding revealed a flicker of interest in the idea of a small business. Gladys raised a little bit of capital for Banura to start up a food kiosk and some funds to send her daughter to school for two terms. When Gladys had no funds for the third term, Banura proudly declared that she had earned enough from her enterprise to cover her daughter's fees by herself. It was a modest but undeniable triumph.

When Banura's older cousin Zam gave birth to her own baby, she came to Gladys. "Mommy, the father of the child abandoned me," she said. "Can you assist us? I am here too."

As Gladys had catered for Banura, it seemed only fair to help Zam. After two months she had gathered enough money for a little stove and some pots, stools, and cooking oil. The young woman did not let her down. Within days Zam was up and running, stirring pots of piping hot *katogo*, a breakfast dish one could sell all day, on a busy Kampala lane.

THE VALUES OF resilience and creativity Gladys held up to those young women loomed large as she planned her own three-acre start-up. The entrepreneurial spirit had infected Esther as well. She purchased a smaller land parcel less than an hour's walk from Gladys's plot. The two friends joked that they were starting their own village.

As Gladys could not afford to make the trip to the plot in Luwero more than once a month or so, she required help in managing her land. And as she knew no one in the area, she had only one choice: the man who had sold her the parcel of land, Jovan Kiviri.

In those parts, Kiviri was a big man, a successful landlord. It seemed that everyone knew Kiviri, and everyone grumbled about him. Gladys began sending Kiviri regular payments through her phone: 150,000 shillings a month to oversee her parcel and hire laborers to tend to the land.

On her visits, the progress was visible to Gladys: the cleared brush and weeds, the rows of grasslike maize shoots, young beans and cassava plants, the lines of saplings that would grow to delineate the edges of her property. It was looking more and more like a real garden.

While it would take many years to realize her dream of a children's home, she was eager to start building something on the land. A simple house. Through some great stroke of luck or act of God, an offering of funds came to her from some Good Samaritans.

Aside from the occasional round at the office, Gladys refrained from personally soliciting donations; if people wanted to help, they would do it on their own. If readers were moved to assist a child, they could call the phone numbers listed in her column. Sometimes people would call her to ask where to send money. Or they would donate goods: books, bedding, clothing. After she wrote an article about a boda driver who had been mangled in a truck collision, a reader even donated a supply of colostomy bags. She never expected to receive any donations herself, though, so she was overwhelmed to receive support from some Americans who had heard of her work with needy people.

The funds were not enough to finish construction, but with Kiviri's help she went ahead and started anyway. After a few weeks a solid cement foundation stood in the middle of her plot, circumscribed by a two-foot-high brick wall, marking the precise point at which the money had run out.

Gladys hoped that such sturdy groundwork would declare her presence to the neighborhood: she was here to stay. One could argue that the stunted foundation only underlined the owner's lack of resources, but Gladys enjoyed gazing upon it. It was a step forward.

As the months went by, though, expenses continued to mount. Labor costs. Bush clearing. Hoes. Slashers. Jerry cans for water. More bush clearing. Spraying for pests. Gladys hadn't known about the need to spray beans!

When she expressed discouragement, Esther assured her, "It is always like that. You can't get money out of nothing. You have to put money in to get money out."

While Gladys did not expect much bounty from the first crops, the prospect of chipping away at her debt excited her. But the first harvest disappointed even her modest expectations: the two paltry sacks of beans did not even cover her labor costs.

Prospects for the next harvest looked no brighter. Some of the crops were growing more slowly than expected. The weather was again unseasonably dry. Most disturbing, though, were the subtle signs of plunder. Beans were disappearing. Ears of maize vanished off stalks.

PROBLEMS DEMANDED ANALYSIS; solutions required creativity. Gladys spent her long commuting hours and sleepless nights thinking on her situation. Everyone knew that the large lady who owned this plot did not live in the village. They could see her arriving on a boda boda, visiting the gardens for a few hours, then moving back down to the main road to catch a taxi. They knew she would not soon return. Maybe not even for a month.

With gardens, Gladys had learned, thieves usually came in the night. But her place was unattended: anyone could pick and choose from her gardens in broad daylight, like shoppers at the market. There was little risk in snatching a few ears of maize or some beans, especially when the theft might go unnoticed for weeks.

Gladys could not hold Kiviri responsible for such setbacks. His own home sat way over near the main road, and anyway, it was not Kiviri's job to monitor who might be coming or going. The gardens needed someone to guard them.

It was then that Gladys started to think about Zam.

RECENTLY THE YOUNG women's food businesses had not been doing well. The police performed periodic sweeps of the neighborhood, overturning kiosks in an effort to clear the streets of informal vendors. In the latest raid, Zam and Banura had lost their frying pans and other supplies.

It occurred to Gladys that Zam might be interested in a job. The girl had shown initiative by acting as her cousin's peer mother and approaching Gladys for help when her own baby was born. She might be the type to make something of such an opportunity. After all, the ultimate purpose behind Gladys's farming enterprise was to support her kids and other disadvantaged people. So why was she paying Kiviri 150,000 shillings a month when she could be directing that money to a needy young mother?

It was not that Gladys believed that Zam could run the place. The young woman might have no experience at all in farming. But Gladys was looking for someone she could trust.

Even if she could trust her, would Zam want to come out to this country place? She was a city dweller, living on the lively, crowded Kampala streets of malls and shops and music and crowds and cars. There were no big buildings out here in the village. The nights were black and quiet. Move here? The girl might laugh in Gladys's face.

Prepared to spend a good amount of time selling the positives of this homely endeavor, Gladys introduced the idea to Zam. But the girl immediately said, "Oh! Yes, Mommy, I am ready! Where is the place?"

"It is deep in the village!" Gladys replied, startled into more candor than she had planned.

"Oh, it is not such a problem," Zam said easily, "whether the village or what."

"But really, can you dig? You, who have been staying in town?"

"I remember digging at my father's place when I was eight years old." The family garden had paid for young Zam's school fees.

"Okay." Gladys suddenly felt like it was she who had just been convinced, rather than the other way around. "I want you to help me."

She invited Zam to the *New Vision* offices to discuss the plan. They sat down in the conference room and compiled a list of requirements for Zam's new home: a mattress, a blanket, saucepans, jerry cans, a lamp, a kettle, plates, a knife, a spoon, paraffin, salt, soap. They wrote down everything they could think of, down to packets of matchbooks. The projected costs were daunting, but Gladys agreed to cover them. She would not dump this young mother and baby in that remote place without basic necessities.

Zam and her baby, Maria, could not live on the plot itself, with only the foundation of the house completed. Gladys rented a small room from a woman with a house a couple of miles away, near Esther's plot. Some kind neighbors there were willing to watch baby Maria when Zam went to tend to the gardens.

The living arrangement did not give the gardens much security from thieves, but at least Gladys now had an ally on the ground.

"THIS IS A good-sized plot, Gladys," Mike remarked. "You can do a lot with this piece of land."

It was a pleasantly overcast November day in Luwero; an early-morning sprinkling of rain had intensified the colors of dark earth and green vegetation. As they walked the length of Gladys's parcel, Esther breathed deeply, appreciatively. Unlike city air, fumy with exhaust and sewage and burning trash, this air was sweetly filtered through trees and bush.

"I tell you, I was overwhelmed," Gladys said. "What to plant here, what to plant there . . ."

"Didn't you want more land, not less?" Esther teased.

The two women had not been able to visit their gardens for weeks, and they were eager to measure the height of the stalks and the breadth of the leaves with their own eyes. They hastened past some thorny branches, ignoring their snagged skirts.

Gladys was eager for counsel. Her land was still a patchwork: there were areas with crops, areas still thick with bush, and cleared sections that had not yet been planted. As with almost all subjects, Mike was quite knowledgeable about farming. As they walked, the trio discussed various options for the uncommitted areas: coffee, jackfruit, papaya, pumpkin, groundnuts, avocado, pineapple, cacao, perhaps mangoes . . .

"My neighbor is growing passionfruit," Gladys commented.

"There is a lot of money in passionfruit."

"Ah-*hah*. But I now can't start copying my neighbor."

Mike blinked, incredulous. "Who tells you you can't grow passionfruit? You are not copying!"

"Is it okay?"

"Yes," Esther assured her with a smile. "It is not copying."

A slight incline led them to a section of maize. The stalks had grown, but like many of Gladys's children, they were small and thin for their age.

"I think the soil is not so good for maize," Gladys observed.

"No, it's not the soil," Mike said, tapping at the ground with a toe of his oxford, which somehow remained shiny despite the dirt. "As long as you put fertilizer in every single hole you are planting in."

"In every hole?"

"Yes. When you plant maize, put fertilizer with the seed."

Gladys sighed. "Ah, I haven't applied any fertilizer."

There was so much she did not know. So much she did not even know to ask. Digging in her grandparents' garden was very different from planning three acres of her own.

A figure came jogging up the path toward them.

"Eh, Mommy!"

"Eh, Zam-u!"

The women greeted each other warmly, and Gladys introduced Zam to Mike. "Zam was pregnant when I met her. And now she has a one-year-old. So this is our baby!"

Zam swiveled around to display the child on her hip. Baby Maria was a serious, long-faced child. Her hair sprouted in wild tufts above her scalp, and her forehead dimpled at the inner ends of her eyebrows. The effect was an air of perpetual consternation. In contrast, her mother radiated self-assurance. At twenty-three, Zam was full of an energy that was youthful but not giddy; she could stand perfectly erect even with twenty pounds of baby on one arm. Hers was an earthy attractiveness; she had full lips, strong teeth, and a smattering of bumps on her cheeks. Her best feature was her eyes, with their sleepy lids and subtle feline slant. A rose-colored knit cap covered her hair; a small stud decorated her nose. Her words flowed out in bright, measured bursts, like the songs of birds that have already claimed their territory.

"I have no problem working in the gardens," she said. With her free arm, she squeezed Gladys to her side. "Because my mother Gladys is here. I did not imagine that I would be in this position, but God has got his own ways. He has got his miracles."

Disengaging from each other, the women wasted no time in turning to the business of the day. Zam presented her needs with the orderliness of an accountant.

Baby Maria was sick. She was suffering from fever and diarrhea; Zam needed money for antimalarial medicine. In terms of the garden work, her progress on the bean planting had been slowed by the thorny bushes. She only had plastic slippers; she needed boots. Her panga was too dull to slash the weeds; she needed a file for sharpening the blade. The second panga was missing, and Kiviri had not delivered the two hoes he had promised.

Then there was the issue of the *matoke* planting. Gladys had sent Kiviri money to purchase and plant 140 of the banana seedlings. Zam claimed the lot was short by two dozen.

"Did you count them?" Esther demanded to know.

"I counted them. This man is not doing the right thing." Since Zam had arrived, she had reported many problems with the landlord: unfinished work, undelivered supplies, and pilferage.

"But as I tell you, that is what you must expect when you are not around," Gladys said with a sigh.

Mike nodded. "And that's when you have to weigh the balance of, do you raise hell?"

"Also, look there." Zam pointed out a section of field where there were ragged holes interrupting neat rows of crops. "The rain was very heavy and loosened the soil around the cassava, so people could come and just pluck them out."

Gladys gasped. With the cassava still a year from harvest, thieves had stolen entire plants.

"There is one I suspect of stealing the cassava," Zam declared. She had followed a trail of muddy footsteps to a neighbor's door. "I will deal with them. But I am really praying that the house will be quickly finished so I can start sleeping here. Then I can keep an eye on things, and they will never again be able to trespass."

"Ah-*hahh* . . ." Gladys seconded.

"They watch me," Zam said, annoyance tightening her mouth. "I leave at eleven a.m. to go and cater for the child, and by the time I come back they've already slipped in here and raided the maize."

At Gladys's feet, the remaining cassava plants looked vulnerable, their broad, flat leaves reaching up like open, trusting hands.

"So your biggest problem is people who are stealing."

"Yes. But I will deal with them," Zam said again, almost cheerfully.

"If you know that thieves are after the maize, can you sell it before it is stolen?"

"What I think: we shouldn't sell the raw maize," Zam replied. "We should grind it into flour. We need to sell the processed flour, not just the maize itself."

Listening a few paces away, Mike gave a grunt of approval.

Most of all, Zam went on, she really needed a bicycle, because her rented room was a long walk away from both the gardens and clean water, and she could not always borrow the neighbor's bike.

"Can she ride a bicycle?" Mike asked Gladys, noting the girl's long skirt.

"I hold the baby in front and carry the beans on my back," Zam answered, her smile wide, almost cocky. She shrugged. "It is the only way to manage."

Gladys absorbed Zam's narrative without challenge or protest; the girl's requests were reasonable, if beyond her employer's current resources. As they moved back down the path, the ransacked fields behind them and the foundation of the house before them, Gladys paused.

"Now, Zam, I want you to know that your money will be made from here. You know I can't look after this place from far away." Gladys spoke deliberately, she and the young woman holding each other's gaze. Even Maria stared unblinkingly at her big *jjajja*, this grandmother who had entered her young life. "So you are in charge here. I want you to be developmental. Be creative."

Zam allowed a moment to show that she had absorbed this message, then launched into a series of proposals: the best path for the road was here; the sandy soil over there was good for potatoes. She pointed to an area with some spindly trees. "Those are of no use to the garden. You should cut them down for charcoal."

Gladys agreed that the trees in question were unproductive, but added, "If we get rid of those trees, we have to make sure we plant other ones. You don't just cut trees down without replacing them."

"If you burn those trees for charcoal, the byproduct will provide nutrients for the soil. You can plant small eggplants," Zam suggested. "The ones that bring a lot of money."

"Yes," Mike concurred. "It's a good idea."

Esther stood a few feet away, hands clasped behind her back, observing the conversation. Mike gave her an appraising glance, perhaps detecting in her some coolness toward Zam, a bit of skepticism that the girl could deliver on all she promised. Or perhaps just impatience to visit her own garden.

They paused by one of the trees slated for the ax; the garden, with its young plants, provided little shade. Gladys mopped at her face with a damp square of handkerchief.

"Mike, tell me what you think of this." Although he was hired to assist on these journeys, he had become her friend, and she valued his wise and worldly counsel. "I didn't make a mistake, coming out to Luwero?"

"Not at all." Mike's tone was emphatic. "Not at all. It's a brilliant idea, and this girl, she's a gem. I'm telling you. She's knowledgeable, and she's got a force. You know, the *A* she has got from me right away is when you asked her to sell the raw maize. But she said no, it's best to make flour out of the maize. That is very brilliant. Because when you make and sell flour, you get three times the price. I like her. She'll be fantastic."

Gladys glowed. "By the way, Mike, I am also happy that she loves what she's doing."

"It is rare," he said admiringly. "It is rare to get a girl like that."

"A girl from the city, too!"

Mike nodded, gesturing toward a large patch of earth bordered by uprooted weeds. "Do you know she dug all this place today?"

"She is a very hard-working woman," said Gladys. "I want to encourage her to take responsibility, and make some money out of this place."

. . .

THEY SOON REACHED their second destination, a couple of miles down the road. Esther went off to survey her gardens, which, being directly adjacent to decent neighbors, had not suffered significantly from theft. Gladys gazed wistfully at the neighbors' compound, with its shady huts and plump red chickens and furry black-and-white goats and bougainvillea so pink and bright it made the eyes water. It was a vision of what she hoped for her own land.

The small building with Zam's rented room stood nearby. How was her city girl getting along in this out-of-the-way place? With no family, no husband to help her with the child? Would she soon complain of exhaustion, of loneliness, of boredom?

"Zam-u!" Gladys called. "I want to see where you and the baby are sleeping. Show me."

The girl led the way, setting Maria on the veranda before opening the door to her room. As Gladys stepped over the threshold, what she found there both touched and astonished her.

She explained the discovery to Mike as they waited at the car for Esther. "Zam is a serious girl, Mike," Gladys said. "I gave her money to buy one mattress. But in that tiny room are two mattresses! I asked her, 'Where did you get the second one?'

"She said, 'Mommy, you said I need to get in partnership with you. You said we need to get serious about making money for the children. So when I went back home, I carried all of my belongings here. I am now a village girl! I no longer have anything in town, not even my mattress.' I was left with no words." Gladys shook her head, marveling. "I was speechless, you know? What do you say—'the ball is in your hands'?"

"'The ball is in your court,'" Mike corrected.

"It will be up to me to fail, is that what it means?"

"Yes. The ball is in your court."

"So it is up to me to fail the project, as she has shown me that she is ready. My God. Do you know what it means for someone to . . ." She fumbled for words.

The room had been neatly furnished with mats and sheets and even a lacy white curtain. Gladys was accustomed to others looking to her for resources, not entrusting her with their own. This girl was investing in her as heavily as she had invested in the gardens. Even more so, as Zam had a child!

"Her last comment to me: 'You see, I've come with everything! Just help me by completing that house, for me to be near.' Oh my God. She has given me a challenge. Oof!"

"You have the right person," Mike concluded. "You have the right person."

AS THEY PUTTERED down the dirt path to the main road, Mike seemed as energized as if the gardens were his own project. Assisting Gladys was no ordinary job; he could not help but feel invested.

"Gladys, so, you have kids that need support, right? That means that whatever you put on that land must be so smartly done."

"You mean like you were telling me to add fertilizer to every planting."

"Yes. Whatever you put on an acre, make sure you get at least eighty percent full yield. Even from one acre you can get a good profit. You can get four million shillings a month from an acre in this place here."

"What a great dream this sounds like." Gladys sighed with delight.

"So the only task now is to cultivate smart," said Mike, tapping the steering wheel for emphasis. "You must plan. A half an acre of this, half an acre of that. And all your problems about your children's support will be history. Those kids will never lack."

"That's some good advice. I will be fierce — I must be focused!" Gladys thrust her jaw forward and snorted. "I will be the second person in Uganda with vision — as you know, we have only one person here with a vision."

"Museveni." For years the president's supporters had promoted him as Uganda's "man with a vision."

"The only vision bearer. Until today!"

They giggled like primary school kids.

"Well now, Mike, you have seen Gladys's project in Luwero. We will very soon be looking at a house there! Imagine when the house is completed. It will be celebrations!" Gladys sang. "Mike, we will sit and eat cassava, eat what-what."

The Volvo sailed down the main road. What a good road it was, blacktop as smooth as a church pew.

"Finish the building quickly," he urged, laughing. "Quickly!"

The Lost Smile

It was a Sunday, so the traffic on the way to Jinja, some fifty miles east of Kampala, had not been too bad. Still, in the towns the vehicles collectively slowed, as though weary of dodging potholes. Ferrying Gladys and Esther, Mike's trusty Volvo rolled by chapati stands, a colorful army of dress-shop mannequins, and hand-painted wall advertisements for Fun All the Time soda. In front of a furniture shop, bored young men perched on a wooden bed frame like refugees stranded on a raft.

Abruptly a blast of sound shot through the car's open windows. "He can't find it!" screamed an amplified voice. "He is looking, but he can't find what he is looking for!"

A *bibanda* proprietor had positioned a speaker outside his video club, hoping to entice passersby to peek through the dark door. Gladys glanced over at the old wooden speaker, which vibrated with urgency and bursts of antiaircraft fire. "He found it! Rambo is firing!" the translator shouted in Luganda. "He has hit one! He has shot down one plane! Rambo! Rambo!"

"Rambo is still fighting," Mike said, chuckling. Though it was the middle of the day, no doubt there were patrons inside the club. The towns offered a variety of escapes for young men with a few shillings: action movies; sports betting; *waragi,* the cheap, potent alcohol that could be bought in small plastic packets like children's juice; and khat, the herb that was both stimulant and appetite suppressant.

Chewed with a wad of Big G bubblegum, a handful of leaves could make a mealtime — indeed, half a day — pass with little notice.

Gladys paid scant attention to the ruckus of Rambo's bad day. Her life contained too much excitement already. With all the dumped babies and defiled girls and hostile administrators and corrupt officials and kids with abusive parents and hydrocephalus and AIDS, there was no corner of her mind that required the arousal of exploding fighter jets. Life was not boring, if one did not shy away from the type of drama that lasted for longer than two hours.

With today's case, the drama had started a year ago.

THE CHILDREN, two girls and a boy, had come to the *New Vision* offices in Kampala with their mother, Susan Nabugwere. Unfortunately, it was a Sunday. The family encountered only security personnel, who told Susan, "There is only one person who can help you. Her name is Gladys. But you will have to come back tomorrow."

With one blanket and no money, mother and children spent the night outside, on the veranda of Club Silk, a nearby disco.

When Gladys arrived at the office, she was shocked to learn that the gaunt old woman waiting to meet her was only thirty-five. She looked closer to fifty-five. Between coughing fits, Susan explained that three weeks earlier her husband, a stone quarry worker, had died. She was acutely ill with TB and probably, as her husband had been, with AIDS.

After her husband's coworkers buried him, they realized that if Susan died as well, three orphans would be left on their hands. They took up a collection to send her and the children back to her hometown of Njeru.

It had been almost two decades since Susan had lived in Njeru. For days she wandered and slept on the streets with her three kids, but she could locate no path to her past. Finally she found the widow of a witch doctor who had treated her when she was a teen. The widow took pity on the exhausted family and took them into her home.

As her condition worsened, Susan insisted on traveling to the *New Vision* offices in Kampala to plead for assistance for her children: her son, Alex, nine, and her daughters, Annet and Mercy, six and five.

What gave Susan Nabugwere the strength to make that last journey? She must have accepted that her time was running out. One week after telling her story to Gladys, she was dead.

OVER THE FOLLOWING YEAR, the three children remained with the witch doctor's widow, and Gladys wrote about their plight. One day she received a call from Pastor Frederick Shimanya of Young Hearts Orphanage in Jinja District, not far from Njeru town. The pastor said he would take the girls, Annet and Mercy, but his home did not accept boys. He thought he might be able to find an American couple to adopt Alex.

Gladys demurred on the adoption point and requested that he take all three siblings. Pastor Frederick eventually agreed, on the understanding that he and Gladys would discuss the children's future when she visited Young Hearts. Not knowing this pastor, she did not wish to conduct such an important conversation over the phone. One had to see what was what with one's own eyes.

So here she, Esther, and Mike were now, branching from the highway onto sketchy back roads near Jinja. Gladys tossed her thoughts back and forth in the creaking car, musing over Pastor Frederick's adoption suggestion. Many people seemed to feel that for a Ugandan orphan, securing a foreign adoption was the equivalent of winning the lottery. Pastor Frederick had said as much when she had not embraced his plan for Alex: "Don't you think that you might be denying him a better life?"

Admittedly, Gladys's opinions on adoption were colored by a recent case. Over the past two years she had repeatedly profiled a lost boy held at a government home. A boda driver had found the crying toddler near the Northern Bypass and taken him to Old Kampala Police Station. No one could get much out of him, not even a name. As with many lost children before him, the boy became Mukisa, for "lucky."

Perhaps he could be considered lucky, in that he had not been abducted for child sacrifice. Every year dozens of children across the country were killed or mutilated by witch doctors who convinced wealthy clients that the body parts of a child could be used to bring wealth, cure impotence, even win an election. "He could have been picked by a kidnapper who changed his mind along the way," Gladys speculated.

"Do you know if the boy was circumcised?" Mike asked. It was an astute question. Witch doctors insisted that sacrifice victims be unscarred, their flesh pure. Some fearful parents preemptively pierced the ears of their baby daughters to advertise their "impurity," but a boy's circumcision might be discovered only after the fact of the kidnapping.

"That might be," said Gladys. "And then he was considered damaged goods and dumped."

Whatever the reason, the lost boy had languished in Amahoro, a dingy facility in Kampala that was more holding pen than home, for two years. It was only after the fifth listing in "Lost and Abandoned" that Gladys received a call from the police telling her that Mukisa's parents had shown up. His father, a policeman in northern Uganda, explained that their son had disappeared from a baby class and that they had been searching for him ever since.

On the heels of this good news came the dismaying discovery that Amahoro, the government home, had given Mukisa away to an American couple. The outraged parents demanded the return of their child, but the adoption had been executed through the courts. In the eyes of the law, their son now belonged to the American couple. They had missed the chance to reclaim him by two months.

"That Mukisa surely is lucky," some would say. "He lives in America now." But Gladys felt sick for the boy who would never know the culture or the family into which he had been born, and for the parents who would feel his loss for the rest of their lives.

The situation of Susan Nabugwere's three children was different, of course, as their parents were dead. But concern over foreign adoption had settled into Gladys's stomach. One might soothingly insist that an adopted child belonged to two countries, but the reality was different. When oceans separated old and new homes, the connection quickly frayed. Once broken, where would the tug be stronger? Did anyone really believe that poor Uganda could pull as hard as rich America?

GETTING OUT OF the car at Young Hearts Orphanage, Gladys surveyed the area with cautious approval. The grounds were flat and expansive, with several large red-brick buildings, their green roofs complimenting the stretches of grass below. There were no kids on the battered wooden gym, but a few were climbing on piles of concrete pipe. On one side stood a long new dormitory-like structure lacking only a roof. Young Hearts, it seemed, was a place with some means.

An unfamiliar children's home presented important questions. Were the children well treated or neglected? Was the management caring or mercenary? The signs were usually obvious, but sometimes they were only scents in the wind.

First she needed to see her kids, these three children of the deceased Susan Nabugwere. They came to her shyly, led by a matron. Alex, the boy, did not meet her gaze, but Annet and Mercy grinned happily in recognition. Gladys greeted each in Luganda with a smile and a touch, then stepped back an admiring distance.

"Eh! They seem good," she remarked to the matron in English. She petted little Mercy's head. "This one, she used to look so miserable!"

The children looked a bit bigger and less malnourished, although their stomachs still protruded slightly from their slim frames. They stood together, Alex wearing a pair of pink plastic slippers, the girls barefoot. The older one, Annet, had a runny nose. Mercy plucked at strands of grass with her toes, trying to keep still as the adults chatted away.

Gladys had made little of the siblings' closeness when she met them. The trio had huddled silently in the corner of the widow's tiny house while Gladys interviewed the mother, her coughs slapping sharply at the unfinished brick walls. Their clinginess made sense then: they were in a stranger's home, and their last parent was dying. But one year later they still moved as one, not three.

"So what can you tell me about these children? What is their condition? Are they getting used to the place?"

The matron, a young woman in a frilly blue blouse, carried a cell phone in one hand and a stick in the other. She pointed at the children with the stick. "When they first came, they were not social. They only stayed with each other. Now, after a couple of months, the girls have made some friends here."

"Ah, they feared to join. Why do you think they were like that?"

"Maybe because they were strangers."

"Hm. Do you have children?"

A shake of the head.

"Okay. But have you noted that when you move with a child somewhere—I'll give you a simple example. You take a child to a party. By the time you think of looking for him, he'll be over there, playing with other children. How come these ones were not mingling with the other children?"

The matron looked puzzled, as though the question had not occurred to her. Gladys prompted: "Could we say that they were still traumatized? By the death of their mother?"

"Maybe it was the death of the parents," the young woman said, then added brightly, "but right now they think that Pastor Fred is their father. And they are so comfortable with that. And if they see his wife coming, they say, 'Mommy, Mommy!'"

Alex, glaring, stood to one side, arms folded across his chest, in apparent defiance of this cheerful assessment. Gladys pulled out her notebook, fixing her eyes on the matron. "What's your name?"

"Wakisa Joan."

"Wakisa means 'kind.' Are you kind? Are you really someone kind?"

The weight of the reporter's gaze squeezed a nervous laugh out of the young woman, who poked the ground with her stick.

"Are you kind?"

"I am kind!"

The pen hovered. "And your telephone number?"

• • •

PERHAPS IN RESPONSE to Gladys's scrutiny, Wakisa Joan proved solicitous and efficient, leading Gladys, Esther, and Mike to the office and displaying the children's files in a neat pile on the desk. She appeared relieved when a dark-blue SUV pulled up at the open door.

Pastor Fred emerged from the driver's side, a knot of keys in one hand and a smartphone in the other. He was large in the way of a man who is not born to be thin, a baobab tree among the acacias. Everything about him was thick and rounded: round belly, cheeks, chin, and jowls, a Ugandan Buddha.

"Call me Freddy," he informed his visitors.

Unlike many first encounters in Gladys's daily life, this was one in which the parties shared a hope of cooperation. In the office, Gladys and Freddy seemed physically matched, each providing ballast for her or his side of the office. They exchanged brief pleasantries, Freddy apologizing for his lateness.

It had been a tiring week, he reported. They had just taken in a three-day-old girl who had been dumped into a pit latrine. A young man, hearing crying below, had run from the toilet and summoned the police. "The police got the baby out of the pit and poured water over her to remove the poop," Freddy recounted. "They didn't clean her properly. It was drizzling, and they just wrapped her in clothes."

"What was the condition of the baby at that time?" asked Gladys, scribbling quickly.

"She had the eyes closed, she was not crying, but the maggots were coming out of the ears and the nose."

Gladys emitted a high-pitched squeal of horror, like air escaping a stomped-on football. Two toddlers standing in the doorway looked up at the noise, one swiveling her head so quickly she almost fell over.

"Big maggots—you could just see them coming. So we cleaned her with disinfectant, bathed her, and gave her a tetanus injection. That night we didn't have milk, only glucose and water. The whole night she was here, crying."

"Because she was hungry."

"She was hungry, and also the maggots were coming out of her ears."

"What do you mean! They kept on coming?"

"Yes, the whole night. And out of her nose, falling on her neck. They were irritating her."

"Oooh!" Gladys covered her eyes with a hand.

They discussed the impending police investigation, and how an article in Gladys's paper might prompt someone to come forward with information on the child's abandonment.

"What name have you given the baby?"

"Charity."

"Charity . . . Why Charity?"

"She has been shown much charity in being retrieved from that pit. God has been so charitable."

GLADYS WAS EAGER for the briefing on Susan Nabugwere's children. Were they healthy? Wakisa Joan assured her that they had been declared healthy. They were still catching up in school but were faring well. Alex, now ten, was proving especially bright.

"And plans for these three?" Gladys asked. "As the parents are now dead."

Freddy thumbed through a file. "What of the old woman — their grandy?"

Gladys explained that Nabukonde, the witch doctor's widow who had taken in the family, was not actually kin. "These kids don't have any relatives around." She paused before adding, "I was told the children think of you as their father. But you don't keep boys in this home."

Freddy nodded. The girls could stay; their brother was another matter. He had asked Nabukonde if she could keep Alex, but the old woman declined. "So I said to her, 'What about if we get somebody who can adopt the boy, take him to America, provide an education? Maybe in the future, you never know, he can come back and help his sisters.'"

Young Hearts was serious about adoption, Freddy maintained. "We are not like other homes." They had placed three children in America so far. In addition to making regular phone calls, Pastor Fred visited them every year.

"Who pays?" Gladys asked bluntly. "Who pays for those visits to America?"

"I pay!" Freddy responded, then amended: "The home pays. So we monitor them. And we give the children to a Christian family. We don't just want to give them to people who are drug addicts, who go to disco and dance."

"So strictly it must be Christian."

"Yes."

The picture was coming into focus. Most likely evangelicals abroad were supporting Young Hearts, assisting with funding for things such as the new construction outside. It was the only way a home like this could have such resources.

"Alex is growing up," Freddy was saying. "In Africa we need to give boys land, we need to see that at least they have some place to be, at least they get a job. With the girls, it's okay. They can get husbands, they can find somewhere to live." He leaned forward in his chair and rested his chin on thumb and forefinger, eyes on Gladys. "But what about Alex's future? I have been waiting on you to tell me your heart."

"Um ... what is your ... how many classes do you have here?" she began, fumbling. She was grateful to this man for taking care of the children, but she was determined to speak firmly. "Your school goes up to P Seven. That's very good. You can accommodate Alex up to P Seven. Then, God willing, if I'm still alive, we will again discuss. I don't want to separate this family. They don't have any relatives. I don't want someone to keep on telling the girls, 'You remember your brother? He's in America. Maybe when you grow up you'll see him.' No!" She screwed up her face and spat out the word, as if she had tasted something bitter. "I'm not ready for that. I'm sure by the time he is in P Seven I will have come up with a solution."

Freddy pursed his lips and nodded, more in resignation than agreement.

"The moment you feel you can't handle these children, please let me know," Gladys added appeasingly. "Let me take them and maybe we will get some other place."

• • •

OUTSIDE, GLADYS SNAPPED pictures of baby Charity, saved from the latrine. She was a tiny, still creature whose medicine-encrusted eyes had still not opened. This was worrisome — three days on earth, and no glimpse of the world? Given what this newborn had experienced in her short life, one could not blame her for being afraid to look.

The veranda was crowded with babies. At one point Gladys nearly stepped on a two-year-old who had been abandoned by her prostitute mother. How would that be, to survive such cruel treatment, only to be trampled by a reporter?

From behind the office, Joan emerged, leading Susan Nabugwere's children to stand for Gladys's camera. Annet and Mercy clearly enjoyed the special attention. Their cheeks, as round as passionfruits, rose high on their faces. Only their brother still wore his mask of a frown.

"Alex is a bit reserved," Gladys commented to Freddy. "Why do you think that is so?"

"I don't know why he's reserved, but he's a clean boy. A very clean boy."

Freddy beckoned the kids to join him in front of his SUV. The girls beamed, safe in the generous shade of their protector. Freddy hoisted Mercy up in one arm and rested the other on Annet's shoulders.

"Girls, keep looking at me. Yes, please!" Gladys sang. "Alex, get closer."

The boy remained a half step to the side, chest thrust forward, his slight body flexed like a bow.

"I can't understand this one," Gladys mumbled. "He doesn't have a smile. The girls, they have beautiful smiles. Are you hungry, Alex?"

"He doesn't know how to smile." Freddy shrugged.

Gladys quickly scrolled through the pictures she had taken. She still needed a happy one. When her readers responded to a story, it was important to give them the next chapter. Susan Nabugwere's children's lives were not perfect, but for the moment they had a safe home here, and that was something worth reporting.

"Now I want to take a nice photo," she announced.

The boy looked at the camera, his manner less defiant than bemused, as though he did not comprehend the language being spoken. Off to the side, Mike observed the standoff, the boy's small, hard frown mirrored on his own lean, lined face.

Gladys coaxed, "Please put your arm around your sister. I need your smile." Mechanically the boy draped an arm around Annet.

"Smile like your sisters, Alex," prompted Joan. "Cheese!"

"Okay," Gladys called out, her camera clicking. "This is now the family. Alex, be happy. You are next to the father."

Alex smiled the grimace of one being blinded by sunlight.

IT WAS GETTING LATE, but Gladys was set on visiting Nabukonde, the witch doctor's widow in Susan's hometown of Njeru who had taken in the family. It was not so far away.

"This thing of smiling . . ." Mike began, turning onto the main road. "I understand what that boy is going through. My father died when I was in my thirteenth year."

"Ee-ehh!"

"I was so injured, it took me a while to really put a smile on my face."

"Ah," Gladys said sympathetically.

Alex was injured—that was the correct word for it. Like a patient, he needed time to heal. The precariousness of his situation worried her. What if Freddy decided that the boy could not stay at Young Hearts through P7 after all? She needed to have a plan ready.

Nabukonde was central to that plan. The witch doctor's widow, now a born-again, had selflessly housed Susan's family for many months. The children were no longer in her home, but surely she still felt some connection to them. If worse came to worst, perhaps Gladys could shift the three back into Nabukonde's home and raise money for them to attend a different school.

As they drove, Mike, Gladys, and Esther agreed that Freddy was doing good work at Young Hearts Orphanage, but they questioned his rationale for suggesting that Alex be given to another family.

"You tell me just because of the African way of doing things, a boy has to get someone, a parent, to leave him land?" Gladys snorted. "Who told you Kalibbala's children got land from their father? Oh my God. Hee-hee-hee!" Her laughter pierced the roof of the car.

"'The girls can just get married,'" Mike quoted. He had a college-educated daughter living on her own in England. "That to me was nonsensical."

"These days men are looking for women who have something," Esther put in.

"Ee-yeh, women who work!" said Gladys. "What he's telling us is old theory: 'Marry a man who is well-off so that you will be well-off.' No way. It can't work today."

Arriving at the town, Gladys, Esther, and Mike walked up the dirt path to Nabukonde's home, only to find her door locked.

"Perhaps we can call her," Esther suggested. There were several handwritten phone numbers on the door of the house, but the digits were smeared. Esther and Gladys pulled out their mobiles and guessed at the numbers, their efforts leading only to recorded error messages.

Gladys clucked in disappointment and glanced around. Across the path was a larger brick house with a cluster of five children staring from its doorway. Nearby a skinny calf nipped at the rope tied to its leg.

"How are you people?" Gladys called out. "Where is the lady of this home?"

"She went to the tailor. We don't know where."

Mike was looking at his watch. The way back to Kampala was long, and Gladys knew he preferred not to drive long distances when it was dark. But they had come all this way. It wouldn't hurt to give Nabukonde a few minutes to appear.

Gladys used the time to explain why the old woman deserved special consideration. "As you saw as we were driving, there are many big houses in this area. So I was humbled to find it is only this poor old woman who would give this family accommodation." She gestured at the tiny, unplastered, loose-brick box of a house. "Nabukonde has only two small rooms in there. They were all sleeping on the floor. She really struggled, you know—it was not easy to feed everyone. I was really humbled.

"Nabukonde even took the trouble to take the mother to hospital, but Susan ran away from there after two days. You know what she told the old woman? 'I want to stay close to my children. My children don't know anyone here. I have to keep close to them.' Within a week she was dead."

A speckled white hen appeared at the patch of greens near the side of the house, a line of chicks darting and peeping in her wake.

"Unfortunately, Susan died when the old lady was not around. Alex had been sitting with a candle, watching her, getting very little sleep. His mother was now fighting, struggling to breathe her last. The poor boy was trying to bring her arms down, to get a hold of her. She was too heavy for him."

Gladys sighed and looked down, taking no notice of the procession of hen and chicks. When she spoke again, her voice was almost a whisper. "I think it's the worst experience, watching someone die. You always hear of people dying in their sleep, peacefully. But watching someone fighting . . . she fought for her *life*. And Alex was there."

"Eh-eh-eh!" a voice sang out. It was Nabukonde. She came waddling up the path, arms weighed down by grocery bags, her *gomesi* a shade of light blue favored by born-agains. As she knelt in greeting at Gladys's feet, her shopping bags spilled *matoke* and tomatoes onto the ground, prompting peals of bright laughter.

"I'm so happy to see you! I was so annoyed because I did not see you here!"

"I'm so happy to see you. God be praised!"

As Nabukonde gathered her groceries, Gladys handed her a bag of sugar and a loaf of bread, pleased to have something to offer this time. On her last visit she had been so broke she hadn't even been able to bring sugar.

The old woman accepted the gift with flustered gratitude. "In my house, there are no chairs. We must sit outside," she apologized, slipping through the door. A moment later she emerged with two plastic jerry cans to sit on.

Gladys considered them doubtfully. "It must be for someone

light. Otherwise the jerry can will be . . ." She made a flattening gesture with her hands, as though she were squashing a mosquito.

The jerry cans disappeared back into the house. Mike, Esther,
and Gladys perched on some large rocks in front of the house while
Nabukonde dragged out a mat and sat on the ground.

Gladys stretched out her right leg, slipping a shoe off a swollen
foot. The sun was dropping, the air growing cooler. For a moment
the two older women simply smiled at each other. The speckled hen
and her chicks took advantage of the peaceful interlude to parade
boldly through the open door of the house.

"Where is your daughter?" Gladys asked Nabukonde.

"She got married. And now she has moved away."

"So whom do you stay with here now?"

"Nobody."

A stranded chick appeared, crying piteously at the sound of his
brethren in the house. He scurried back and forth in front of Gladys
and Nabukonde, having spotted the open door between them. Inside, the hen clucked shrilly back at him: *Come in already.*

"Have you ever gone to visit Alex and the girls, now that they are
with Pastor Fred?"

"Three times. And during the end-of-term holidays they will
stay here."

"Good, that's good."

Gladys felt reassured by the old woman's response. There was no
need to press her into future commitments. It was enough to know
that Alex and his sisters were still welcome in this home.

The hen in the house was still clucking loudly to her errant
chick, who dashed about at the women's feet. Finally he emitted a
mighty *peep peep peep* and sprinted through the doorway, his small act
of bravery unnoticed by the women. And then all was quiet.

NABUKONDE WALKED her visitors back down the lane. "Thank
you for coming all this way to see me," she repeated to Gladys. "You
like me so much, God be praised."

As they reached the car, the old woman again dropped to her
knees. Gladys looked down at her in surprise.

"So you have seen the children now and they are fine," Nabukonde began, reaching for Gladys's hand. "Now will you help me finish my house? I've handed those three children over to you. Build my house for me."

Around them, neighbors stood on their verandas, idly watching. Gladys resisted the urge to pull her hand away. "I've seen the kids, and I've seen you, so I'm ready to go," she said simply. "We are leaving now."

As soon as the doors of the old Volvo were shut, Esther and Gladys erupted.

"Can you imagine?" Gladys cried. "She wants me to build her house for her now. My goodness. Ai-yi-yi!"

"'I turned over those children to you. Now what about my house?'" Esther mimicked.

"Oh my God!" Gladys's voice descended three octaves in those three words, the last one landing with a thud. "These people are mad. And what I know, none of them thinks of Gladys living in a rented room. They imagine Gladys sleeping in a big house with some huge wall around it. With a very large gate, where you have to reach up and ring a bell."

They shared a laugh, but in truth Gladys's disappointment was deep. The chatter was tinged with embarrassment for that woman kneeling in the dust. Had Nabukonde adopted the born-agains' "prosperity doctrine," the belief that good deeds should bring personal benefit? Did Gladys's token gifts of sugar and bread make the recipients see her as a rich woman?

When Gladys introduced herself to the parties in a new case, she often told them, "I've come to see how I can help these children." She had begun to wonder whether *help*, that friendly word, labeled its user as "one with money." Had things become so bad that everyone — even this kind Nabukonde — believed that a person giving assistance would do so only if she had great wealth herself?

All this complicated the situation of Alex, Annet, and Mercy. If Freddy could not keep Alex at Young Hearts, could Gladys be assured that Nabukonde would take the three children back into her care? It might just be a matter of money, of course, as such matters so often were, but Gladys had hoped for more. She had hoped for family.

If Alex was adopted and sent to America, money would be no problem there. School fees, clothes, transportation, soda, Kentucky Fried Chicken — he could have anything, anytime. He might even have his own room.

Alex's chances for adoption, at ten years old, were already slim and would diminish every year. Was this, as Pastor Freddy asserted, his one great opportunity? It would be hard to find prospective parents interested in a teenager, and it would be harder for a teenager to adapt to a new home, a new culture, a new country. A baby like Charity of the pit latrine could easily accept America as her world. She hadn't even opened her eyes yet. But Alex had seen so much.

Alex should be given a say in these matters, but it didn't seem right to force the decision on one so young, so recently orphaned. The boy needed time to breathe.

How much could she give him? How long would he need?

THEY HEADED WEST back to Kampala. The car rumbled along, its passengers silent. Full night had fallen, and they had not eaten a meal all day. Between Gladys's feet slouched a plastic sack containing a carton of biscuits, but no one expressed any hunger.

At the wheel, Mike stared out at the road. With his strong cheekbones and long chin edged in the red glow of taillights, his profile was intimidating. It was hard to imagine him as a boy.

"Mike, you went through Alex's experience," Gladys began. "You lost your parent when you were young. How long did it take you to come out of your grieving?"

Mike paused, shifting in his seat. "I was thirteen when my father died. He was Festus Wawuyo, a senior police officer who investigated some very prominent cases. There was the murder of Brigadier Okoya. This man was shot dead by Idi Amin. My father investigated that case in 1970, so naturally when Amin took over the government, he came after him."

"Eh . . . ," the women uttered in acknowledgment of Amin, the bogeyman of many such stories. This tale would be as long and dark as the drive back to Kampala.

Mike began. "It was January twenty-fifth, 1971, the day that soldiers attacked our home. My father had just left on the road they came in on. So my mother went to the doorway to talk to the soldiers. The neighbor who led them to our home didn't like my father. He thought he would be malicious and show them where our house was. But as soon as he stepped out of the soldiers' VW, he was shot spot in the chest."

Gladys gasped. "They shot the neighbor?"

Mike nodded. "The guy died. I was standing in the window looking, and that scared the hell out of me. I ran back into my bedroom. My mother was screaming. They shoved her into her bedroom, banging her with the gun butts, shouting, 'Where is your husband?' Two soldiers pushed my mother toward the bed. My bedroom was next to that bedroom, and the door was open. They were kicking my mother so brutally. Then I could see those guys dropping their trousers. I was just horrified.

"The maid was in the bedroom. She tried to resist, and the men pushed her down. One guy stepped on her with such force, he stepped on her thigh and broke it. So when I saw this happening, I slipped through the window. You know those old government houses, they had those old-fashioned windows with the space in the middle of them, and I squeezed through one of them. The dead neighbor was lying there in our compound. The man who shot him was outside, with another guy who was shooting all of our dogs, all of our chickens. They didn't see me.

"I ran to all of our neighbors. No one would open the door for me. But there was one American neighbor, Mr. Howard, a lecturer at the university. I banged on Howard's door. And he opened it!"

Gladys and Esther exhaled as though they had been holding their breath. If that door had not opened, would Mike be with them in this car tonight?

"When the gunshots stopped, I went back to the house. I found the maid crying—she was in the kitchen, wriggling on the floor with her broken leg. They had taken my mother away. Maybe they raped her more. I don't know." Mike paused. "She lived to be an old woman. But we never discussed that day. Ever."

Oncoming headlights shone in streaks on the bug-splattered windshield. Mike took one hand off the steering wheel and touched his temple. "Do you know what it means when you are the only boy who was at home at the time? When you know and your mother knows that you know what they did? You understand that kind of feeling? Men taking turns at your mother. That really traumatized me."

The women sensed the grown son's enduring shame. "If they had known there was someone watching, they would have killed you," Gladys pointed out.

"While I was in the house, they returned with my mother," Mike went on, not pausing for solace. "I saw the car. They shoved her out and she fell. And they said, 'We are coming back this evening. So your husband had better be here when we return.'

"After they left, my mother said, 'Okay, we'll sit here and wait.' I was young, but I said, 'We are not going to wait. We are going to get away from here.'

"I went back to Mr. Howard. He said, 'It's five forty-five p.m. And curfew is at six o'clock. How can I take you anywhere?' But this guy was so courageous." Risking arrest or worse, Howard agreed to drive the family to a safe place.

"I went and got the maid. I got this piece of wood and tore a sheet and tied her thigh to the wood. We wrapped her thigh and tied it as tight as we could, but all the same, the ties were so flimsy I could see the leg shifting around. And how the girl cried!

"There was a eucalyptus forest nearby, where there was a small cave near a pond. I knew that place, because we used to play there. So Howard dropped us there, and we stayed at that cave for three nights — me, my baby sister, my mother, and the maid."

"And you had no food?" asked Gladys.

"Well, the day the soldiers came, my mother was baking a cake. And the cake was in the oven. So the next day I went back home, climbed through the window, and picked it. It had almost burned. But I brought it back and we ate that."

In the pause that followed, the image lingered: the ragged family huddled in a cave around a burned cake. The three travelers looked out into the darkness through different windows.

"I was at home when the soldiers came because I had just finished primary school. So I saw everything that my brothers never saw," Mike continued. "But I also saw my father one last time."

"Eh! You saw again your father?"

"Yes. He turned himself in. He asked for permission to return home to take me back to school. So they let him come, but Idi Amin put some plainclothesmen to follow him. My grandmother asked him, 'Why don't you just escape across the border?' And he said, 'If I do that, they will come back and kill everyone. Let me go back to Kampala and see if I can work it out.' My father gave me a hug, told me to study hard, and got into the car. That's the last time I saw him."

MIKE VEERED LEFT to avoid a stalled Toyota, expertly riding the road's crumbling edge. Night intensified the usual hazards of driving: the potholes and bad drivers and reckless pedestrians and wandering animals, most rendered invisible save for the shining coins of their eyes. But Mike did not falter in his narrative; on the contrary, each distraction seemed to tighten his grip on the thread of his past.

"Two years after my father had been pronounced dead, a certain man came. From Kenya. He told my grandmother, 'You know something? Your son didn't die. Your son is in Nairobi! I met him!' So he gave us some ray of hope.

"In my village there is a rock. A small, funny rock. But when I was a kid, I thought it was a very big rock. After that man's visit, I would sit on that rock and I would look toward the Kenyan border, saying, 'My father is going to come back.' When I lived with my grandmother, I sat there every day. I would sit in the morning, at least two hours, and in the evening until the sun went down. I would be looking, looking, imagining that I could see my father coming from there, that I would run and give him a hug. I had so many plans about it! But each day I would walk back home alone.

"My grandmother, she knows I'm going to the rock to look out at the border. And every time I came back, she would look at me. And I would look at her. And my eyes would say, 'He is nowhere to be seen.' And my grandmother's eyes would say, 'I told you.'

"I didn't want to give up on my father. I sat on that rock for about six years."

For a long moment there was no sound in the car but the wind from the open windows.

"The last time I sat on the rock, I was angry. I yelled from that rock, 'Stupid man! Stupid man!' I was cursing and screaming at the border. 'If you are out there, if you are in Kenya and you haven't bothered to come back after this long, *don't come back!* Don't *ever* come back.'

"I never sat on that rock again. And he never came back."

Gladys let out a heavy sigh. The boy had turned into a man, waiting on that rock. But it had happened too soon.

"My grandmother died from my father's death. He was her heartbeat. My father had joined the police because my grandparents were so poor. His whole life, he devoted it to try to better their circumstances. He built them a house, got them cows. He would bring them to the city, to Kampala. My grandmother watched the TV for the first time, you know?" Mike half smiled. "My father lit up her life. And so when he was gone, she cried for nine years. Nine *years*. She stopped digging, all her gardens perished. She stopped caring for the cows, all the cows died.

"Every night, after I would come in from sitting on the rock, after we would look at each other, she would go inside and sing from her hymnbook and cry for three hours. And then she'd get into bed with her *waragi*. Five-liter *waragi*, with a tube coming up to her bedside."

"Eh!" Gladys uttered in sympathy and alarm. *Waragi*, the "war gin" that British colonials had used to control their Nubian conscripts, regularly felled grown men, leaving them curled up on the ground like victims of sleeping sickness. One could only imagine what such a quantity could do to a grieving old woman.

"She would drink that poisonous liquor until she fainted out. I'd go to her room, drop a cover on her, and wait for the next day." Mike shook his head. "It was a long, long suicide."

Gladys knew that feeling of pain and impotence, of watching the person responsible for your welfare retreat into oblivion. Even now her own father could go for three days consuming nothing but alcohol.

There was a brief pause as Mike gunned the engine to pass a lumbering fuel truck. The air through the windows buffeted the passengers' ears, then subsided.

"After the overthrow of Amin, I said I would hunt for every killer of my father. I had so much anger. I joined the army, just to take revenge. I was taken to Nigeria with some of those elite forces, and I trained so hard! In training I met four men. They heard my name, Wawuyo, and they said, 'Wait a minute! There was a man named Wawuyo in Mutukula Prison. He was a very talkative person, and he kept up our morale. He kept fighting for us and fending for us, making sure we were not mistreated. He was so, so, so assertive.' I knew immediately: 'That was my father!' That's when they gave me the whole history of what happened.

"My father was taken to Luzira Prison, where he was kept for one full year, 1971. At the end of the year they took fifteen hundred detainees to Mutukula Prison, including my father. They transported them in trucks. Threw them in, hog-tied, like sacks of grain. In Mutukula, the orders were to kill all of them. They were killed systematically over two months. Sometimes, for the guards' amusement, they were made to fight each other with hammers. Sometimes guards threw grenades into the ventilators of the cells. Out of fifteen hundred prisoners, only forty survived. The four men I met in training were among them.

"Those men said they couldn't believe that my father would stand by them, by whoever was in his cell. That woke me up. That he tried to stand for them in those hard circumstances. But eventually he was done. My father was brutally murdered. Chopped to pieces. He was thrown into a mass grave."

Gladys could hear the pain in Mike's words. It was not only that his father had been butchered. His family had not been afforded the dignity of burial.

Kin must be brought back home for final rest. How could Mike not be tortured by the thought of his father discarded in an unmarked patch of earth overrun by weeds and litter? Pedestrians treading over it, unaware that beneath their feet lay the body of a man who had defended so many others, a man missed by a boy who sat on a rock for six years, waiting for his father to come home?

THROUGH GLADYS'S WINDOW, this stretch of night seemed especially dense. The headlights penetrated only a few feet into the blackness. Beyond the highway, the shadowy shapes of buildings and trees and huts were amorphous and scattered, nothing adding up to anything nameable like a town or a garden or a forest. Everything out there seemed on its own.

Alex and Mike. Though more than four decades separated them, they bore similar scars. Like Mike, Alex had a father buried in a place he could not visit. The stoneworkers had left Alex's father's body somewhere near the quarry. The boy had not had a chance to say goodbye.

Like Mike, Alex bore guilt over his mother's suffering. After his mother's death, he had wept for many days. Perhaps he was tortured by those last, terrible moments, by his failure to wrestle his mother's spirit back into her body. His sisters had only stared at their crying brother. Insulated by youth, they could not yet fathom a well deep enough to feed that stream of tears.

"With your story, Mike, I really have realized why Alex can't smile."

"I'm telling you, that boy—when you tell him to smile, he just can't understand it. It's like his face is going to get torn. His smile has been wiped out of his system," Mike said, slicing the air with one lean hand. "After what happened to my family, I couldn't see how to smile, you know? I had so much anger for Amin's soldiers. When they had checkpoints going into Kampala, when they turned everyone out of the bus, they would always single me out. Because of the look on my face, out of the whole line of people, they would pick me. And they would traumatize me."

"My goodness." Gladys sighed. "You understand better what Alex is going through, because what you went through is double what he has experienced."

Big-hearted Mike, whose grin was so radiant it could charge a mobile phone, had once worn a face like Alex's. Gladys recognized that face now. It was the face of a child who has not forgotten anything.

FOR YOUNG MIKE, the nightmare had continued on other fronts. As a result of family infighting, he and his siblings were split up among an uncle's several wives.

"The moment that we kids were not together, I just could not think. I had one brother here, one brother there. I spent all my time moving from place to place to go check on them. They were starving. You see, each of those wives had her own children, and they were minding their own children's welfare, so my siblings were not fed."

A *matatu* stopped short in front of the Volvo. Mike braked hard, muttering under his breath. Traffic stood at a standstill, the vehicles puttering listlessly in the dark.

"My father was a highly placed person. When he was declared dead, it was going from glory to rags, you understand?" He raised a hand up to the roof, then let it drop to the seat. "In the flip of a page, we were suddenly down there. So deep, so instantly. My siblings were being persecuted, and I just couldn't concentrate. Each time I thought about their situation, I would be crying. My brothers and I decided we would move out together. So I had to get a job. I worked as a truck loader, carrying a whole load of *matoke*. Because I didn't want us to be split up."

"Ah-hah," said Gladys. "And when you got all your siblings out, your mind got settled."

"Very settled. All four of us were crowded in one small room. One of my brothers started drinking recklessly, but all the same, we were together. You know? All of us felt, like, *whew!* We felt we are someone." He chuckled abruptly. "You know *kamongo,* that fried fish? For the poor people."

The women nodded. *Kamongo,* a slimy, salamander-like creature, thrived in swamps and lake bottoms.

"In Idi Amin's time you would have to be the lowest of the low to eat that fish. In the evening we would go and buy that *kamongo,* about three pieces or so, and then get yams and cassava and boil them. The four of us ate, and you know, we felt happy with ourselves."

"And you felt it was delicious," said Gladys.

"Yes." Mike laughed.

"That's how it works. You find it delicious and you enjoy the meal. Just because you are together now."

"Yes!"

Gladys pounded a fist on the windowsill like a judge wielding a gavel. "My decision is now *right.* This has been running in my mind. And now I've heard everything from the experience of Mike. And I was *right.* You can't separate Alex and his sisters. You can't. If you want them to overcome all the trauma they've had, they must be together. To give support to one another. That's why those kids don't like to play with others, they just want to stay together."

Her words tumbled out now. "I can't buy what Freddy is telling me. Freddy will think he is doing Alex a favor by giving him out to a very rich family in America, so that they send him to expensive schools, give him land, or whatever he's talking of. But I tell you, people, it would hurt Alex so, so, so, so badly! Alex will arrive in America, they will drive him in big, posh cars, but he will not be happy. You will have a very disappointed couple that will wonder: 'Look at this African. We have done everything for him, but Alex doesn't appreciate it. The boy is always gloomy, the face is gloomy.' Alex has been through too much. And his sisters need him."

Mike jumped in belligerently. "If you want those kids, take the three. If you can't take the three, leave them. Don't even think about it!"

"And you know what? I thank you, Mike, because your story has given me more satisfaction that Alex can still go through with the life. Yes! I'm sure that boy will be determined to go through. I don't expect him to give up. He may be like Mike, who went to load *matoke* in the name of assisting his siblings."

Mike laughed. "I've done everything under the sun, I tell you."

Gladys continued to refer to him in the third person, as though recounting the tale to another. "Mike did not want his siblings to suffer being divided among those other families. No! As he tells it, they didn't have money, he didn't have a good job. But they were together, and their minds got settled!"

Having reached loud and jubilant agreement, the companions relaxed. Gladys reached down into the footwell for the *kavera* containing the snacks. The plastic sack made its way around the car, adding to the journey's theme of meager meals: burned cake, fried *kamongo,* a carton of biscuits. The carton made its way from passenger to passenger until it was empty.

THE TRAFFIC GREW thick as they entered the heart of Kampala. That was the thing about a long story told in a traveling car: at its end, one found oneself in a different place from where the story began. Around them people milled about the city, walking and hawking and haggling and chatting and begging and loitering as though it were the middle of the day.

One question lingered. How had Mike thawed the anger that had frozen his expression for so long? The young man had vowed to punish those responsible for his father's death. What had come of his thirst for retaliation?

Heading toward the taxi park, Mike delivered the epilogue.

After he had learned his father's fate from the four men who had survived Mutukula Prison, the target of his revenge narrowed to one man: Major Mududu, the officer responsible for killing the fifteen hundred prisoners, including Mike's father.

"After Amin's overthrow, this Mududu was sent to prison to await trial. I was twenty-one, I had finished my army training, and now I was going to deal with this man. You know how young guys watch too many war movies . . ."

"Like *Rambo,*" said Gladys.

"Yes, like *Rambo* today." Mike nodded. "Well, I went to the High Court every day with a bunch of kids, all armed to the teeth. With grenades, with guns, waiting for this Mududu to come out of the bus for his appearance at court, so that we can attack him." There was a matter-of-factness to Mike's tone that erased any doubt of his ability to carry out such a plan. "I fantasized about cutting off every one of his fingers and then killing him. Even when I was practicing shooting at the range I was seeing that man's face.

"I didn't know when his trial would begin, so I went to the court every day. For six months. Each time I watched to see if Mududu was getting off the bus, my adrenaline would be so high, my heart pumping so hard. I wondered how many other people I might have to shoot to get to him.

"Every day for six months I imagined killing this man. As it went on and on, I realized I was becoming sick from this head trip. So I called the contract off. I told my friends, 'I think I'm giving up on the revenge.' They said 'No! You must kill this guy!' They called me yellow, said I was a disgrace to my father's body. But I realized, if I don't stop, I will live in such bitterness I will never survive the void I feel inside."

"Eventually you would have run mad," Gladys agreed. That's what revenge was: a fire that kept you warm, then burned down your house.

"I tell you, if you do not move on, you will have so much pain. You don't have to forget. But you have to be able to move on." Mike shrugged. "So I said, 'To hell with it. I'm not going to hunt him anymore. I will let this be.' I closed that chapter, and I quit the army. And I felt peace with myself."

Outside, Nakasero street market came into view. Weary fruit vendors knelt on mats battened down by perfect pyramids of oranges or tomatoes or avocados as big as human heads. Shoppers gathered around the candlelit altars of produce like worshippers.

"Does he still live?" Gladys asked.

"Mududu? Yes." The officer was an old man now, spent and faded, lingering on a sugar plantation somewhere. "But I don't want to look for him. I just want him to live with his own conscience. There is nothing worse than having a terrible conscience. That, you can't eradicate."

"Ah-*hah*," Gladys voiced in assent. Surely the nightmares of the guilty were worse than those of the weary.

THEY ARRIVED AT the glowing perimeter of the taxi park. Rows of light-bulb vendors rimmed the sea of white-topped minibuses. Lo-fi pop music blasted from both sides of the street, colliding inside the Volvo. Boda bodas weaved through lanes, passengers blithely texting, cell-phone screens glowing blue. Mike navigated the stream of vehicles and bodies and pulled to the curb.

"I think it was a good day," said Gladys.

"Thank you so much, Gladys." Mike checked his mirrors for traffic as the women exited from the car. "Safe journey."

He watched Gladys and Esther cross to the park, where they would board a taxi and ride another couple of hours back to their home in Entebbe. There Gladys would sleep for a few hours before rising to take the long ride back into Kampala again. The lengths to which this woman would go to help complete strangers—it amazed him.

That young boy, Alex, could not know that the course of his life had taken a turn for the better today. That he had someone watching over him, and over his family.

Mike steered back into the street, away from the memories of his past, away from the young man who had once believed that guns and grenades could restore equilibrium to an upturned world. If you lived long enough, you discovered that a steady hand, not a fist, kept things from spinning out of control. You didn't need a Rambo. You needed a Gladys.

The Boy with Seven Names, Part One

Mugerwa Junior

I WANT TO QUIT THE STREET
Mugerwa Junior, 11, cannot remember his parents' names, their home, or how long he has been on the street. He remembers going to ease himself on the day he arrived in Kampala with his parents and failing to trace them thereafter. He resorted to washing dishes at food kiosks as his means of survival. Now he says he feels tired. He turned himself in to Old Kampala Police.

Hello, Rebecca." It was Sunday evening. Gladys had just finished a long day of reporting out in the field, and by all rights she should be sitting down to her first proper meal. But she had answered her phone, knowing that Officer Araba of the Child and Family Protection Unit of Old Kampala Police would not be calling to chitchat.

"I've been meaning to call you about a situation," Rebecca began, with uncharacteristic hesitation. "But I am not sure how we can discuss it." A situation like this could be troublesome if it was leaked to the papers, she explained. Some might accuse the police involved of negligence. Including Rebecca's boss.

Like Gladys, Rebecca was tall, stout, and staunchly professional. She returned calls promptly, and she always wore her uniform while on duty. Gladys appreciated officers who did not wear street clothes to work, since this made for poor photographs. When she ran a picture with a story about a lost child, how were her readers supposed to know that the lady in the dress was a policewoman and not some relative or bystander? But Rebecca wore her police cap even on the hottest days.

While Rebecca and Gladys cooperated on children's cases, their responsibilities to their respective jobs sometimes placed them at odds. A year before, Gladys had written an article about how abandoned children at Old Kampala Police Station were engaging in illicit activity. A lucky kid might find a space to sleep under the office counter, but most sought shelter in the wrecked cars behind the station. In the rusted husk of a minibus, a twelve-year-old girl had had sex with three boys who promised to buy her a chapati and a soda, and she feared she might be pregnant or infected with HIV.

The story put Rebecca in a difficult position, but as a fellow professional, Gladys felt compelled to report on the situation. The article was embarrassing for Old Kampala; communication with the media was temporarily strained.

But the freeze thawed between Gladys and Rebecca, as it always did. And now, again, the policewoman was appealing for the journalist's discretion as well as her assistance. Gladys made no promises about the former, but Rebecca sorely needed the latter.

Rebecca took a breath and delivered the bad news. There had been an accident at the station. A fire. Some boys had suffered burns. One was a street kid who had been hanging around the station for weeks. His name was Mugerwa Junior.

Of course Gladys remembered him. He was the boy with the bloodshot eyes who had told her he had been on his own for years. She had interviewed him at the station three weeks ago. While the length of his homelessness was notable, the boy's circumstances were not unusual for a street kid. She ran his profile and photo in her column, but no one responded. No parents, no relatives made contact with Old Kampala Police. Gladys ran the profile a second time; again nothing happened.

Mugerwa Junior's intention to quit the street was a positive sign, but Gladys had been reluctant to get involved in his case. Street boys lived lawless lives, and many places would not accept them. She had proposed Amahoro Home. The government facility was a bleak, rundown compound, but if Junior wanted to sleep under a roof, he would find one there.

No one had followed up on Gladys's suggestion that the boy be taken to Amahoro. And now he had been burned. At the police station.

"How is it that this boy ends up being here for almost an entire month," Gladys demanded, her voice rising like a sudden storm, "and no one has resettled him? And how did he get burned? These are children. They were not cooking. Where was the fire coming from? I want you to tell me! What were you doing with him? What kind of police are you?"

"It was not me! I didn't even know about it," protested Rebecca.

"That child is under your care! How can you not know about it? Those kids are your responsibility! Tell me how such a thing happened!"

Withering under the assault, Rebecca stammered out the details. Three boys who had been hanging out at the station had been performing small tasks for some of the police on staff. An officer had sent them to burn some trash behind the station. Tossed into the rubbish pile were exhibits from past cases, including some tins filled with chemicals used in counterfeiting. The tins exploded in the fire, burning all three of the boys. Two of the boys had families that retrieved them, but the third was the lost boy, Mugerwa Junior.

The fire had occurred on Friday. Two days ago. "And he has received no medical care?" Gladys's outrage funneled into Rebecca's ear, searing like sunlight through a lens. "How can adults not be able to dispose of chemicals you know nothing about, and make kids do it? How do you allow police to do this to children? Someone must be held responsible!"

Rebecca was not happy about the situation. Of course the boy required medical attention, but some were concerned that the doctors might ask questions. They would want to know what burned him, and under what circumstances. So the boy had languished at the station, untreated.

"No! That's wrong!" Gladys insisted. "Of course the doctors are entitled to know the answers. They want to give proper medicine!"

For a few minutes Gladys hammered Rebecca for information, and then the two hung up. There was nothing more to do but to wait for the morning, when Gladys would be able to see the boy's situation for herself.

GLADYS'S MONDAY SCHEDULE was typically full, so she was disappointed to discover that Rebecca was not present when Mike delivered her and Esther to Old Kampala Station. As Rebecca was the officer responsible for the children at the station, it would be harder to push forward Mugerwa Junior's case without her there.

Gladys walked around the compound of faded yellow buildings. Some male officers leaned against the guard hut, chatting and laughing. A woman and her half-dozen small children sat by a bush, sharing the meager shade with a resting goat.

Gladys found Junior waiting on a bench outside of the Child Protection Unit building. He was a dark boy with rounded features: a moon face, a soft hill of a brow, full lips forming a perfect circle of a mouth. But it was difficult to pay attention to such subtleties today. Gladys's eyes were drawn to the terrible ruptures of skin along his right arm and hand and across his cheek, chin, lips, and neck. His swollen forearm and hand looked wrapped in tree bark, the amber-colored pus weeping forth like sap. The skin on his face had already started to split in places, exposing raw pink flesh underneath. The boy wore a girl's polka-dotted camisole dress trimmed with lace, the feminine garment adding a touch of humiliation to his plight.

"He has no other clothes?"

"The ones he had were burned," an officer explained. This sleeveless top had seemed the best choice to avoid aggravating the blisters.

Gladys noticed that the boy's feet were bare. "What about shoes?"

"Everything was stolen." Junior spoke Luganda in a husky whisper.

"Stolen?"

"When I ran away from the fire, I left my slippers there. Someone took them."

"Ehhh . . . So when that thing exploded, everyone started running away. Show me, where did it happen?"

Junior pointed toward the back of the station, where the children often loitered around the wrecked cars. The half-dozen crushed and rusted heaps, one perplexingly upside down, had been there as long as anyone could remember. Between them, in the open area where sewage and other refuse was dumped down the slope to the street, a dark circle of black ash stretched across the dirt.

"The place where you were burned? It was right there?"

The boy nodded, his voice quiet but matter-of-fact. "The officer, he told us to clear some stuff out of storage for him. And then he told us to light it up and to make sure it burned completely. I was standing near there and something exploded."

"What exploded?"

"It was a tin."

"So when it exploded, it sprayed something on you."

"Yes."

"How about the other boys? How were they burned?"

"One on the face, the other on the leg."

"Badly?"

"With one kid, the eye nearly came out."

"Eh!" Gladys's exclamation rose sharply, as though she herself had been burned. It was outrageous, the negligence! But it would not do to rant and rave. To assist the boy, she required the cooperation of the police.

Mugerwa Junior gazed into space while the adults talked over his situation. He seemed frozen, as if even the movement of air on his skin might bring pain. There were grooves of fatigue under his bloodshot eyes. Those red eyes had been another reason that Gladys had originally declined to place the boy. Perhaps it was irritation from living out in the elements for so long, but it could also be a sign of drug use.

Another officer, a young man also with the family name Mugerwa, tried to assist in getting more information from the boy. "Junior, is Mugerwa your father's name?

The boy's voice was barely a whisper. "No."

"Yes, but if your name is Junior," said Esther, "then you must have your father's name."

The boy shook his head. He did not know it.

"How can he not know his father's name?" Gladys wondered aloud. He claimed he had been on the street for so long he could not name his father or his mother, nor any place he had lived. How could she resettle such a child? Whose past contained no A to B but only endless wandering?

"Has he been given any medicine?" Gladys asked.

"Yes," responded Officer Mugerwa. "We gave him some pills at the clinic."

The boy produced the plastic bag he had been given. The adults held it up in the sunlight and took turns squinting at the three types of pills inside.

"Amox . . ." muttered Gladys, recognizing the antibiotic. "This one?" She pointed to a second group of capsules.

Officer Mugerwa shrugged.

The third medication was Panadol. "Eh, Panadol is no longer issued to people," Gladys noted, clucking. There had been a move to ban the painkiller because of safety concerns. But the police clinic was little more than a desk and a couple of boxes of supplies; it provided what was on hand.

"Has he taken his medicine yet?" Esther asked.

"I don't think so," Officer Mugerwa replied. "He is supposed to take it on a full stomach."

Gladys suppressed her dismay. Of course the boy couldn't swallow medicine. There was no breakfast at the station. No food was available until the afternoon, when the maize flour was mixed into *kawunga*. And there was no guarantee that a street boy would get a share of the porridge, especially if Rebecca was absent. Eh! The clinic just tossed these pills to the boy, never questioning how he would achieve "a full stomach."

Junior confirmed that he hadn't eaten anything since the previous day, so Mike took him to a nearby food kiosk. As they waited in line, the boy maintained his still posture, eyes unblinking, his blistered arm held slightly away from his side. There was a sense of vigilance about him, as if he were monitoring a radio frequency too high for anyone else to hear. A black-and-white kitten crouched by the kiosk, meowing loudly, its cries histrionic next to Junior's stoicism.

When they returned to the bench, soda and cake in hand, Gladys had already sprung into action. She held one phone to her ear while she pressed the keypad of a second one on her lap. "The Mango lines are down . . . Esther, can you try the number on your phone? Do you have MTN or Mango? Try MTN. Why isn't Rebecca picking up? Eh! I'll try Caring Hands now. Okay, it's ringing."

Gladys finally reached Dr. John Mundaka, a physician associated with Caring Hands, an NGO that offered support to critically needy patients at Mulago, Uganda's largest hospital. "How come I can't reach you?" she cooed into the phone, her voice mock flirtatious. "You do not love me anymore!"

Pleasantries, even brief ones, were important to maintaining such relationships. When you turned to someone for help, it would not do to burst in with your demands. A moment of friendliness showed appreciation and smoothed the way. It was like Junior and his pills. You had to give a bit of food before the medicine.

"So the reason why I am calling you today is that I am in urgent need," she began. "I have a boy at Old Kampala who was involved in some kind of an accident. I can't explain it right now. He needs to go to Mulago, but I don't want to dump him there and leave him on his own. That's why I wanted to alert you."

A boy of eleven or twelve could not navigate Mulago Hospital by himself. In that crowded place, how would he know where to go? Which line to stand in? How would he understand what the doctors said? Plus he had no money for food or medicine. He might wander off into the street again.

Dr. John told Gladys to take the boy to the social worker at Mulago Hospital. Gladys scribbled in her notebook and again attempted to reach Officer Rebecca. Neither she nor Esther had any luck on their phones.

"What do I do?" Gladys mumbled, rubbing her chin. "I do not want to make all my decisions while Rebecca is not here. But her number does not go through."

Beside her on the bench, Mugerwa Junior nibbled at his large square of yellow cake, a bottle of cola held between his knees. The lap of the camisole top was littered with crumbs. Flies hovered around his uncapped soda bottle. One landed on the seeping burn on the back of his right hand. Junior tried to wave it away with his left, and his finger grazed the wound. He inhaled sharply and quivered, as though someone had slapped him awake. It was his first visible acknowledgment of pain.

"Can he take the pills now?"

"The soda takes some time to settle," Esther said.

"He should have had water." Gladys shook her head reproachfully. Of course a child would choose soda.

At last the call went through. "Ah, Rebecca. I've been at your place here for an hour and I'm about to leave," Gladys said. "I couldn't leave without talking to you and making some decisions. The burns are turning to sores now. The boy needs to be checked."

After a brief discussion, Rebecca authorized the young Officer Mugerwa to stay with Junior once Gladys got his situation cleared up at Mulago Hospital. Gladys hung up and gave a satisfied laugh. Good. She had arranged the first step of the plan.

And now it was time to rearrange her original plan. What appointments would she fail to make today? "Now this is the problem with Gladys," she said, staring down at her keypad again. "My schedule of work keeps changing. 'You said you would be here at noon!' she mimicked in a high, irritated voice as a ringtone sounded in her ear. "Oh my God . . ."

MULAGO HOSPITAL, a challenge to navigate under regular circumstances, was undergoing major renovation. Trucks and workers weaved through paths already congested with regular hospital activity. Departments were temporarily relocated, sending disoriented clients from building to building. Traffic entering the complex was redirected through different gates, the route changing constantly.

"We'll have to go through the back," Mike said. "Through the mortuary side." It was hardly an auspicious sign, entering a hospital through the mortuary.

"No, that way is also blocked," Esther disagreed.

While Mike and Esther quibbled over where to enter, Gladys thought about the impending meeting with Faith Karamagi, the principal medical social worker at Mulago. She had not worked directly with this Faith before. It was the social worker's job to assist patients with challenging issues; no doubt many cases landed on Faith's desk each day. Even in that stack of files, surely Junior—with his physical trauma, his youth, and his abandoned status—warranted particular attention. Gladys would do her best to press his case, but one never knew what to expect. Would she find a like-minded ally or someone who could not be bothered?

THE MEDICAL SOCIAL WORKER'S office suggested an orderly inhabitant: the walls were free of posters, the floors uncluttered by boxes, the desk tidy, with files lined up in three straight stacks. Faith was about Gladys's age—early fifties—a neatly composed figure in a beige business suit. She greeted her visitors, her manner courteous but watchful. Along the side wall, two coworkers sat quietly in observation.

Gladys introduced herself as a journalist from *New Vision* and Mugerwa Junior as a boy whom she had profiled. "You see, I put those missing children in my column."

Faith rested her hands on her desk. "I know. I have been following your column for some time."

"Thank you!" said Gladys, encouraged. "Now, I published this one's story, but no relatives have appeared yet. And then there is this accident." She waved at Junior, who was standing stiffly by the door. "Come closer!"

All eyes fixed on the boy as he made his way to the empty chair centered in front of Faith's desk. Junior sat down gingerly, careful not to touch his arms to the chair's arms. He tucked his bare feet under the seat as though to hide them.

Faith's brow furrowed as she looked him up and down, perplexed by the lacy camisole top. "It's a boy," she said finally.

"Yes, it's a boy." Gladys briefly explained how the three boys had been injured in the chemical fire. "The other two were burned badly. I'm not a doctor, but I think this boy is also burned badly. Police are now asking me who will be caring for him. I told them, if we get in touch with these people at Mulago, they have been so good to us whenever we have taken a child over there."

The social worker gazed steadily at Gladys, her expression unreadable. Gladys pressed on.

"Dr. John at Caring Hands advised me to get in touch with you. He told me, 'She will work it out for you.'"

"You have to go to Acute, and they will probably refer you to Burns," Faith said.

If this was a note of dismissal, Gladys chose not to receive it as such. "Ah, so Burns may be another department," she said, taking this as the pertinent information. "Of course I would like to turn him over to someone directly."

"We are not the ones who admit the patients," the social worker clarified. "With these cases, sometimes they need you to get in touch with the police office."

"Madame Faith. I understand what you are saying. In fact, a police officer who has been involved in this case will be meeting us here later. I was able to get him out of the office briefly."

"Which one?"

"Officer Mugerwa of Old Kampala."

"But he's supposed to come with the child." Faith gave a skeptical chuckle. "It is not 'getting him out of the office.' He's supposed to bring the child."

Gladys had overplayed the point, and she laughed too. No sense in trying to cover.

Another worker entered the office then. He frowned and gestured at the child. "So he is a boy?"

Everyone tittered.

"Yes," Gladys said. "This is Mugerwa Junior."

"Junior?" questioned Faith.

"It seems he must have the father's name, but he doesn't know it." The answer dissatisfied Gladys even as she offered it. The boy needed a proper name. He could not just be the "junior" to a man whose name he could not recall.

"Call him Godfrey," she added, impulsively offering the name of her own beloved brother who had passed away. "Godfrey Mugerwa."

"So he does not know his parents."

Gladys shook her head. "He told me that he only recalls one time that he was moving with his parents. They reached the park and he needed to relieve himself. So instead of telling his parents where he was going, he just—you know, as a small boy, he could just sneak out and do his thing. But by the time he came back, he couldn't see them anymore. And you know, with such a place, the more you keep running around to look for someone, the more you get lost."

The social worker nodded. This happened often in Kampala. A child could disappear in a city crowd quicker than a pebble in a sack of beans.

"So that's how he parted from his parents. When you ask him how long ago, he says, 'I don't know, I've been here for so long.'" Gladys imitated the boy's small voice. "'I don't remember how many years, but I've been on the street all the time.' On reaching Old Kampala Police Station, he told them, 'I'm tired of the street. I want to go to school.' That's why they called me.

"At first I was hesitating. I don't trust street children. But for the more than three weeks he has stayed at Old Kampala, the in-charge, Rebecca, has confirmed that he has not been behaving like street children. You know how those street children always appear there? Within three days they disappear again."

Faith nodded. "Here, after you treat them, they will run away."

"By the way!" Gladys agreed. "That's what the in-charge was telling me. So she was trying to study this one. She knew that within a week, if he was not serious, he would run away. He has not. And it's coming up to a month. So I'm now trying to see if I can get him treatment and then take him out of police hands."

"I understand," Faith said, her tone neutral. It was hard to gauge the impact of the boy's story on her. She did not chime in with affirmations or exclamations; she did not even straighten files or fiddle with a pen. She only listened and watched.

"I think he would be better off if I can get him in a boarding school. My suggestion would be Entebbe Early Learning School. I need him in a friendly environment. And the director there is so friendly. I have not taken there any children from the street . . ." Gladys gestured at the boy. "But this one needs love. He has not been loved for so many years. He missed that age, you know, where your mom pampers you." The half smile that had softened her face was shaken away by a confident nod. "If he gets cured, I can connect him to Early Learning School."

Faith allowed a short pause to confirm the end of Gladys's testimony. Then she unfolded her hands and placed them on the desk, as if to push herself up. "Let's get him to Acute. And let them advise us what we are going to do."

"Okay," agreed Gladys, inwardly rejoicing at the social worker's use of *we*. "We will follow you."

AS GLADYS, ESTHER, and the boy trailed Faith to the Acute Care Unit, the disruption from the hospital's renovation became more evident, as their way was blocked and rerouted around construction materials, vehicles, obstructed entrances, and makeshift waiting areas.

When they crossed from one building to another, a man in a lab coat spotted Junior and did a double-take. He nudged his companion and gestured. His companion gasped audibly as the burned boy passed.

Entering a courtyard, Faith led them along a dispirited line of people snaking down a very long hallway. Junior Godfrey started at the wild-animal squeal of a passing gurney. A young man in a bloody shirt was sitting upright on the gurney, pointing in different directions, trying to help the orderly navigate.

"The main building is being renovated," explained Faith, "so almost every corner is turned into a treatment area."

As they walked alongside the queue, more battered gurneys rattled by, full ones going in, a couple of empty ones coming out. The line terminated in a knot of people pressed up against a glass reception window. Above a doorway was taped a handwritten paper sign: CASUALITY UNIT.

"This is our emergency room," Faith said.

Watching Faith move to the head of the queue to speak directly to the man at the desk, Gladys felt a surge of relief. Thank God the social worker had agreed to assist them. All around, clusters of people lined the walls: women and babies, grandmothers, a man curled on the floor in a fetal position. Some might have been there since seven in the morning. They might spend the whole day waiting in line, in all levels of distress and pain and hunger and fatigue.

This is why Gladys had begged. Her approach had been light and respectful, but really she had begged. Junior Godfrey was just a boy. You could not send a boy to a hallway like this and tell yourself you had helped him.

NOW THAT THE boy would be examined here, they would need to enter his name on the admission forms. Names were a concern for Gladys, as her editors always demanded proper identification for the people she wrote about. That was not always possible for, say, a nine-month-old baby found by a roadside or a teenager with mental deficiencies. Given that Mugerwa Junior Godfrey was clear of mind and at least eleven years of age, she was irked by the lack of clarity over his true name.

"You don't even remember your parents' names?"

The boy shook his head.

"That's not extraordinary," Faith observed. "It's possible he could not remember the parents' names. Because here children call their mothers Mommy, they don't call them by their names."

"No! But how can they not know the names?"

"Gladys," Faith said, almost gently, "I was shocked. It is not just the children. If you ask a woman, she may not know the name of the father of her children."

Gladys wrinkled up her nose and shook her head as though passing an overfilled latrine on a hot day. "Ah, no. No, Faith. No way. No, no, no. Whoever says that—"

"And she doesn't have only one child. One, two three ... She doesn't know the name of the father."

In previous generations it had been inconceivable that a child would not know his people, his family, his clan. Today many couples met in the city and cohabitated without bothering to find out where each other's village was. But not even to know each other's names!

"Shocking."

"I was very shocked," Faith repeated. "But it is normal. There are very many people who don't know those details."

"So it is just, 'Sweetie ...'" Gladys imitated a high, flirty voice. The women laughed together.

As she and the social worker exchanged cordial farewells, Gladys was buoyed by the feeling that she had gained a colleague. It seemed clear now that Faith had not been giving Gladys a hard time in the office; she had been prudently observing, to assess this journalist's conduct. And that was fair.

Soon Officer Mugerwa arrived to take over the task of accompanying Junior Godfrey through Acute Care. The boy had been standing near the wall; now he raised his head, happy to see the officer. The flap of skin on his face had split further, revealing a startling meat-pink slash underneath. Gladys winced internally. If it hurt simply to look at him, what kind of pain must the boy himself be experiencing?

Still, Faith had reported that he would be seen shortly, and Gladys felt it was safe to take her leave.

"Godfrey." It took a moment for the boy to respond; he had owned the name for only an hour. "Officer Mugerwa will stay with you now. And I will come to check on you later, okay?"

The boy nodded at her as the young officer rubbed his head. Mugerwa Junior and Officer Mugerwa.

Weeks ago, when Gladys had first interviewed the boy for her column, Officer Rebecca had commented that the boy might have chosen the name Mugerwa simply because he liked Officer Mugerwa. Lying about one's name was something a typical street boy would do. Was this street boy typical?

She made her way back down the crowded hallway. There would be time to discover the answers to these questions. She and her colleagues must attend to the burns first. Then they would attend to the child.

The Boy with Seven Names, Part Two

MUGERWA JUNIOR GODFREY

Then he said, 'I'll give each child five thousand shillings to go for treatment.' Can you imagine? Can five thousand get you treatment in Uganda?"

Gladys shook her head, allowing Officer Rebecca's rant to flow. The two women were sharing the bench outside Old Kampala Station. The morning sun provided a wide spotlight for Rebecca's indignation over the colleague who had dropped Junior Godfrey's fiery accident into her lap.

"He tells me, 'Your children are burned. Take care of them.' Just like that. I said, 'If they are our children, why do you make them do that work? You have these suspects here. You have some idlers. Why not have them do the work?'"

It did not seem quite proper to place prisoners in the path of explosive chemicals either, but Gladys let the point slide. Just as Gladys had erupted at Rebecca when hearing about the boys' accident, now it was Rebecca's turn to blow off steam.

"These are the problems I have every day," Rebecca said forcefully. "Because that is child labor. And after the incident they did not even take them to hospital!"

Given the circumstances, the higher-ups preferred to wash their hands of the affair, and of the children involved. Without the official support and resources to handle the boy's case, Officer Rebecca had had little recourse but to involve Gladys.

Gladys appreciated her friend's predicament. "So then you call me, and I blast your ear off," she said.

"Yes, I also felt fire!" Rebecca quipped, and the two bellowed with laughter.

A young male officer peered curiously at them from around the corner, then quickly ducked out of sight again.

What these men must think of them, thought Gladys. On Monday the two big women might shout and argue and hang up on each other. On Wednesday they would be huddled on the bench, giggling like conspiring schoolgirls.

They could always get themselves sorted out, Gladys reasoned, because they understood each other. They were both practical women. What other Child and Family Protection Unit officer besides Rebecca kept a spare uniform hanging in the office? Here was a colleague with whom she could speak freely, argue honestly, and strategize realistically. They might exchange a few bruises, but they would hammer out a plan.

Gladys did not fear Rebecca, nor did Rebecca fear Gladys. But together the two women frightened others, particularly their male colleagues.

"Do you remember when we were talking in your office together one time," Gladys asked, "there was an officer who said, 'If you take these two women into your home, it will be on fire'?"

"'It will be on fire!'" Rebecca echoed, and they both hooted with laughter.

"What—what did—" It took a few gasping starts for Gladys to complete her question. "What did he think of us really? Why did he make such a comment?"

"Because, as you know, we are not easy. We are principled. When we make decisions, it is not easy to change them."

"Yes. By the way"—Gladys was laughing again—"you don't just tell us, 'This is done like this,' and we follow. No! No way!"

The banter went like this for some minutes. The shade retreated across the bench while the sun's heat increased.

Rebecca glanced around. "I don't know what is taking Officer Abdullah so long. He should have finished with Junior's bath by now."

"Abu!" Gladys called out, in no particular direction. "We want to see our boy!"

THOUGH GLADYS CHATTED easily with Rebecca, her mind had not fully rested since she had last seen the boy, two days ago. Her relief at getting him assistance at Mulago was short-lived. That night had found her sleepless. With the burns already starting to fester, she worried that the boy had not had a tetanus shot. *That child, I've left him at that hospital,* she fretted to herself. *Has he been examined? What did the doctor say? Has the boy eaten?*

She called Officer Mugerwa, who told her that Junior was now back at Old Kampala Police Station. A doctor had examined the boy and given him a tetanus injection. He would need to be seen again in two days. In the meantime he was to be given frequent fluids. The doctor recommended passionfruit juice. Gladys thanked him for the heartening news.

As night fell, her relief again evaporated. It was the cursed juice. Where would you expect a boy like that to get drinks, let alone passionfruit juice? She could not blame Office Mugerwa for failure to provide. Police officers were paid very little. He could not afford additional expenses like juice. Who knew if he even had enough money for his own children at home?

Now the boy was again stuck at the police station. Did he have food to prepare his stomach for medicine? Or even water to swallow with it?

Such thoughts buzzed around her head like the flies around Junior's weeping hand, circling the most vulnerable parts of the wound. How could she swat these worries away? How could she drift off to sleep in her bed knowing that the boy shivered in a filthy wreck of a car?

Her children, they really suffered, and at night she suffered with them. This irrepressible empathy sometimes frustrated her boss, Cathy. "You take the issues of these children too much to heart," Cathy would scold. "You must learn to stop it."

Gladys knew that Cathy spoke out of concern. But it was never so simple as flicking a switch; she could not turn off her feelings along with the light. It brought to mind the inn sign she always passed when going to Old Kampala: FOR SIMPLE REST. *Simple rest?* Gladys would scoff. *What is that? I may need a complicated rest! And you are telling me you are offering only simple.*

The only effective cure for her worry was to solve the problem. She had to find a home for Mugerwa Junior Godfrey.

HER FIRST CHOICE was still Early Learning School, but she had no tuition money to offer. The garden project was not yet profitable, despite Zam's energetic efforts. The young mother called her almost daily to report on the crops' progress, new expenses, hassles with Kiviri the landlord, and her own hard work. Unfortunately, the income from the occasional harvest was still minuscule compared to Gladys's outlay.

Expenses aside, would Director Agnes even accept a boy who had lived on the streets for so long? And could Gladys ask her to?

The nine children Gladys had sent to Agnes were innocents. Life had betrayed them, and they deserved refuge. Street kids, on the other hand, often ran to the street willingly, kicking off supervision like a pair of too-tight shoes. Their unruly habits could be a damaging influence.

Gladys did not turn to homes like Early Learning School with every needy child. Reunion with a family member was a case's preferred outcome. For those without families, like Junior, Good Samaritans could often be found to assist with school fees and medical bills, and there were other facilities she could call upon. But Early Learning School was special. A child under Agnes's care could receive not only education and a place to sleep but also love.

The last time Gladys had called Agnes on behalf of a child, the director had turned her down. She was very sorry, but the school had just relocated, and there was simply too much to handle. Although Gladys understood, she felt hurt. She had gotten her hopes up.

With the urgency of Junior Godfrey's case, Gladys was again prepared to press. But she had to know that her footing was solid.

"I REALLY NEED to convince Agnes to accept this boy," she confessed to Rebecca as they continued to wait for Junior to return from his bath. "But I am still a bit worried. Can he behave? He is coming from the street. How do you see it?"

Rebecca spoke without hesitation. "This boy has turned out to be very humble," she said. "You know, we get these kids turning up. If they are from the streets, we just ignore them. That is their first 'interview.' Most boys who have been on the street, they will disappear that day. Junior passed the interview. He came back the next day. And the day after. He is consistent. In the morning he comes to see me in the office. He cleans for us. I asked him once, where did you learn how to clean? He said, 'I watched people. And I learned from that.' So he may have earned a little money or food that way."

"Ehh . . ." So the boy was willing to work.

"It really seems he's tired of the street. And he says he has no parents." She shrugged. "Maybe the mother abandoned him at a tender age, so he didn't know the father. Which is typical of some of these ladies in the slums."

"So he could be from one of the slum areas," Gladys said slowly, seeing the logic.

"At times, you know, these women die and leave children behind," Rebecca went on. "The neighbors do not know her village, where she's coming from, and they just take the body to the city morgue. The boy could be a victim of that."

Junior Godfrey emerged then, unescorted, from behind the buildings. This morning he wore his usual dark-blue pants, but replacing the girl's camisole was a plain white T-shirt. The shirt was in good condition, with only a few pinholes at the collar. He answered the women's greetings politely, his posture less rigid but his manner still solemn.

Mike joined the group at the bench, and the three adults surveyed the boy's injuries. The burns on his arm had continued their gruesome metamorphosis. Some blisters had burst and shriveled; others were leaking. The larger boils along his arm were distended with fluid, looking to Gladys as though they would burst at the touch.

"The water, it will come out," Rebecca advised. "You don't want to disturb it, as it will cause a lot of pain."

"Let it come out naturally," Mike concurred. "The skin under the boil must be able to heal itself."

The burned areas on Junior's cheek, nose, earlobe, and chin had mostly fallen away. Large patches of tender skin stretched the length of his face, tongue-pink against his normal deep brown.

"Do you have pain?" Mike asked in Luganda.

"I feel much better than before," the boy reported. "Although the place where the shot was given is very sore."

Concluding the medical review, the grownups noticed the boy's feet. They were clad in new plastic slippers.

"Look," Mike said. "The other day I gave him some money to put in his pocket, and he went and bought himself slippers."

The purchase of these shoes told Gladys something about the boy. He had walked across the street in his bare feet, and he had spent his money because he did not want to have bare feet when he crossed back again. Most young boys would have used their shillings on soda and candy. Some would have stolen slippers from someone else. But it seemed that this one was thinking maturely. Spending money on shoes demonstrated a willingness to invest beyond the hours of the given day.

The adults all stared down in appreciation at the bright blue slippers. The boy ducked his head, the gesture only partly hiding his grin of satisfaction.

REBECCA RETURNED TO her office, leaving Gladys to the next step in her plan: calling Director Agnes at Early Learning School.

Gladys did not like to force people to do things. It was unpleasant, and in the end it did not work. You could not make someone do what he or she was unable to do. A person might say yes to escape the pressure of the moment, but the next day, would such a person follow through?

There were those who would not help and those who could not help. Then there were those who were inclined to help but who were very busy or distracted. With those in the last group, you needed to capture their attention. To inspire their support.

It was fair play to plead a child's case. And plead she would.

Agnes was inclined to help; she had a big heart. If she refused Gladys again, it would be out of practical or financial concerns. Taking in a street boy would be both a risk and an expense. Early Learning School already supported a lot of indigent children, most of them delivered to the home by one Gladys Kalibbala.

It took a half-dozen tries, but Gladys finally reached Agnes on the phone. Jumping in, she summarized Junior's history from the time of her first profile to the burning accident to his treatment at Mulago Hospital.

"I was so, so, so scared that the boy didn't have a tetanus shot. But he got the shot and some medicine and now he's doing much better. Of course, he can't stay here at Old Kampala Police, where the only place to sleep is those old vehicles. I really want to see this kid get off the street. Please help me, Agnes."

It had been a lengthy monologue, but here she dared to pause for a breath. In the moment of silence, Gladys braced for the dreaded words: "Sorry, Gladys . . ." But what came was not words, only a choking sound. Agnes was sobbing.

"Okay, okay, okay, you bring him. Bring him here," she managed. Her tearful reply was so loud, even through the tinny phone, that Mike glanced over curiously.

With her phone still pressed to her ear, Gladys swayed her body from side to side, waving her fist in a silent victory dance that made the bench rock beneath her. She pushed out her lower lip and wagged her chin. *Woo-woo-woo!*

"Thank you, sweetie!" she squealed, sending a delighted peal of laughter into the receiver. Her huge grin revealed every one of her perfect white teeth. "Thank you so much, dear. We will bring him Thursday!"

AFTER SHARING THE good news with Rebecca and Officer Mugerwa in the office, Gladys went to find Junior.

He was sitting on the bench, tugging at the corners of a checked hankie that Mike had given him to keep the flies off his arm. The boy listened as she told him about Early Learning School and the other children she had taken there.

"You know, I feared taking you on since you've been on the streets," she admitted. "I don't want to send you to a school where you will teach the children bad manners."

"I won't," the boy protested. "I want to study."

Gladys scrutinized the boy. His eyes, those bloodshot eyes, were round with hope. She wished she knew what made them so red. But it was too late for second thoughts.

"Okay, Godfrey, I am going to take you on."

The boy blinked at her, as though unsure of her meaning.

"You see, my request has been granted, and I will be taking you to Early Learning School." She bent down to stare directly into his eyes. "You will be going to school."

A smile raised every feature in Junior Godfrey's round face, and the effect was that of watching the moon turn into the sun. The joy in his face eclipsed his injuries.

"The minute I hear you are acting badly, we will come to the school and take you out."

"No, no, Auntie, I will be good."

"Okay." Gladys attempted a stern expression, but there was no steel supporting it. "I will keep studying your behaviors. Behave."

"I will."

Surely that smile must have strained that poor face. Those wounds had never been stretched so wide! But the boy kept beaming, and Gladys beamed back.

The Boy with Seven Names, Part Three

MUGERWA JUNIOR GODFREY VICTOR

The morning they went to pick up Junior was not a cheerful one for Mike. It had started in Kampala with Gladys's rounds at Jinja Road Station, where she had interviewed a sixteen-year-old mother with two children, aged three years and six months. Fleeing an abusive uncle who liked to hang kids from a tree to beat them, the girl had been taken in by a couple whose grown son then defiled her. Pregnant at twelve, she was now HIV-positive. Her toddler looked reasonably healthy, but her infant was emaciated. While Gladys discussed the possibilities for medical treatment, Mike watched in pity and horror as the girl's baby struggled and failed to hold his head up.

"Gladys," Mike announced when they were back on the road, "I can't take any more!" He chuckled without mirth. "That girl . . . the baby . . . really, Gladys, I want you out of my car!"

Gladys's laugh was simpler; she had heard such sentiments before. "That is what my boss Cathy tells me sometimes. 'Please, Gladys. Not today. Spare me today.'"

Life spared no one, though, so one had to savor the small triumphs whenever they came.

Like this one: their return to Old Kampala Station to retrieve Junior Godfrey. Mike could not sit back to enjoy the moment, as the roadway was even more congested than usual. While he muttered under—and over—his breath, Gladys relished the sight of Junior sitting in the front passenger seat. He was finally leaving the police station. From now on this boy would ride in vehicles, not sleep in them.

In his lap the boy clutched a small plastic bag of pills. In addition to his white T-shirt, his blue pants, his slippers, and the checked hankie Mike had given him, this was all he owned in the world. Gladys knew she could not take him to Early Learning School with so little. She did not have money to buy him a mattress, but they could find him a cheap blanket on the way to Entebbe.

"Godfrey, how do you feel, leaving this place?"

The boy didn't answer.

"Godfrey?" He turned and blinked at her. "Don't forget your name now. You are Mugerwa Junior Godfrey. I want to know, how do you feel being taken away from this place now?"

"I feel so good, leaving here."

She offered him a biscuit, which he accepted with a clear "Thank you."

"Eh!" Gladys uttered. "You know some English."

He reverted to Luganda. "I know a little. I hear how people greet each other."

"Have you ever been to school?"

"No. Never."

She had feared as much. "What do you want to study? What kind of work do you want to do?"

"I want to be a policeman."

"Eh! Like Officer Rebecca." This was an uncommon aspiration for a street kid. Most boys his age dreamed of becoming football stars. "What you must know: to be like Rebecca, you must study. You must study very hard. Because you've never been to school, you will find yourself in a class with very young children. So you will be bigger than the others. But you should not worry about that. Just study. Do what you have to do."

Junior nodded. This one was not too old to catch up, she thought. Not like poor Ezra. When she had taken Ezra to Early Learning School, he had been about seventeen years old. In a class with seven-year-olds! And unable to count to fifty. He had made progress, but the gap between him and his peers still loomed large.

This boy, though, seemed primed for the challenge. His hands were small and his voice high, but there was a hard seed of resolve planted in that soft ground. Although he had been living the street life, he identified less with his peers than with the police. Perhaps he had, as Rebecca had suspected, taken the name Mugerwa after Officer Mugerwa.

"Why do you like the idea of becoming a policeman?" Gladys asked.

The young voice answered swiftly. "I want to stop instability in this country."

Mike released a snort of admiration. "That is a very sophisticated answer," he said in English.

"I wouldn't expect such a one to give me that reason," Gladys agreed.

Mike glanced over at his small passenger, following up in his language. "How do you judge 'instability' in your own mind?"

"When people like to fight each other. They kill each other, they torture each other. That's what I want to stop."

"Where have you been seeing that?" Gladys asked.

"The street. They have been beating the weak people. Or even beating their friends. To the extent of killing them."

"Okay." Gladys absorbed this with a sigh. "That's good reasoning."

"What did you experience on the street," Mike pressed, "that made you want to leave?"

"Wherever we slept, people came in the night and beat us, chased us." The boy worried the corner of the checked hankie, which he wore knotted about his neck. "So it was a very difficult life."

"Who was beating you?"

"The city authorities. And other children, of course. The bigger street boys. They move with sharp objects in the night, and they stab you when you are sleeping."

"Why would they stab you?"

"Because they want your money. If you have anything, they stab you and take it."

"How did you get money?"

"We would collect water bottles, or mop and sweep people's homes. Wash their porches. Or if someone needed us to carry something, we would get a few shillings."

Mike waved at a taxi driver to let him into a traffic circle. "How much money have you ever held in your hand, since you've been on the street?"

"It might be a thousand shillings," answered the boy. Then, recalculating, "No, three hundred shillings."

A paltry sum, Gladys thought. "I think he would only be able to buy a cup of porridge."

"It takes five hundred shillings for a cup of porridge," Mike said. How many verandas would the boy need to wash for that cup of porridge?

The *matatu* ahead of them abruptly slowed, jerking toward the side of the road. "Ah!" Mike muttered as he hit the brakes. "These idiots don't want to live."

The taxi conductor leaned out of the open door and began waving and shouting at a potential customer. Another *matatu* had stopped to hunt the same game, and soon the two conductors were waving and shouting at each other. As the Volvo pulled past, the motto on the back of the second taxi was revealed: JESUS FIRST.

"The street. You can't believe the street." Mike made it sound like the name of an incurable disease. He knew that many boys entered the life giddily, enticed by the thrill of freedom and unruliness. Sooner or later the street would hit them back, hard. "You see those boys becoming hardcore creatures in order to survive the street."

Mugerwa Junior Godfrey, though, did not seem the least bit hardcore. Somehow his vulnerability remained visibly intact. Most street kids developed a leathery exterior—weather-beaten faces, reptilian skin—to match their callused natures, but Junior's skin was still smooth. There were white-line scars here and there, perhaps from the nighttime knife attacks he had mentioned, and there were those bloodshot eyes. But there was a sweetness to that round face, an underlying softness.

This presented a bit of a puzzle. Gladys had seen how the street divided its inhabitants into predator and prey. Junior said he had been on the streets for many years. If he had not crossed into the predator category, how had he survived as prey?

"Well," Gladys said, "let's give this one some new life. And see what comes out of it."

WHEN THEY REACHED Entebbe, intermittent showers began to fall, so that Mike had to keep switching the wipers on and off.

"Can you see Lake Victoria?" he asked Junior.

The boy turned to look. Here, with the road running close to shore, the beaches stretched across the expanse of his rain-dotted window. The big blue field of water went on and on. The boy stared and stared.

"Have you seen it before?"

"No. I have never seen a lake before."

The grownups laughed, enjoying the boy's astonishment. His life was about to open up. He would be living in a new city under a new name. His past would become a place visited only in bad dreams.

But still Gladys wondered. There must be some trace of that past he could carry into his future. "If you were to meet your parents, would you remember what they looked like?" she asked him.

"No, I can't remember their faces."

Gladys gave a sad, heavy sigh. "Is there nobody in your family you remember? No relatives?"

"No," the boy said plainly. He was still transfixed by the lake. "I am alone."

Imagine, Gladys thought, forgetting the faces of your own parents. How could a child of Uganda have no relatives? In this country, where a woman typically gave birth to six children, a child's world should be filled with siblings, cousins, aunties, and uncles. How could this boy have no one?

Well, she mused wryly, he was not completely alone. He had gained Mommy Gladys.

"You know," she remarked to Mike as they turned onto the dirt road to the school, "maybe this burning accident was a blessing in disguise."

Mike's eyes flicked up at her in the rearview mirror. She nodded, realizing how improper it sounded. "I had not wanted to take this one on. But it made me change my mind. I felt so sorry for him. With those burns, and just left there like that." The corners of her mouth drooped, pulling her face down with them. She added softly, "I felt so bad."

THE LAND WAS flat and open near the school. They could see small figures jump up at the sight of the car and run back toward the compound like termites retreating to their mound. By the time the Volvo pulled into the driveway, the self-appointed sentries had reemerged, bringing Agnes with them. The school director wore a white-and-red damask blouse, a pearl-gray skirt, and a knitted brow.

Agnes rounded the front of the car and opened Junior's door. As soon as he stepped out, she enveloped him in a hug that was warm, tight, and a threat to his open wounds. If the boy was startled, no one could tell, as his face was trapped against Agnes's breast. After a long moment she released him, keeping one arm around his shoulders and her head lowered to his.

"How long have you been on the street?"

"I don't remember. I think since I was four years old."

"Where did you stay all those years?"

"I stayed in unfinished houses."

Agnes's interrogation was gentle but direct. As Junior responded, his index finger wandered toward the car door and began picking at a chip in the dark-green paint.

"Were you stealing?"

"No."

"Are you lying?"

"No."

"You must not lie."

"Yes."

Small kids crept up on either side of the car, hoping for a glimpse of the new boy. Agnes shooed them away with a quick wave of her hand.

"How did you end up at police?"

"A security guard who was Indian escorted me to the police. He told me they would help me," Junior answered, flicking away another speck of paint.

By the end of the interrogation, the bare spot on the car door was the size of a cashew. "Well, I'm glad to see you here," Agnes said finally, holding him a moment longer. "It will be okay."

She waved over an older boy who had been standing a polite distance away. He was perhaps fifteen, stretched out tall and skinny by adolescence. "See this boy? This is Dennis. His mother died, and he was on the streets for over three years. He's here, and he's well behaved. He doesn't steal. Children here don't steal, do you understand? They don't fight. And they know God. Have you ever been to church?"

"No," answered Junior. "I am too dirty for church."

Agnes's face crumpled, her eyes welling up instantly. "You have got a home now. You will never have to sleep outside again. You will sleep under this roof." Then she asked, almost as an afterthought, "And what is your name?"

"Junior. And now they call me Godfrey."

Gladys came around the car with Junior's medical record and papers authorizing the boy's placement at the school. Agnes scanned the letters from Community Services and the Kampala CPU. The heading of the probation officer's letter read:

RE: TEMPORARY PLACEMENT FOR MUGERWA JUNIOR (11 YEARS)

Agnes gave a throaty chuckle. "You know, in this letter here, the police say 'temporary placement.' But the police never come back!" The two women erupted into cackles.

"They don't know English!" said Agnes, snorting.

"None of them!" Gladys roared.

"They say 'temporary placement' and they stay away forever!"

It took them a full minute to regain their composure. They patted their chests and wiped their eyes as the children stared at them.

"It is always a 'temporary' issue, but no one from police comes." Agnes sighed. "No one there ever checks on these children again."

Gladys placed a hand on Agnes's shoulder, feeling such affection and appreciation for her colleague. How would she have managed, if not for Agnes? It was a never-ending struggle for Gladys to produce the money for school fees and expenses for the children she had brought to the school, but she knew that Agnes would never kick them out for lack of funds.

What did Agnes think of her, she wondered, bringing another boy to the school while there were already several at the home with unpaid fees? Here was another needy child lacking clothes, a mattress, what-what. Gladys did not have much, but she contributed what she had. Surely Agnes recognized that?

Well, she could not say for sure what Agnes thought of her. But she knew what Agnes's husband thought. He was not happy with her at all. When he saw these two women together, his face grew as stony as that of a father watching his teenage daughter touch hands with a boy. He knew something bad must be taking place. That Gladys woman was probably leaving a basket of quadruplets on his doorstep! The school was a family business, and nonpaying orphans did not help with the bills. No doubt he viewed Gladys as an ever-heavier weight sinking his bottom line. And really, could she disagree?

Two boys appeared, bearing clothing for the new boy. "Hold them up, let me see."

Junior Godfrey posed with the two shirts, his wardrobe effectively tripled. He did not smile; he wore the slow, stunned look of someone who has just awakened from a dream.

"His eyes are so red," Agnes commented. "Is it from the fire?"

"No," said Gladys. "They were that way when I met him the first time. It may just be a result of living outside."

"I don't like it," Agnes said suddenly.

"What do you not like?"

"Godfrey is not a good name for him." Agnes was very opinionated when it came to names. "He needs another name. A strong name."

Gladys waited. She had her own opinions of Agnes's practice of changing students' names, but it did not seem appropriate to voice them now.

Holding one open palm flat, Agnes began to shrug her shoulders up and down, as though she were trying to catch the tempo of a song played at low volume. "Like ... like ..." She bounced an invisible ball on her palm, conjuring up the name. "Like Victor. *Victor.* That is a good name for him. It means someone who wins." She was in a groove now, bobbing in place. "'I'm a winner,'" she chortled, trying it on for size. "'I'm Victor!'"

"That's fine," Gladys acquiesced, her voice neutral. So on top of the new city, the new school, and the new home, the boy had another new name. "Victor."

Ezra, who often acted as a kind of student captain, offered to show the newcomer the sleeping quarters. The boy would have to share a bed with another student, as he lacked his own mattress. Still, it was a step up. When was the last time this one had slept in any kind of bed? Had he ever?

Gladys was quite certain he had never celebrated his birthday, as he could not even confirm his age. Of course, he would be included as a guest of honor at the Early Learning birthday party. It was a pleasurable feeling, to think of the good things in store for one who had endured so much.

Gladys watched him shuffle off behind the other boys. Although he was now Mugerwa Junior Godfrey Victor, she would still think of him as Junior. And for the first time she felt that she was leaving Junior in safe hands.

AFTER VISITING THE DORM, Junior-turned-Victor followed the other students to class. Over sixty bodies packed the room, filling every bench. He sat next to his new friend Dennis, by the wall near the back. In the light of the window, his pink wounds fairly glowed.

The chorus was summoned to the front of the classroom to perform the Early Learning School song, which Agnes loved; she was fond of saying that its lyrics contained all her aspirations. Even if Junior Victor did not understand the English words, the song was an important part of the welcome ritual.

The boys and girls of the chorus assembled in two rows. Ezra was the tallest of the bigger kids in the rear; Deborah, his size by half, stood front row center. Right hands raised to chins, fingers pointing up, the singers began:

> *The aim is helping learners realize their skills and*
> *Developing confidence in pupils, and make them accept themselves.*
> *Encouraging each child in areas where they can excel later.*

What the lyrics lacked in cadence they made up for in sincerity. The children's pure voices lifted them with the agility of roots growing around rocks.

> *Helping children to be law-abiding citizens who respect their land*
> *By protecting their environment and community.*
> *To help those who have missed parental love and care . . .*

As the students around him swayed to the music, Junior bobbed along intermittently, then gave up. By the third verse, his eyes began to glaze over.

> *Our mission statement tells us to bring up children who will change*
> *this nation through love,*
> *And who will excel in all areas of their lives.*
> *God bless Early Learning School!*
> *God bless Early Learning School!*
> *Now and forevermore!*

The singers took their seats, and Agnes resumed her place at the blackboard. "We have a new student," she announced. "Come, Victor."

The children turned to look at the boy, who reflexively lowered his blistered face. If he had dared to meet their eyes, he would have seen that their curiosity was simple, not morbid.

Most of the students had homes and supportive families who paid their fees, but some, primarily the ten who had been brought by Gladys, lacked both. The school was their home, the staff and classmates their family. Here the tall teenager with the lopsided face was a leader, the little girl with the hunchback an ambassador. Not knowing all this, Junior kept his head bowed as he shuffled to the front of the classroom.

"This is Victor." Agnes took the new boy's hand and briefly explained his past on the street. "He was there eating in those rubbish places. And sleeping outside. For a long time. Finally he went to police, and he was burned by something. Now Auntie Gladys asked if he could come here.

"Many times I've said, 'I don't want any more children in the school, I have enough! I don't have *posho,* I don't have beans. And now you are bringing in more.' But this time, when she told me Victor's story, I said, 'Let him come.' Here he can rest, and have peace. So he has come to us. We can't send him away."

A few of the children stood. Agnes pointed to one boy.

"I will give him clothes," the boy said. The kids all clapped.

"I will buy him something to eat," offered another student.

"Who else among the boys wants to give him something?" Agnes called out.

One said he had a pair of shoes that might fit Victor. A girl raised her hand, saying that she would like to donate her 100 shillings for a haircut.

"Thank you very much," Agnes said.

Deborah stood up. "I would like to give him one of my shirts," she piped up in her high, musical voice. It was hard to image that anything small enough for her frame would fit a boy of eleven or twelve, but Agnes smiled and thanked her.

"As you can see," she said, addressing the whole of the class, "we are here on this world to give." She looked down at Junior and spoke quietly in Luganda, relaying to him what his classmates had pledged.

"So don't take what's not yours. When you were living on the street, when you were hungry, you had to eat some horrible things. Still you need not take what is not yours."

The boy looked up at the rows of expectant faces. He swallowed, then said in Luganda, "Thank you for helping me."

"You need to speak up," Agnes urged. "They have not heard anything."

The second attempt was only marginally audible, but Agnes took pity and released him. Junior sank onto his bench. If the flood of goodwill had buoyed him, he lacked the certainty to float along; he seemed still to struggle with the current.

He stared blankly at the words Agnes had written on the blackboard: *Wisdom is the application of knowledge.* With so many bodies in the classroom, the air had grown warm. Placing an elbow on the desk, he rested the good side of his face in his palm. For a moment he looked like any other boy in a stuffy classroom at the end of a long afternoon. A hand rose to his mouth just in time to cover a yawn.

Silver Sandals on the Yellow Line

NAKINTU MISTREATED

Nine-year-old Olivia Nakintu was born with a swelling on her back. She was found loitering the streets and is currently at Kawempe Police Station. She claimed her mother, Agnes Mbabazi, had been mistreating her and she revealed a big scar where she reportedly burnt her with a hot knife.

In tears, she said her mother discriminated against her because of her disability, so she had decided to look for her father, Misuseera Sebutali of Ndegi village near Lukaya town.

In some of Gladys's cases, all the names were known. Each star in the family constellation had been identified, along with its location in the galaxy: child, mother, father, village. On the surface, the reconnecting of kin in such cases should be a simple matter.

But as with many things in life, particularly life in Uganda, a matter was rarely simple. Even when Gladys knew the names and village of a child's relatives, reunion was no certainty. Maybe the family members had moved. Maybe they lived in a remote area where no one could read English or afford the newspaper. Maybe the parents had moved on to new families. Maybe they were dead.

While she could continue to publicize the children's existence through "Lost and Abandoned," the fact that Gladys lacked the means to chase down every lead meant that children might languish in police stations or children's homes or some other limbo for weeks and months. Sometimes, as in the case of Olivia Nakintu, years.

GLADYS HAD FIRST encountered Olivia two years before, when she was making her rounds at Kawempe Police Station. Passing by the recycled shipping container where kids were held overnight, she saw an image she could still vividly recall: a girl in a light-blue school uniform, the hump on her back giving her the profile of a question mark. She appeared to be around ten years old, although she was shorter than average because of the compression of her spine. Her face was wet with tears.

"What is the matter?"

"I'm trying to get back home."

Gladys placed a hand on the trembling shoulder. "Come, my dear. I want you to tell me everything. Tell me the story from once upon a time to the very end."

Indeed, the story was like the hardship in a fairy tale. Her mother had stolen her from her father's home and had brutally mistreated her. The girl had run away to look for her father. "Because he used to love me," she said simply. "And my grandmother too."

Florence, the Child Protective Services officer on duty at the time, told Gladys that Olivia had been picked up on the road. She told the police that she was trying to walk back home to her father's village somewhere around Lukaya—a town over sixty miles away! There was no way that a child, particularly one with a malformed spine, could make such a journey on foot.

The other children at the station were eating the single daily meal of *posho* the police could provide, but Olivia had arrived too late to share in the porridge. *Who knows when she last ate?* Gladys fretted as she crossed the street to buy her some *matoke* and meat.

After finishing her other interviews at the station, Gladys went to check on the girl, only to discover that other children had eaten her food! Maybe it was a misunderstanding, or maybe they had taken her food because she was small and misshapen and weak. Whatever the situation, Officer Florence told Gladys not to worry. The problem of the girl was solved. By a stroke of luck, a policeman who was coming by the station happened to be going in the direction of Lu-kaya, the town the girl had been walking toward. "We'll just give her to this policeman," she said, "and he can drop her there on his way."

That was not right. They were just going to dump her in Lu-kaya somewhere? So the girl could be stranded there instead of in Kampala? The child had already spent several nights in a couple of police stations, and she was terribly stressed. You couldn't just pass her along like an empty bottle for someone else to dispose of.

"No," said Gladys. "They are not taking that girl and leaving her like that."

"Then where do we keep her?"

"Don't mind. Give me one day, and I will find a way for her." In convincing the policewoman, Gladys had trapped herself. Now that she had made the promise, it would somehow have to come true.

Since that day Gladys had done everything she could for Olivia. She had run her profile in the paper repeatedly, but no relatives had come forward. That was not so surprising, as the father's family lived in a remote rural area. Gladys managed to get Olivia placed in Early Learning School in Entebbe and contributed to as many of the girl's expenses as she could afford.

As with so many of the displaced kids at the school, Director Agnes promptly rechristened her. Olivia would now be known as Deborah.

Under her new name, the new girl blossomed. In this alter-nate world, Deborah's infirmity was an identifying feature but not a negative one. Every visitor to the school remembered the winsome, hunchbacked little girl with the brilliant smile; she became the school's unofficial ambassador. It amazed Gladys that Deborah was always the first to greet her when she stepped out of the car. How could the girl spot vehicles before anyone else? With her shortened body and her little legs, how could she consistently outrun the boys?

The hump on her back seemed to cause her no awkwardness as she chased friends around the yard or offered one of her frequent af-fectionate hugs. If anything, the way her shoulders bunched up gave her an attentive air; she seemed permanently oriented forward, like an eager student leaning on a desk.

Her voice was honeyed, flutelike. In the school chorus, her clear soprano shimmered like the iridescence on a rooster feather. She was also bright. The teachers reported that Deborah was the most frequent user of the library. In contrast, Ezra had not once been spotted inside its door.

Gladys had entreated Deborah to assist Erza in learning English, as his progress was achingly slow. The girl saw nothing odd in leading the teenager to study after class, although she was half his size and age.

Other children might have felt jealous of the attention she drew, were it not for her generous nature. A fellow classmate could always turn to her for a share of food or a spare garment or a turn in a game of jump rope. She was in all ways a charming girl.

Deborah was happy in Entebbe. But Gladys knew she still longed to visit her father's home. The problem, as so often, was transport. The expense was a problem for everyone; even the police did not have access to vehicles. How many times did Gladys come across a case and think, *Surely such a child can be resettled,* only to realize with a sigh, *But now how can I take the child there?*

It would take a half day just to get to the town near Deborah's village. With new obligations to new cases landing in her lap every week, Gladys could not place such a costly journey at the top of her priority list.

So Deborah waited. She smiled, she sang, she studied, she played. But Gladys knew she waited. And how the father and grandmother must miss their girl! Where might they have looked for her? Were they still looking? They must have endured restless nights worrying over how this child, a born victim in the eyes of the world, had survived. Or did they assume she had not?

THROUGH HER OWN scrimping and some donations, Gladys finally had the means to take Deborah home. Gladys's dress reflected her sunny mood: a long sheath of blue-green with a gold trim, in a light and airy weave.

This time when Gladys reached the school, Deborah was not

alone in greeting the car. Friends held each of her hands, and an entourage of well-wishers trailed in their wake. Knowing Deborah's story, they were excited that she was getting her turn. Some looked on a bit wistfully. Little Rose, who longed for family attachment, peered into the car as though scouting for a place to stow away.

Deborah slipped into the back seat of Mike's Volvo. She wore a neat black blouse with white polka dots, a black skirt, glittery silver sandals, and the irrepressible smile of one who has won an unexpected prize.

"Pray for us!" Gladys called to the children out the window. "We are hoping for a successful outcome!"

The car headed west on the Kampala-Masaka Road. It would be a long drive, about four hours. As Esther chatted with Mike in the front, Gladys took advantage of the rare opportunity to talk to Deborah alone.

"I don't know if you still help my boy as I asked you to," Gladys said.

"I do," the girl chirped.

"You do? You take Ezra to library? But how come he has not learned English well, like you?"

With Zam at the garden, Gladys had concocted a way to light two candles with one match. Ezra needed money for school expenses; Zam needed help with digging. If Ezra spent the month of holidays working under Zam's supervision, he could make his own money. The boy was certainly up to the task, having endured his difficult childhood through his practical and hard-working nature. But Gladys sought reassurance that his studies would not suffer.

"He talks English when we are at school."

"He talks English now? But he still has a problem of writing it. He doesn't know the tenses."

Deborah did not refute the point but answered patiently. "Every time he's in class, I give him my book. He studies it, and every word he doesn't know, I help him."

"He points out the words he doesn't know?"

The chatter eventually petered out, and after a while Deborah started to feel ill. Unaccustomed to long car rides, she was nauseated by the start-and-stop of the traffic and the smell of exhaust. Gladys patted the girl's shoulder and encouraged her to sleep.

With her head lowered over her folded arms, the scars on Deborah's scalp were clearly visible, lines and patches where hair would never grow. Given her sweet and sunny nature, it was easy to forget that she had been so injured.

Some children wore their hardships like shackles. Alex, for instance, whose ability to smile had died along with his tubercular mother. But Deborah possessed unusual buoyancy. She did not behave like a child who had lived through hell.

UNLIKE SOME CHILDREN'S stories, Deborah's had not changed since that day at Kawempe station two years ago. As she had explained to Gladys, her mother, Agnes Mbabazi, left home when Deborah was a toddler. She did not reappear until Deborah was about eight. It was school break, and Mbabazi announced that she wanted to take her daughter to Kampala with her. The family agreed, but when the break ended, she did not bring Deborah back.

In the city, Mbabazi's decision to repossess her daughter quickly corroded. She complained that people were mocking her for having a deformed child. Her humiliation sparked an escalating cruelty, as Deborah's scrapes and bruises were soon followed by cuts and burns. "Why don't you go back to your father?" she would yell at Deborah. "He's the one who produces disabled people like you."

After Deborah was seen with stab wounds on her head, neighbors reported the mother to the police. For a few days Mbabazi was held at Wandegeya Police Station. When Deborah was taken to see her, she was greeted not with remorse but with hot bile. "I wish I hadn't produced you, you bastard," her mother hissed at her. "Why did I have to produce a lame one like you? I wish I had known what I was producing. I would have killed you before you came out."

That night Mbabazi escaped from her cell. She headed straight back home to beat Deborah again, hatred guiding her blows in the dark.

The next day Deborah started off in search of her father. Instead she ended up meeting Gladys.

"I THINK THIS girl may need some fresh air," Gladys told Mike. Deborah's eyes were closed, and in her lap she clutched a *kavera* in case her stomach turned over.

"I know—it is a long journey," Mike sympathized. "But we will soon reach a place to take a break."

They entered a shopping area where the signs seemed bold and bright, where vendors swarmed a parked bus like ants on a dead grasshopper. Mike pulled up in front of a green-roofed building, beside a billboard with UGANDA EQUATOR LINE RESTAURANT stenciled over a drawing of a roasted chicken. Closer to the road stood a twenty-five-foot-tall ring fashioned of cement, like a thin slice of a road tunnel, emblazoned with the words UGANDA EQUATOR.

"As I said, it is a long journey today," Mike said, eyes twinkling. "It has even taken us to the other side of the world!"

Gladys, Esther, and Deborah followed him into the restaurant, where they purchased cold drinks. Mike, who could not walk ten paces anywhere in the country without running into an acquaintance, heartily greeted one of the employees, a man named Kalungi.

Kalungi pointed down at a painted yellow line leading out the door. "That yellow line is on the equator. It is at zero latitude. Come, I will show you what that means."

The yellow line ran right through the center of the cement ring. About twenty yards to the left of the line, a metal basin stood atop a stand. It was painted yellow, with a white spiral leading to the drainage hole at its center.

"On this side of the line, we are standing in the Northern Hemisphere," Kalungi explained, filling the basin with water. He floated a small white flower facedown on the surface and unplugged the drainage hole. The group shadowed the basin, watching the flower spin around along with the water.

"See here, it is spinning clockwise, yes? That is because the north is pulling." The observers nodded, then followed him back across the yellow line to a second metal basin twenty yards on the opposite side of the ring. Kalungi produced another white flower and repeated the experiment.

"Eh!" Gladys remarked. "It is now going in the other direction."

"Yes, counterclockwise," confirmed Kalungi. "The south is pulling the other way."

At a third basin, positioned directly on the yellow equator line behind the cement ring, the water sucked the flower straight down, like a lizard gulping a butterfly. Deborah yelped in delight, her motion sickness forgotten.

"Ee-ee!" exclaimed Gladys. "It could not rotate."

"No, because both the north and south are pulling."

"Is it true?"

They wandered back and forth between the hemispheres, their heads spinning along with the flowers. Could the two halves of the world really act so oppositely, existing side by side?

Kalungi walked them to the concrete ring, where they could take a picture of themselves under the UGANDA EQUATOR sign. "You can stand with your right foot in one hemisphere and the left in the other," he suggested.

While the others played at straddling the waistline of the earth, Deborah set her shimmery shoes neatly on top of the yellow line, a beatific smile on her face. It was as though she felt the pull of the earth running directly through her body, a tree anchored by its roots.

BACK ON THE ROAD, it was impossible to shake the feeling that they were indeed crossing over to the other half of the planet. As Mike drove through the Rift Valley toward the Katonga River, the roadside vendors shifted from selling charcoal to sponges to fish, both smoked and fresh. Men stood with one foot on the tarmac, brandishing their wares. In the heat of the day, fishermen dipped their biggest silver perches in water and jostled them like puppets, trying to make them look "fresh from the net," or at least "not dead yet."

The Volvo rumbled past sports-betting parlors and inns and churches and bars and mosques. The passengers noted perplexing business names, like the God Is in Control Dairy Farm and the Mild Beauty Institute and the Executive Butchery Shop. They crossed the papyrus-filled Katonga River, a battleground during the Ugandan Bush War, now the burial plot for the soldiers whose bodies would never be retrieved from the swamp and its traps of quicksand.

Compounding the sense of distance was the fact that they didn't really know where they were going. Deborah claimed her home was somewhere "around Lukaya," but her dot of a village would not appear on any map. Gladys would have to navigate using the girl's memories.

"Deborah," she said, "what I want to know—do you still remember Lukaya town? Because now we don't know the place we are going. We have to find out where it is in relation to that town."

Deborah sat up, alert as a front-row student.

"Your village called Ndegi, what is its landmark? What is the sign of it?"

"It is in Kalungu District."

"Is there a government school there? Or close to there?"

"No."

"Did you know the LC chairman of the village?" Members of the local council would know who lived in their area.

"No."

"Where did you go to church? Where did you go to pray on Sundays?"

"The church was at school."

"What was the name of the pastor?"

And so it went. With the interrogation yielding little in the way of concrete information, Gladys resorted to her tattered address book. Perhaps there was someone in the area she could call. Whom had she met from Lukaya? From Kalungu District?

"So, Gladys," Mike called back, "do we know where we are going?"

"Unfortunately, Deborah doesn't know Lukaya town, and that is the only town I know around there."

"I passed there once," offered the girl.

"You passed there once. Okay, what I want to know is, do you pass there on the way to your home? Or do you branch at the town? Or what?"

"You pass through town."

"Is your father very well known? So that if we stop in Lukaya, people know him? If so, it means your village is not very far from that town."

Deborah gave an uncertain nod.

Gladys shifted tactics. "To get home, would you move on foot? Or use bodas?"

"Bodas."

Despite the girl's vague responses, Gladys concluded, "I think we can find the place."

"Okay." Mike sounded doubtful. But if he was surprised by the lack of a destination, he knew Gladys well enough by now not to be surprised by the journey.

IT WAS ALREADY midafternoon when they entered Lukaya, a highway town whose inns and bars catered to passing truck drivers and fishermen. Street vendors hovered at the edges of the road with *muchomo,* skewers of roasted meat hoisted in fists like heavy bouquets. Some held flat baskets of fruit and vegetables and roasted plaintains and dried fish. A few dangled live chickens at their sides. All were poised to pounce on any vehicle that stopped, or even slowed.

Gladys knew what she needed. "Look for boda-boda drivers," she instructed Mike. "You know, when you see them together — there!" She pointed to a corner where a congregation of young men and motorcycles lounged by a meat vendor's stand, its sign reading SMART BUTCHERY. "That is the place."

Mike pulled over, and in moments the loose circle of men was breached by a large woman and a little girl. A few drivers glanced at Deborah's unusual form, but Gladys's strong voice quickly pulled their attention.

"Who knows the village called Ndegi?" she called out. "Who knows a man named Sebutali?"

There were a few murmurs. A couple of the men claimed to know the area.

"Can you take us there? How far away is it?"

"Seventeen kilometers," said one young man in a gray shirt. "Or maybe fifteen."

"About twelve kilometers," offered another, in a green shirt.

Gladys snorted. A distance was not an item to be bartered! "If you know where it is, how come you can't give us the correct distance?"

"I know where it is," insisted Gray Shirt.

Gladys pressed the drivers for another minute, letting each vie for the job. This could be a tricky business, as it was common for boda drivers to get into fights over customers. It was a testament to the remoteness of Deborah's home that there were not more candidates in the running.

Finally Gladys nodded at Gray Shirt. "Okay, I want you to lead us to that place."

They followed the boda man through a side street, where they waited for him to put fuel in his bike. Two young mechanics leaned in the shade, staring at Mike's dusty green car.

"Even if you were to give me that to drive for just one day, I'd be so proud," one remarked. "Driving a Volvo . . ."

Gladys laughed, amused. The Volvo was a fine car, but she was simply pleased to have transportation. How good it felt to be able to get somewhere!

AS MIKE FOLLOWED the boda boda, he explained that he had given the driver half of the agreed-upon fee; the balance would be paid when — or rather if — they arrived at the destination.

"We will get there," Gladys assured him.

"I'm glad you think so," Mike quipped. Gladys and Esther laughed.

It was true, Gladys embarked on these journeys with the confidence of a bird migrating across water: fly long enough, and you will reach land. "You know, my boss Cathy always wonders how I get to these places without knowing first where I am going. She says, 'Give Gladys the names of those far, unknown places, and she will go!' One time she got so worried. I went on a case out to some place called Kyaggwe."

At the name, Mike sucked air through his teeth.

"Cathy was so worried. But she became even more scared when I came back and narrated my experience. I went there with only the boda-boda man to guide me. Cathy said, 'That's very, very bad! How can you trust a boda-boda man when there are only two of you with those bushes up there? Something can happen to you! And those people there, they can kill you. Some can even eat you!' You know, that place has those, those . . ."

"Cannibals." Mike supplied the word.

"Yes. So Cathy said, 'How about if they had eaten you?' I said, 'No, they can't eat me.'" Gladys gave a dismissive laugh. "I am a big woman."

"If they get a body like yours," Mike teased, "they will be so happy. They will eat for at least four days!"

Gladys squealed like an overheated kettle. "Eeeeeeee! You hear this man?"

"Have a party, for four days!" His chuckle was low and slow, like the honks of an unhurried driver. "Ha. Ha. Ha."

"Hee-hee-hee! Enjoying the flesh." She wagged a finger at him. "But with you, they will be very disappointed, Mike. They will say, 'We have caught this big one, but there is no meat!'"

"'So much trouble to catch, but this one is only bones!'"

"Hee-hee-hee-hee-hee!"

"Ha. Ha. Ha!"

"The bad thing is," Gladys mused more soberly, "when I am chasing something, I don't care where it is or what it takes. I must have it! Someone will be telling me, 'There is this woman, she is suffering, but she is in a very remote area. There is no transport, there is no way you can reach there.' I tell them, 'Just give me the name. I will reach there.'"

· · ·

AS THEY BOUNCED behind the boda for several miles, the scenery offered few distinguishing characteristics: sparse bush occasionally broken up by patches of crops.

Deborah pointed to some rows of trees on either side of the road. "They are growing coffee there. My father is a coffee trader."

When they moved through an area with a few scattered buildings, Deborah pulled herself forward to peer between the front seats.

"I remember this road," the girl announced, her voice quickening.

"Is this the place?" Gladys asked.

"No, not yet."

"Do you know this place?"

"I know this place."

"Are there people you know here?"

"No."

"Are we near your home?"

"Yes!"

Ahead they saw people: some children playing, watched by a woman with a baby on her back.

"Let us talk to these ones," Gladys said.

Mike honked for the boda man to double back, then pulled over.

Leaning out of her door, Gladys called cheerfully to the woman. "Hello, Madam! Pardon us for disturbing you. How are you?"

The woman hesitantly returned the greeting.

"We are asking for Mr. Misuseera Sebutali," Gladys continued. "Is this a village called Ndegi?"

"No, this is someplace else." The woman pointed to the way they had just come. "You have to go back."

Mike, the boda man, and the woman embarked on a complicated discussion of directions. It seemed they were close, but the route was difficult to describe. There were many indistinct roads and paths. Outsiders never used them, so none were marked. Giving directions was like trying to describe a particular row in a field of sugarcane.

They returned to their vehicles and retraced their paths. They meandered this way and that, they plowed ahead, they slowed and stared. At this point the boda man was no longer the leader; he was just sticking with the Volvo in the hopes of being paid.

"I remember this place!" Deborah piped up, on a road that they had clearly traveled down before.

She doesn't know the way, Gladys thought. She was beginning to worry over the time. Like the heroine in a fairy tale, Deborah needed to find her castle quickly. She was supposed to be back in Entebbe by nightfall.

On one narrow lane their progress was halted by a herd of An-kole cattle. The Volvo had to stop in the middle of the road to allow the animals to pass on either side.

"Look at those ones!" Gladys exclaimed. Despite everything, she enjoyed the sight of the big, slow beasts lumbering by, their magnifi-cent pronged horns bobbing up and down like outstretched arms. There was no reasoning with these creatures; with their density and their simplicity, they ruled the moment. No one, not even a cabinet minister with an entourage and sirens and military jeeps and soldiers in the lead, could insist on the right of way. One might as easily hold back a river of mud.

As the last meaty flank swayed past, Gladys took a breath and gave Deborah an encouraging nod. "I think we must be near your home. Just keep looking."

BY AND BY they rolled down yet another rutted path, with a couple of brick houses set back from the road on either side. A girl and a boy drew in the dirt with sticks, while a man in a white shirt and a fellow with a bicycle stood chatting.

"Oh, I know that person," Deborah said, the words popping out of her mouth almost casually.

"What?" asked Gladys.

"That man. I know him!"

At that, Mike halted the Volvo and, with a movie stuntman's efficiency, reversed through his own wake of dust. The boda-boda man puttered ahead, oblivious, but this was not the moment to worry about him. He would double back.

Gladys spoke to the men through her window. "Do you know Mr. Misuseera Sebutali? This child says she knows one of you."

"That one," said Deborah, indicating the man in the white shirt.

"She knows me? Who?" The man squinted into the dark car. Then his face brightened. "I know this girl. She's Sebutali's daughter."

Deborah beamed at the man as Gladys's heart jumped. "We are trying to find Sebutali's home."

"If you just go to that corner, you turn and take a . . ."

"What about you get in and take us there?" The proposal popped out of her mouth.

The man considered for a moment, then nodded.

Gladys leaned toward Mike, speaking quietly. "How do you see it? Is it an inconvenience?"

"I mean, there is no other option . . ."

". . . other than going on like this."

And so the man got into the back seat, and the boda fell in behind the Volvo.

From there, everything was easy. "The road that goes by church," directed the man, "that's the one you have to use."

They turned past the church. "I know this road!" Deborah cried, her voice high with excitement. "I used to come and collect firewood here."

"We are on track!" Gladys declared triumphantly. "I tell these people, Gladys does not fail."

Mike's foot pressed a little more eagerly on the gas pedal, stirring up the air in the car. Gladys tingled with anticipation. From the beginning Deborah had told everyone of the father and grandmother who loved her. She had been trying to walk back home. It had taken two years, but she was returning at last. Just as Gladys had promised.

THEIR ARRIVAL UNFOLDED exactly as Gladys had imagined it. The moment the car pulled up, faces appeared at the window and turned shiny with joy.

"Olivia! Olivia!" People shouted Deborah's original name. The news of her return spread instantly through the village, like lights coming on after a blackout.

Sprinting down the footpath from the bush came a young woman, screaming and crying. Clapping her mouth with a flat hand, the woman emitted a ululating call as she scooped up the girl in one arm.

"Woo-woo-woo-woo-woo-woo-woo!"

In a flash, an old woman came running from behind a small brick home, the sleeves of her yellow dress tied hastily under her arms. The dress was nearly falling off her body, but she did not slow down to adjust it.

"Olivia! My girl!"

"Where have you been?"

"We are so happy to see you!"

"We thought you were gone forever!"

"Woo-woo-woo-woo-woo-woo-woo!"

Deborah was spun around from person to person. As they wept and wailed, she said nothing; she just hugged them back, a delirious smile on her face. Gladys looked on, laughing, her camera snapping away.

A strapping, handsome teenager in a red football jersey picked up Deborah as easily as he would a baby.

"Is that your brother?" Gladys asked.

"Yes!"

Gladys turned to the old lady in the yellow dress. "And you are the grandmother?"

The weathered face contorted with emotion. "Yes. Yes!" The first words dropped like pebbles, then came the avalanche. "Thank you for keeping my grandchild. I'm so happy! She is back! Just last night I was talking about this child. I was saying this child has died. But Olivia has come back!"

Around them the happy shouts continued as more and more people came running up through the bush.

"Look who is home!"

"We missed you!"

"When someone is lost, never say the person is dead!"

"Woo-woo-woo-woo-woo-woo-woo!"

Gladys looked around. The whole village was running out to greet its returning child. But there was someone missing. "Where is the father?"

"We were so worried about this girl." The grandmother bent down to look directly into her granddaughter's eyes. Her voice was frail and hoarse, as though she had been thirsty for a long time. "Welcome back. My child, my girl!"

UNDER THE SHADE of a tree, Gladys sat with the grandmother and brother while Deborah floated about, chatting with everyone.

"Where is the father?" Gladys asked again. Had something happened to him?

The grandmother did not answer, but a voice chimed in, mentioning that the father was somewhere nearby.

"I hope someone is getting him." The clock was ticking on their visit. Gladys would start her interview with the others and hope for the father's arrival.

The old woman was Deborah's paternal grandmother, and just as Deborah had always maintained, she doted on her granddaughter. When the news had come that the girl had run away from her abusive mother, the grandmother had become frantic.

"Did you try to find her?" Gladys asked.

The grandmother shook her head. "I have not been well, as you can tell by looking at me." It was true: her fifty-eight years hung heavily on her. The whites of her eyes were yellow and red-veined; her mouth was missing many teeth. "And I had no funds."

Gladys's pen worked quickly. "What about the father?"

"I told him he should look for her, but he said, 'The mother took the child, and that is her business now.'"

So they hadn't looked for the child. "You thought the girl was lost all this time."

Again the grandmother shook her head. When Deborah had been picked up on the road and taken to the first police station, an officer had called one of her uncles. "Her father—my son—was given the phone. The police asked for confirmation that this was his daughter. With the swelling on her back. The father said, 'Yes, the child has got a hump.'"

Gladys's pen hovered in midsentence. The police had called the family? The family had known where Deborah was? Her mind reeled. This made no sense. "You knew the child was found."

"Yes."

"Why did you not get her?"

"The father told the police that he didn't have money for transport, they would have to bring the child here. But the police said no, that's too far."

"You understand, the police do not have money. They may go months without salary." Gladys's voice grew hot with disbelief. "Did you really think that they could get the child from Kampala and bring her back to you? Of course you would have to get her yourselves. You have the grandmother's love for the grandchild, do you?"

"I do," the old woman insisted. "But as the grandmother, I have no authority. The parents are the ones who have authority over the child."

This was true. So where was this father, this Sebutali?

"It is very unfortunate that I have not seen the father," said Gladys. "Because from what I now hear, he did not care that this child was alive. That's really bad. I never knew that someone had communicated with you people. That you knew the child was there, and you just sat down and didn't even take the trouble to come and get her."

The old woman winced. "I told my son when his wife took the child away, 'Go and get money. Go and look for your wife.' But as you know, a father can be lazy."

A shout went up from the footpath, and every head turned to see a man approach, his hands waving in greeting. He was neatly dressed in a long-sleeved blue shirt, cuffed gray trousers, and black loafers. Deborah ran to him.

The man hugged her, patting her head affectionately. Then he looked up, taking in the visitors: the two well-groomed ladies and the tall, thin man. Gladys, Esther, and Mike returned his stare. If this was Deborah's father, his manner was oddly restrained for such a reunion.

With Deborah clinging to his hand, the man started to walk toward the visitors. Then a wail rose up behind them. It was a wavering, squeaky sound, like the failing brakes on an old car.

Stumbling down the path was a thin figure carrying a radio. His brown pants were covered in dirt. As Deborah dashed up to meet him, he staggered toward her, weaving from side to side as though he were trying to corner a chicken.

This, Gladys knew instantly, was Misuseera Sebutali. "The father has come," she said, her insides crumpling. "But he's drunk."

It should have been a happy scene. For Deborah, it should have been beautiful. The father should have been the first one to greet her, his embrace as wide as the wings of a crane in flight. He should have swept up his daughter in strong arms, full of gratitude that his two-year search was finally over.

Instead, this wobbling scarecrow gripped Deborah like a sack of beans he was about to drop. His face leaked. Tears streamed out of his squinting eyes. His nose dripped. A string of saliva dangled from his slack mouth.

"Why don't you come bring the child here?" Gladys urged, pointing toward the bench under the tree. "Sit down."

The father appeared not to understand. "My child, my child!" he wailed.

Deborah sagged on his shoulder, her silver sandals dangling above the ground, her smile faded like a dried flower. Off to the side, her brother turned away, his face hardening with reproach.

Mike glanced at Gladys. This was really bad.

"Yeah, he's very drunk," Gladys muttered to Mike. To Sebutali, she repeated firmly, "Sit down. I want you over here. Put her down."

After a minute the father let Deborah slide down to the ground, the movement nearly toppling him. Still sniveling, he blew his nose into his hands, and in the next moment extended them to Gladys and Mike. "You brought my child . . ."

Gladys avoided the wet handshake and moved right to the point.

"Two years ago, when the police called and told you that this child was found, what did you do?" she asked. "Did you come to get her?"

"How could I come?" He was instantly defensive, his speech shooting out in spurts. "I didn't have money. How could I have come?"

"What do you do?"

"I'm a farmer. And a trader."

"What do you trade in?"

"Beans, maize. But I have no capital."

"What I want to know: why didn't you go to get her?"

"I didn't have money!" he shouted, eyes flashing. With anger as his lens, he suddenly focused. Indignation wiped the slur out of his words.

"Where do you think I got the money from to come here?" Gladys retorted. "Please answer that for me."

Gladys had witnessed firsthand the ugliness of a parent's surrender to alcohol, and she was not about to let this one off the hook. Mike looked on, marveling at the way she was nailing the man with her sharp, sharp questions. Sebutali was losing his cool.

"You want to lock me up?" The man thrust out his arms theatrically. His gestures were loose and abrupt, like the marionette of an unskilled puppeteer. His head bobbed as he yelled, "I don't have money! Not even one shilling! You want to lock me up right now?"

"What happened with your wife? Why did she leave you?"

Gladys did not flinch, even as the man lurched toward her, his breath as toxic as car exhaust. "You know, I had money once. A lot of money. I was a businessman. I got money and I bought some land. I was trying to grow coffee. But then when I lost my money, I lost everything, she walked away on me. And I brought up the kids myself. Then she comes back and picks the child. What should I have done? I didn't have money! Not one shilling to go and pick the child from the police station."

"Huh," Gladys scoffed. A man who had really raised his daughter by himself would have found a way to retrieve her.

The man dropped to the ground, his puppet strings severed. "I don't have money! I don't have anything! I am a poor man."

"Get up," Mike hissed, his voice low with disgust. "Get up. Stand yourself up."

"I'm poor," he whined.

"You have been drinking the money?" Gladys said mildly.

"I knew my child was dead. I gave up on her. That's why I drink so much."

How convenient to justify a vice through tragedy. But more likely the real reason Sebutali had declined to make any effort to retrieve Deborah was her hump. Even if he cared for her, he also cared for money. A girl with that infirmity would not fetch a good bride price, if she could be married off at all.

AFTER MUCH WRANGLING, Gladys managed to get the father, the grandmother, the young aunt, the brother, and Deborah to sit with her on the benches under the tree. Around them a few dozen people, probably the entire population of the village, sat in loose groups to watch the show.

"I need you to listen to me," she began. "It's been a long journey and we need to discuss. Now, I'm called Gladys. Gladys Kalibbala. I work with *New Vision*. You know *New Vision*?"

The aunt nodded her head.

"Ah-hah. Do you know English?" Gladys asked.

"I don't know English."

"It is bad that you are eating mangoes instead of studying." Gladys sighed. "The newspaper is written in English. In my column, when I find a child who has been lost, I take her picture, and I put it in the newspaper. When someone reads about it and sees it? They come and collect the child."

Gladys related her involvement in Deborah's case and her efforts to help the girl over the past two years. The grandmother and aunt stared at her, struggling to absorb the improbability of a complete stranger offering such assistance. Only Sebutali appeared unattentive, his eyes as glazed as those of the fish dangled by the roadside vendors.

"I'm not a minister. I'm not an MP. I'm not anybody. So I don't have money," Gladys explained. "Still, I have come to this place with this girl. But she is your child. And now I know that one of the police officers who found your child called you."

The grandmother started to reply, but Sebutali slapped at the air in front of her face. She flinched, her chin quivering.

"Shhhhh!" he sputtered, spittle flying from his mouth, before turning to shout at Gladys. "I don't have money to take me to Kampala. The police should come here."

"The police who work with children, they don't have transport," Gladys said, her exasperation flaring up again. "Pity them as well. It is irresponsible, as the parent, to say, 'I don't have money, I won't come.'"

"I don't have even one shilling."

She gave him a stony look. "Don't repeat that to me one more time."

"Lock me up, put me in prison," the man persisted childishly. "But the truth is, I don't have money."

Gladys's silence ended the volley. He sniffed, raising his chin as though he had won. Next to him, his mother sat working her tooth-poor jaw as though she were chewing a piece of gristle that she could neither swallow nor spit out.

"With the children I work with, I do the best I can to look for the family. But when I find a person like you, who does not even show any . . ." Gladys raked Sebutali up and down with her eyes. "You want me to shake your hand when you have been blowing your nose in it."

Sebutali thrust out his bottom lip and frowned, as though he couldn't choose between self-pity and anger. "I'm going to leave, because it seems that you don't want me here."

"Don't leave," Gladys ordered. "You should stay here to discuss your child."

He wobbled into a standing position. "Me, I'm going."

They watched him stagger up the footpath, where Esther tried to intercept him. The neighbors witnessed Sebutali's exit with interest but little surprise. Behind him a toddler in baggy men's shorts waddled in pursuit of a ball made of rags and string. The ball rolled like an egg when he kicked it, his giggle the only sound in the village.

Mike glanced at Deborah. Disappointment veiled her face. As soon as she felt Mike's eyes on her, though, she attempted a smile. Then she left the bench.

Many adults assumed that children, having little or no say in serious matters, were oblivious to such dramas. But this one saw everything.

"We would not have sent for him," said Deborah's aunt. "That's how he is. He drinks all the time. He is a very angry man."

"Has he always been this way?" Gladys asked.

"He has always been stubborn," the grandmother replied. "Sometimes he even beats me."

"Beating you! His own mother?"

Sebutali was gone, but the fumes of shame lingered. How one man could contaminate a family, even a whole village. Mike shook his head, muttering, "That one is in trouble with his creator."

"That son is the eldest of my surviving children." The grandmother's voice was wistful, a breeze over a dry riverbed. "I had twelve children, but six died."

Loss. It could make one cling to a rotten plank and call it a boat.

Gladys spoke gently. "Grandmother, you agree that your granddaughter should stay in school where she is? From what I see, it is not so easy here."

The grandmother nodded, eyes moist. "Even if I said we should keep her here, I could not take care of her in the way she is cared for now."

GLADYS INFORMED DEBORAH that she should begin her goodbyes. Down the footpath, Esther was still crouched across from Sebutali, having calmed him into conversation.

Suddenly Gladys felt a tug on her arm. She turned to find Deborah's grandmother thrusting something into her hand. Gladys glanced down. It was a 10,000 shilling note. "Oh my God!" she gasped.

"I've been sick for one year," said the grandmother. "I don't have more money. Just take it."

Surprise was not the word. Gladys was shocked. Maybe it would not seem like much to some people—you could not buy the newspaper for a week with that amount—but for a woman this poor, with no visible income, it was a fortune.

"Please take it," the grandmother said, her tone almost pleading. "And before you go, I need to put some herbs on my granddaughter. For blessing."

Gladys and Deborah followed the old woman to a line of dried maize stalks by the house. There, in a plastic basin, shredded green leaves floated in shallow water. The grandmother squatted by the basin and circled her hands through the mixture.

"What is this called?" asked Gladys, framing the scene with her camera.

"It's called *omwetango*," said the grandmother. "It's used for when a person is found. Once a lost person is declared dead and you have cried for them, if you get that person back, you must do this to cleanse the spirit of the tears you have shed. So this person should never again be lost."

With cupped hands, the old woman released the leaves over Deborah's head, over the lines where her mother had cut her, over the swelling ridge of her back. "I used to cry so many tears for you. We thought that you were dead! I'm sending you these blessings, now that we see you are back. I just hope that this herb will give you all the luck through your life."

She bent to the basin again, spreading more damp leaves onto her palms. Deborah held still as the old woman caressed her cheeks. A patient smile peeked through her grandmother's trailing fingers, like the sun shining through clouds.

THE BODA LINED UP to lead the car away from the tiny village. A farewell party gathered. There were shouted goodbyes and thanks and promises to call. Deborah pledged to visit again soon. Esther had managed to coax Sebutali out of his sulk, and when he appeared in the crowd, Gladys offered him a cordial, if not effusive, smile.

The people were still waving, the car just pulling away, when Gladys could contain herself no longer.

"Did you hear such statements? What the father was saying?" she blurted out. Quoting Sebutali, she whined, "'The police called, saying come for your child. But I told them I didn't have money. If they want, they can bring her.' Oh my God!

"When I'm under such circumstances, there are times when I come to think twice. Am I really stupid? Because it seems I'm behaving differently from other Ugandans."

Mike and Esther chuckled, but Gladys cut them off. "I'm not boasting! I mean, here comes Gladys, a stupid woman, she keeps on trying, tracking, tracking, tracking all the time, looking for opportunities to trace Deborah's people, thinking that they didn't know that the girl was somewhere. How do you feel if you are Gladys, coming here to find that people have known long ago? Am I stupid?"

Mike clucked sympathetically, but sympathy was not what Gladys wanted. "I am posing a question!" she insisted, her voice sharp with frustration. "I am asking! Maybe people look at me as someone who is not thinking right." The words erupted from her, a lava flow gaining in speed and heat. "All along I've been so worried, and because I didn't have transport, I couldn't come and look for these people. At least to let the family know that the girl was still alive. But on reaching here the father says, 'Yes, they called me, they said she was at the police, and I told them they better bring my girl here!' And for two years he doesn't give a damn. And this is Gladys, who has been thinking, praying hard, that one day I will get transport to reunite this girl, to look for these parents, to tell them Deborah is alive. How do you feel, if you are now Gladys reaching this place?"

There was a soft thump as Mike drove through a pothole too shallow to warrant diversion. He shrugged. "When I see the father, I just relax. Because I can't waste my time even giving him a second thought."

There was a pause. Then a giggle trickled out of Gladys, bubbling slowly into a belly laugh. "Eh-eh-eh-ehhhhh! Oh my God . . ."

Mike had given the right answer. You could not fight mud.

Through all of this, Deborah appeared unperturbed, calmly picking bits of her grandmother's herb from her skirt. The adults had not censored their conversation on her behalf; after all, the girl had seen everything that they had seen, and she had lived through far more.

"Deborah, tell me. How are you feeling?"

The girl beamed instantly. "I feel very happy. I first saw my auntie. Then when she hugged me, everybody started coming out." Her lilting words came out like a song. "I was most excited to see my grandmother and my brother. I was very happy to see my grandmom. I thought she died. I felt so good when she embraced me."

"That moment was greeeeaat." Gladys drawled out the last word, then fluttered her hand on her mouth, howling against her palm. "Woo-woo-woo-woo-woo! She couldn't believe!"

"My grandmother said to me, 'We thought that you were dead!' And then she said, 'Your mother is a monster!' And I told her that even though she's a monster, she is still my mom."

After that, there was only the rumble of stones under tired tires.

Deborah leaned back, her head resting on the swell of her own back, her upturned face parallel to the roof of the car. A few specks of herb poked up through her short hair like shoots in dark earth.

Within a few minutes the bumpy road rocked her to sleep.

"THESE KIDS. THERE'S a traumatic story with each one, but each one is different," Mike observed. They were nearing the equator, heading back northeast on the Masaka-Kampala Road. "Each has got its own twist."

It was true. In Deborah's case, it was the two halves of her world rotating against each other. In the clockwise world, Deborah was a promising student. A leader among her friends. A girl who charmed visitors. She would go on to secondary school, certainly, and perhaps even college. In her old counterclockwise home, she was ostracized for her disability, tortured by her mother, and abandoned by her drunken father. There was no school for her there, and little future.

But this small girl had ballast. In the same way she had accepted the limits of her father's love, Deborah had weathered her mother's cruelty: with an innate understanding that she bore no responsibility for the failings of adults.

During the visit, Gladys had lined up the family in front of Seb-utali's unfinished brick house for a picture. It had not been the ideal reunion, but who knew when these four would be together again?

The father leaned against the wall, his expression as empty as that of someone dozing with his eyes open. The son stood stiffly, eyes hooded and intense. The grandmother glanced away. But Deborah looked straight at the camera, hands behind her back, her feet perfectly aligned in those glittery sandals, like one might see in a shop display. There was no shame or discomfort in her expression. Her face radiated the same serenity as when she was standing on the equator.

This is my family, she seemed to say. *And I am me.*

"TELL ME, DEBORAH," Gladys asked. They were heading into Entebbe now, trailing a minibus bearing the window slogan NO MAN IS AN ISLAND. "When are you planning to see your family again?"

"After third term."

Gladys cocked an eyebrow. "Then my question is, how will you come back after third term to see them? Who will bring you?"

Deborah turned to her with a smile so confident it could have sold toothpaste. "You!"

"Me?" Gladys yelped, frowning in mock indignation.

"What answer do you want to hear?" said Mike, and everyone laughed.

"Oh my God. Ooh-eeee . . ." Gladys groaned and chuckled in equal amounts. "Because we have even now promised!"

These promises Gladys made! They were like a string of fire-works, with each successful explosion lighting the fuse of the next.

Ah well, she thought. *At least now we know the way. At least that.*

The Boy with Seven Names, Part Four

Mugerwa Junior Godfrey Victor from Karamoja

LOST CHILDREN
The 11-year-old boy who reported himself to Old Kampala Police station about two months ago has changed his story, swearing that the latter was the right version. At first, he claimed he had come to Kampala and failed to trace his parents when he went for a short call without informing them. Now he says his father is the late John Bosco Mugerwa, who left Karamoja and settled in Kiboga District . . . He died of cancer when the boy was in Primary three at Kiboga Progressive School.

His stepmother brought him to Kampala two months ago and abandoned him at the New Taxi Park where he stayed for a week before reporting to police.

Children lied. And not just street kids. Little kids lied because they couldn't remember. Some kids lied because they didn't want to be sent home. Others lied because they worried that their stories would not arouse enough sympathy. Gladys had interviewed one street boy who had tried to warm himself next to a power box when sleeping on the sidewalk. When he got electrocuted, he told police that other street kids had burned him. He did not tell the truth out of fear that he might be held responsible for damaging public property.

Some street kids lied because other street kids had coached them. *Don't say that you were thrown out by your uncle for misbehavior,* the seasoned ones would advise. *Tell them that you got lost trying to follow your auntie through the taxi park.*

Shame was at the root of many lies. House girls lied about why they ran away from their employers. For some, it was easier to explain that they had not been paid than to reveal that they had also been raped.

Gladys had suspected that there was something wrong with Mugerwa Junior Godfrey Victor's original story. He lacked the roughened exterior—and interior, for that matter—of a boy who had survived on the street for years. Given the trauma of his burns, she had refrained from investigating too deeply.

But now it was clear that Junior had lied. And Gladys believed he might still be lying. At the start of the holidays, she had gone to the school to pick up Ezra. There, Junior had come to her. "Auntie, I lied to you before," he confessed. Through Agnes's encouragement, no doubt, he had undergone a religious transformation. "Now I am saved, and I can no longer lie. I am going to tell you the truth."

The story of his accidental separation from his parents had been a fiction, he announced. He didn't know what had happened to his mother, but he knew his father was dead, of cancer. He had survived on the street not for many years but for only one week! And he knew his tribe.

"I am a Karamojong. I was born in Karamoja, and I left my mother when I was very young." He had had a Karamojong family name, but it had been changed along the way by a stepmother who did not like it. "I cannot remember it now."

Gladys strongly suspected this to be another pothole in his story. First of all, the soft, round-featured boy bore little resemblance to the tall, dark, skinny-legged herders of that tribe, with their hidelike skin. Second, Karamojong culture was very strong. There was no way that they would allow one of their sons to take another name.

"How can you say you are Karamojong?" she pressed him.

"It's true, Auntie Gladys. I am not lying!"

She demanded to know everything now. "Have you been to school before?"

Though he claimed never to have attended school, the other kids had noticed that Junior Victor seemed to be following along with the lessons. Recently he had been discovered helping one of the younger boys with math.

"Yes," he conceded.

So he did know some English. What conversations had he followed, pretending not to understand?

"What else have you been lying about?"

"Nothing—that is the truth!"

FALSEHOODS AND OMISSIONS and shifting facts were a thorn in Gladys's side, as they added unnecessary layers of difficulty to her job. It was impossible to provide proper assistance to a child if you did not know the truth. How could the police track parents who did not exist? How could relatives identify a child they had not seen for years if that child had the wrong name? If a child did not reveal that she had been defiled, how could her defiler be brought to justice? How could the girl get tested for pregnancy and HIV?

Then there were the complications of explaining these discrepancies to Gladys's editors and readers. *Yes, I am writing again about that boy I wrote about two months ago. But now he has a different story. And a different name. And we are still not sure if he is telling the truth. Ehhh!*

Corrections were necessary but awkward. Having invested sympathy in a child's plight, her readers might feel a touch annoyed to read that the circumstances differed from what had initially been reported. It was like telling Esther, "I know you are a vegetarian, and you have already eaten the dish I have served you. But I have just learned that it contained meat. Sorry."

In her corrected profile, she faced the problem of how to identify this boy. At this point, he had so many possible names: Mugerwa Junior Godfrey Victor and something Karamojong? She chose to avoid the issue of the name entirely. The photo and the revised information would have to do. Maybe there would be just enough truth in this new story for someone to recognize him.

A FEW DAYS after the *Saturday Vision* column ran, Gladys's phone rang. It was Officer Rebecca. "Someone has called," she announced.

"Called for?"

"For . . ." With all the children that came through the station, Rebecca had a hard time keeping track of names. She never forgot their stories, though, and remembered them that way. A boy abandoned by his father at a fish landing site became Fisherman. A baby left in a *matatu* might become Taxi.

"For Junior."

A woman had called with information. The boy had a mother. And another name.

The Boy with Seven Names, Part Five

MUGERWA JUNIOR GODFREY VICTOR MANANGA

It was a couple of weeks before Gladys had everything arranged, but finally she returned to Early Learning School to pick up Junior. The Volvo's driver today was Osman, Mike's chatty young nephew, who cautioned that they would need to be quick in order to avoid the worst of the midmorning traffic.

However, Gladys could no more speed through Early Learning School than one could speed down Kampala-Entebbe Road on a Monday morning. As soon as she left the safety of the Volvo, children surrounded her, reaching for her hands, looking up at her with hopeful eyes. She did not have clothes or soap or pocket money for them today, but she did not feel too badly, as the birthday party would be coming up soon.

As Junior followed Gladys to the car, she noticed he was wearing a pair of hard-soled black shoes. They were in decent shape, and the broken laces were knotted at the grommets so that his feet could slip in and out as if they were loafers. "Eh, did you get new shoes?" she asked.

"No, I borrowed them from a friend," he told her. The plastic slippers he had purchased for himself had fallen apart.

AS ON MANY a Wednesday, Gladys was operating on only a couple hours of sleep, having managed to submit her column and photos to her editor after an eternity of sitting in the dark, cursing first a power outage, then the poor Internet reception. But with Junior beside her in the car, she felt no fatigue, only anticipation.

Junior was quiet. This was not the hopeful boy who had grinned with pride at his new slippers and gaped in wonder at the blue expanse of Lake Victoria. Sitting in the back, he stared ahead, his look lost somewhere in the space between him and the front seat. Auntie Gladys was taking him somewhere for the day, and he didn't know where. Perhaps her warning from weeks before was running through his head: *The minute I hear you are acting badly, we will come to the school and take you out.*

He had been told not to lie. And he had lied.

Now he found himself again in the car, this time going in the opposite direction, away from Entebbe. Why were they taking him back to Kampala?

Gladys did not tell him. Junior could not know that they were taking them to Old Kampala Station to see a woman who claimed to be his mother.

The boy had not seen his mother for years. If Gladys informed him, "We are taking you to see your mother," the power of suggestion might push him to identify a stranger as kin. She could not take that chance. His reaction must be kept pure.

So if the journey caused the boy apprehension, there was nothing to be done. Perhaps the heat would distract him. For weeks they had had no rain, and the sun had reigned mercilessly in the empty sky.

To make matters worse, the Volvo's power windows had been failing progressively. At present the back windows were stuck in varying states of mid-descent and the front passenger window was frozen—or melted—shut. Osman's window was the only one that still worked, but he was afraid to tax the mechanism, lest they end up with a) two closed windows that would not open, effectively turning the front of the car into an oven, or b) three half-open windows that would not close, increasing the risk of robbery. Thieves, particularly street children, were notorious for dashing through traffic and dipping past lowered windows to snatch handbags, mobile phones, food, whatever was within reach.

The jam intensified as they neared the city, as did the heat in the car. The congested highway became a parking lot and then a shopping mall. Vendors streamed between the idling cars, brandishing armfuls of belts, hats, plastic toys, newspapers, bananas, toothpaste, battery-powered fans, and shiny lenticular portraits of Jesus, whose eyes opened and shut when you tilted the plastic card. The hawkers peered into windows and windshields, fishing for eye contact, while drivers and passengers did their best to pretend the hawkers were invisible. On the edge of the road, two Mormon missionaries stood blinking, faces and necks flamingo-pink against their black-and-white suits, nearly Martian in their otherness.

Amid the fray, a one-legged man on crutches rocked his way from vehicle to vehicle. Gladys clucked her tongue and nudged Osman. "Do you have water? Give to him."

The man, chapped-lipped and grimacing in the heat, accepted the bottle with a gracious nod. Watching him lumber off, Gladys could not help but offer unheard advice. "You can't keep here begging on the street in such weather. Even with one leg, you have to find work that keeps you out of this sun! The water will go, and you will just have to raise another thousand shillings for another bottle. Because there's no way you can stand in such terrible heat all day without taking water. You would collapse, surely."

Her phone chimed. "I really wish I had money or whatever," she muttered as she reached for it, unable to shake the thought of the one-legged man and his Sisyphean labor.

It was Officer Rebecca. "You said you would be here already."

"We are coming," Gladys assured her.

The day had been long in the planning, and Rebecca was worried that everything could be derailed by a late start. This was no time for Uganda time! "My people have been waiting."

"Just keep them there. We will be there!"

TWENTY MINUTES LATER Gladys clumped into the Family and Child Protection Unit office, pulling Junior and Osman in her wake. "I'm melting!" she bellowed.

"Madam Gladys, nice to see you," greeted Officer Mugerwa. He inspected Junior. "His face has healed very well!"

It was true. The shocking pink patches on the boy's cheek and chin had returned to a normal deep brown, and his arm showed only faint outlines of the blisters that had removed half of the skin there. Only the back of his right hand was permanently pink and freckled, like the chest of a sunburned *mzungu*.

Officer Rebecca quickly dispatched with the small talk. Uncharacteristically, she wore a sleeveless dress in lieu of her uniform, but her manner was all business. "They are just outside," she said, her tone low and conspiratorial.

Three people stood on the veranda in front of the office, glancing about with the muted nervousness of caged birds. There was a petite woman in a pale-blue blouse with a white lace collar and a silky blue-and-green skirt. She was young, but weariness slackened her pretty face. Two girls stood with her. One looked Junior's age; the other was only a toddler. Both wore frilly dresses decorated with beads and satin sashes. One had only to glance at their worn shoes to know that these were their best clothes.

"How are you?" Gladys greeted them. The woman dipped her head in response, her eyes fixing on Junior.

Gladys looked at Junior too. The boy glanced at the woman and the girls, but without particular interest. He was accustomed to hanging on the edges of others' affairs, and assumed that this meeting did not concern him.

Rebecca leaned down toward him, asking, "Who are these people?"

The boy shrugged.

"Do you know them?"

Junior studied the woman. His eyes flicked down at the toddler in the flouncy white-and-purple dress. No lightning bolt struck. Not even a candle.

"No?"

Junior shook his head. "I've never seen these people before."

Gladys reached over to take the older girl's hand. "Do you know this one?"

Another headshake.

Gladys pulled the woman closer. "How about this lady?"

Junior began to look embarrassed. Clearly he was failing a test. He looked from the mystery woman to the girl to the toddler, rubbing the back of his head with his left hand.

The mystery woman waited patiently, head slightly cocked, hands held behind her back. Her lips were pressed into a firm smile, as though sealing something off behind them. She could not take her eyes off the boy.

The silence of the moment caught Osman's attention. The young man had not been told anything about the purpose of this visit, and he had not been particularly curious. Now he glanced between Gladys and Rebecca. From what he had witnessed, it was rare for these two bold ladies to be quiet at the same time.

The moment grew awkward, painfully so. Junior fidgeted, raising his brow and drawing air in through his teeth, a perfect pantomime of confusion. Gladys exchanged a glance with Rebecca. *Could they have the wrong woman?*

But the expression on the woman's face — she looked at this boy like a mother.

Junior's head wagged again. "I don't know them."

Rebecca leaned in, nudging him once more toward the older girl. "Not even Marcy? You don't remember Marcy?"

"Marcy?" Junior repeated. He glanced back at Rebecca and then at the girl again. Though he had been looking at her, only now did he see her. A dam burst flooded the fallow fields of his memory. He began to smile, his rising joy held back only by the thinnest tether of disbelief. Could it really be his sister?

Twitching with excitement, Gladys ducked behind Junior to look at Marcy. She peered into that mirroring face with the familiar soft round features, and her smile grew as wide as the boy's. Gladys spoke into his ear with low, quick words, the way a rider might urge on his horse. "Where have you heard that name from?"

"It's my sister's name."

"Is that your sister?"

"Yes."

"Are you sure?" Gladys growled playfully. "Give her a hug!"

Beaming, Junior moved to his sister's side and wrapped his right arm around her.

"Ah-*hahhhh!*" Gladys cheered.

Rebecca laughed. "That is real love."

Transfixed, Osman released a breath he had not realized he was holding.

Gladys pulled the children into the shade of the veranda to take a picture. Through her lens, the siblings looked like twins. They stood, arms draped over shoulders, heads tilted toward each other, like two halves of a walnut. Behind them, their mother hovered on the periphery of their happiness, her smile trembling.

"What about the mother, do you not recognize her?" Gladys asked Junior. The two siblings dropped their arms and turned to look behind them. "You see her now. Do you know her?"

Again Junior stared at the woman. He did not move toward her; he did not speak. But there was distress beneath his silence. The enormity of the moment seemed to be pressing on him all at once.

This was his mother.

He was looking into her eyes.

He did not recognize her.

"You do not know her?" Gladys said softly. "You do not know your mom?"

Junior did not want to shake his head, but he could not nod. Finally he just dropped his chin.

Tears welled up in his mother's eyes. She fumbled for her younger daughter's orange jacket and used its lining as a hankie.

Gladys felt such pity for the mother. How many times had this poor woman dreamed of this reunion, only to have it come to this?

"It has been too long, that's why he has forgotten," Rebecca soothed Junior's mother. "Don't cry."

The woman only buried her face deeper into the little jacket. Marcy too began to weep. Even the younger girl, who looked no more than three, whimpered into her mother's skirt.

"You know that is your mom," Gladys spoke quietly to Junior. "What are you going to do about it? Just look at her over there."

Junior looked stricken. Suddenly he pressed his left hand to his eyes and tears began to seep out from the heel of his palm.

They stood apart for several aching moments. Finally, eyes still closed, Junior lifted an arm toward his mother. At the gesture, she exploded in tears and pulled him tight to her body, her delicate face distorted with emotion. She tried to speak, but raw sobs tangled her words. Her mouth gulped for air, as though she were being choked. Then she closed her eyes, surrendering, and threw her head back with an open-mouthed expression of exultation.

Junior stood stock-still, as though afraid any movement might wake him from this dream.

"You have seen the mom," Gladys murmured, her whisper reverent. "You have seen your mom."

She glanced up at Officer Rebecca. "Let's leave them. Let's let them be." Osman followed them into the office, swiping at his eyes with a knuckle.

And then there was nothing but the wood-dove sounds of soft weeping against the din of street noise. Though they stood rooted in place, a few feet apart, the family seemed connected in that moment: mother, daughters, and son, all standing on the veranda of the police station, crying for everything that had been lost and found.

AFTER SOME MINUTES Gladys went back outside to interview Junior's mother. The rising sun had erased the shade at the bench, so she led the family behind the building, where they could stand in its shadow. The baby girl followed reluctantly, still hiccupping with tears.

"Eh? You see the young one?" Gladys chuckled. "She did not even know why others were crying, and she is still crying. But we are happy now, baby. We are very happy. Oof!"

Junior and his mother smiled weakly, drained by the events of the last few minutes. The boy's eyes, normally red, were positively inflamed.

Like the burning incident, those bloodshot eyes were a misfortune that had become an unexpected benefit. When the mother reached Officer Rebecca through the number listed in "Lost and Abandoned," she revealed that it had been almost a decade since she had seen her son. "Madam, I don't know how my boy looks now," she confessed. "I can't identify him. But the only mark he has, which I think he would still have, is his eyes. According to the doctor, he had an allergy, and his eyes always turn red." That one feature connected her to her long-lost son: his red eyes.

And now here they were together. Passersby might assume that this tear-stained family had just received terrible news and that the large woman with the camera had just won the lottery. You could no more dim Gladys's smile than you could turn off the sun. As she had said to the baby, she was happy.

The reunion had touched her. It had also validated her insistence on rerunning the boy's story in her column. When nobody had responded to her first two profiles, she had had to push to include him a third time. Hilary had balked at first, asking, "Didn't you write about this one the other week?"

She was not ready to give up. But her job, as some colleagues persistently reminded her, required her to move on. "Gladys, you are a journalist. Your work is to get the proper information and write the story. And we publish the story. Are you supposed to do more than that?"

"Not your job" was one song she often heard; the other was "lack of space." But as with Trevor, she had refused to let this one go. It irked her that the world claimed not to know these kids.

So she had written about Junior again. And again. And finally the phone had rung. Woo-woo!

THE MOTHER'S NAME was Rebecca Nakiru. Odd to think that her son came to Old Kampala Station calling himself Mugerwa, like Officer Mugerwa, and here was the mother, Rebecca, like Officer Rebecca. The confusion of names seemed to be a hallmark of this case. At least there was no Gladys among the daughters: the three-year-old, who had a different father from Junior, was named Mary Faith; the thirteen-year-old was, as all knew by now, Marcy.

"Marcy is thirteen?" Junior asked, surprised. He and his sister were practically twins, barely a year apart. But he was the older sibling. "I thought I was twelve now."

"No," corrected his mother. "You are fourteen."

"I am fourteen?" Junior slowly shook his head. Evidently the day's surprises had not yet been exhausted. Where had those two years gone?

Finding out that this Rebecca was twenty-eight years old, Gladys did some quick calculations. She had probably been pregnant with Junior at thirteen and given birth to him at fourteen.

That she was poor surprised no one. Selling local brew on commission gave her a meager income, and she struggled to feed her children. How had she raised the money for the two-day bus fare from Karamoja to Kampala? It would take an eternity for her to earn such a fortune.

Gladys wanted to ask her about how she had separated from her eldest child, but Officer Rebecca appeared then, warning of the time. The next appointment for all of them, Junior and his family included, was at the military barracks, which kept strict hours.

"We will continue the interview later," Gladys agreed, looking Officer Rebecca up and down. The policewoman's black sheath dress, with its pattern of beige swirls, looked more appropriate for a party than a visit to the barracks. "Why don't you put on a uniform?" she asked reproachfully.

It was not really a question. Rebecca moved off without protest.

"Okay, let's move to the vehicles now," said Gladys, zipping her notebook into her bag. Junior fell into step with her, and she rested a heavy forearm on his shoulder. The boy had said almost nothing since hugging his mother. "Tell me, are you happy?"

"Yes," said the boy.

"Have you thanked me? Have you thanked me for putting you in my column all those times?" Gladys's prodding was playful but pointed. Children needed to acknowledge assistance when it was offered to them. "I am waiting. Here I am!"

She cocked her head to hear his soft reply: "I pray for you."

"You pray for me? Oh my God," she said with a sigh, her own

voice dropping so low it was barely audible outside her own head. "I think that is great. Instead of saying thank you, he is praying for me! Which is better. Can you imagine?"

She tightened her arm around the boy, talking brightly now. "Thanks for praying for me. And I also pray that I will be able to give you care, and see you continue to go to school. Okay?"

TWO VEHICLES WERE required to take everyone to Makindye Military Barracks. Watching his newly recovered family follow Officer Rebecca to the other vehicle, Junior caught his mother's eye. They shared an easy, unburdened smile, the expression giving his mother the carefree look of a teenager.

"She is beautiful. Beautifully shaped girl, the mother," Gladys remarked to Osman. "Does she look like Karamojong to you? Or Junior? When Junior told me he was from Karamoja, I did not believe it."

"Karamojong are different, by the way," Osman agreed. "Those you see on the streets, they don't have the structure of that lady. They have tiny legs and rough skin. This mother has nice skin."

The cattle-herding Karamojong were often stereotyped as violent and uncivilized. Following a nomadic life in the remote northeast, they were known for their height and strength, their elaborate scar patterns, and their love for cattle and guns. Although the practice had declined in recent generations, one still heard of areas where a Karamojong man might claim a bride by chasing his intended and fighting her to the ground, marking his prize through "courtship rape" and the subsequent payment of cows.

In recent years, persistent drought was driving the Karamojong into cities by the thousands. Survival on the streets of Kampala was no sure thing, even for these tough people.

Gladys had dealt with Karamojong women before, particularly those who would walk through traffic with babies, begging. Recently she had reported on a Karamojong woman who had "rented" twins to beg with. To prompt more generous handouts, the woman had stripped the babies naked. She took them out on the street when it was raining, and one of the twins fell ill and died. Still, Gladys told

Osman, a crowd of Karamojong women had swarmed the police station, crying that the arrest was unjust. "They are very aggressive. If one of them gets in trouble, ten of them show up to demand her release."

"Will this woman be taking the son back to Karamoja today?"

"No." Gladys looked at Osman like he was crazy. "He has to go back to school."

"But she is the rightful guardian. Junior has to be in the village with the mom!"

Gladys turned to look back at Junior. "Do you want to go back to the village with your mother?"

Junior shook his head. "I want to go back to school."

"You see? This is my boy!"

Osman gave a bemused laugh, conceding defeat.

"What I wanted," Gladys explained, "was to get the mother to know where the boy is. And to know that her son is still alive. That is enough. Whenever she wants to see the boy, she knows where to call."

In truth, this plan to keep Junior at Early Learning School was not yet set in stone. It required three approvals. The first was from Agnes, of course, and that approval Gladys had secured. The second was from Junior's mother. There had not been time to broach the subject with her yet. The third approval was from the person they were hoping to meet at the Makindye Military Barracks: Junior's father.

The Boy with Seven Names, Part Six

MUGERWA JUNIOR GODFREY VICTOR MANANGA ADAMS

In his confession to Gladys at Early Learning School, Junior had reported that his father had died of cancer years before. Was he deliberately lying or only telling her what he believed to be true? She would soon find out.

With information from Junior's mother, Officer Rebecca had been able to confirm the boy's father as John Bosco Aleper, an army captain currently being detained at Makindye Military Barracks. A visit to the barracks was arranged, but detention facilities were sensitive places, and there was no guarantee that they would be admitted.

At the barracks, Gladys, mother Rebecca, and Rebecca's two daughters were signed in, patted down, and asked to deposit their belongings at the security table in the yard. Gladys was not even permitted to take in a notebook and pencil, let alone her camera. As they were led across the yard, Osman rejoined the group, nervously recounting how the frisking officer had found a coin buried deep in one of his pockets.

They waited in a tiny anteroom outside an office staffed by a female guard with the jaded, watchful manner of a cat on a windowsill. Officer Rebecca seemed a bit nervous as she chattered about the case.

"This is the prodigal son," she explained, pointing at Junior, who sat deep in conversation with his mother. "He is returned. Ten years he and his mother have not seen each other."

"And why are you here?" the guard asked, more out of habit than curiosity.

"We are here to see the father."

"He is here? What is his name?"

"Captain John Bosco Aleper."

At this the guard gave a snort and rolled her eyes, a surprising show of animation. "I know him," she said, derision curling her words. She nodded in the direction of Junior's mother. "This isn't his only one, you know."

The women glanced over to see Junior exchanging playful grins with Marcy and his newfound baby stepsister. It was evident that the boy had no idea of what might take place in the next hour, in the next room.

ENTERING THE OFFICE, Officer Rebecca's group was met by several men in uniform. Gladys, Osman, and Marcy took seats by the wall while Junior and his mother sat in chairs in front of the desk.

The level of caution was high, Gladys understood, as the situation was sensitive. John Bosco was being held on charges of treason. The captain in charge posed a few polite questions to Officer Rebecca and Gladys about their visit but offered no details on the case.

Without announcement, two guards entered the room, followed by a figure in a red prison jumpsuit. Junior followed the glances of the others in the room, turning his head toward the door. A paunchy, round-cheeked man stood before him, a smile quivering the ends of his scruffy mustache.

"Daddy!" Junior immediately leapt up and threw his arms around the man. Gladys was startled to hear jagged weeping coming from the boy. He was clinging to his father the way his mother had clung to him: with a joy that looked like anguish.

The room erupted in cheers and laughter, and John Bosco's eyes glistened as he returned his son's hug. Chuckling softly, he set his chin on the smaller head, the arch of his hairline a receding echo of the boy's. Gladys beamed, her heart full. For the second time that day, Osman dabbed at his eyes.

As Junior's crying subsided, John Bosco grew aware of his audience. Like a good host—or a seasoned captain—he scanned the room and made eye contact with the new faces around him. His drooping mustache framed his mouth, giving him a jocular air.

"Here is your son," Officer Rebecca announced, somewhat belatedly.

"God is really great," the man said, shaking his head in wonder. "I had given up hope myself."

Dark tearstains showed on the belly of his red jumpsuit where Junior's face had pressed into him. The boy remained at his side, clutching his arm. His eyes saw nothing, and his breathing was shallow. There was no question in Gladys's mind that the boy had been telling the truth. He had believed his father was long dead.

The captain in charge introduced John Bosco to Officer Rebecca and Gladys.

"Thank you for finding my boy," said the father. Someone had sneaked a copy of the paper with Gladys's last column into his cell. The moment he had seen the picture, he had started crying. "I dropped to my knees and prayed. I said, 'God, now I really believe you exist.'"

Around the room, a few heads nodded.

"Maybe you don't see angels," John Bosco said, breaking into a smile. Even in his prisoner's jumpsuit, he exuded the confidence of someone accustomed to wielding his charm. "But I think I am seeing angels at this moment."

"When was the last time you saw your son?" Officer Rebecca asked.

His grin faded. "If I answer that question, I will start breaking down." He gestured at three-year-old Mary Faith. "I left him when he was a few years older than this one."

After splitting from Junior's mom, he explained, he had taken the boy with him to his new wife. Then he had moved on to another relationship, taking the boy to the next woman. But he split up with her too, and lost track of both her and his son. From that point, the only one who could pick up the story was Junior.

"Who told you that your father had died?" Gladys asked the boy.

The second woman, Junior explained, staring down at his borrowed shoes. "She said, 'Your father died of cancer — you should just forget about him.'"

John Bosco must have left this woman with a great store of fuel to stoke her anger, because she had not been satisfied with the lie about his death. She erased him further by changing the son's name to Mugerwa Junior. The boy's real name was Adams. Mananga Adams.

Mugerwa Junior. Godfrey. Victor. Mananga. Adams. Gladys sincerely hoped this was the end of the list of names for this boy.

The third woman's cruel treatment of Junior had ended with her chasing him from her home. That was how he had come to wander the streets.

Officer Rebecca and Gladys told John Bosco of the boy's arrival at the police station, his repeated profiles in "Lost and Abandoned," the burning accident, and his placement in Early Learning School.

"I am grateful to you people for helping my family," the man said.

"He is adjusting well in school," Gladys said. "I think it is a good place for him right now. How do you see it?"

"I think it is good."

"And you, Mommy? What do you think?"

Up to this point, attention had been focused on father and son. Now all eyes turned to the chair in the middle of the room, where Junior's mother held Mary Faith asleep in her arms. Sitting motionless, with slow tears sliding down her cheeks, the woman did not respond.

"We want to know what is on your mind," Officer Rebecca prompted. "Because you have parental rights as his mother."

For a few seconds everyone waited, but the woman said nothing.

"No one is taking him away," soothed the policewoman. "But if he is in school, then when he grows up he can come back and help take care of his sisters."

"Please let him stay in that school," John Bosco said to his former wife. "He has some chance if he is in school."

Rebecca refused to look at him, or even to acknowledge that she had heard him. She wore the sorrowful, stricken look of someone standing in the ashes of a burned-down house.

John Bosco tilted his head at her, his eyes conciliatory. "Forget about the past."

"It is done," the captain in charge agreed. Apparently he knew something of the couple's history. "Why dwell on what has already happened?"

Gladys glanced from the father to the mother; their features surely added up to this boy and the girl Marcy. By nature, these four belonged to each other as much as fingers on a hand. For the first time in ten years they were gathered in the same room. But their minds were as isolated as trees in different forests. What had happened to this family?

"She has said nothing since we entered this room," Officer Rebecca noted with a sigh.

"Please," Gladys coaxed. "Tell us what you are thinking."

After another long silence, Junior's mother wiped her wet cheeks with the back of a hand, a gesture everyone seemed to interpret as assent.

"It will be all right. You know where your son is now—you can come to visit him," Gladys said reassuringly. "Okay? Are you happy?"

"Yes." The answer was low and unconvincing, like an apology from a child accused of something she did not do.

Marcy began to cry, her head bent into her lap, the top layer of her frilly skirt held to her face. Mary Faith woke up in her mother's arms. She began to wail too, a pup responding to the pack.

Everyone watched Marcy sob. What had made her so distraught? Gladys wondered. Surely all this was good news: her brother had been rescued and reunited with their family, and Good Samaritans were providing for his welfare and education. The day had been filled with joyful tears, but these were heavy and sad.

Finally Gladys could stand it no longer. "Please," she urged John Bosco, "explain to her in your language what is happening, so that she can understand."

Keeping her eyes covered by the collar of her dress, Marcy allowed her father to sit her on his knee. He began to whisper to her.

"I only get to see my brother for a few hours," the girl burst out suddenly, her words broken and hoarse. "And I lose him again?"

For the first time since he had entered the room, her father looked at a loss. "She thought her brother would be coming home with her," he explained. "She is worried that he will be taken away forever."

After some words of reassurance, Marcy's tears subsided. John Bosco sensed the visit's end. "If I could fly out of here and be with you, I would," he said wistfully. "But I can't."

"It is unfortunate that you are in this place," Gladys commented. "You must pray that it will not be for long."

"I am not a robber," John Bosco said. "I did not kill anyone, but maybe I am here because of my conduct. God willing, I will be free and I can rejoin this new family." His chuckle returned. "But if the devil is here, maybe I will not be there." He looked appealingly to Gladys and Officer Rebecca. One could imagine that such a look had been applied to other women, under very different circumstances. "Please, you are my new family now. Do not forget about me."

Gladys offered him a benevolent smile. "We just hope that when you get out of this place, you will now be able to be a part of your son's life again, as he has not had the benefit of a father for all these years."

Junior embraced his father one more time as the group was ushered out. "Be good. Grow up to be great," the man said, patting the boy's head. "Discipline."

The visitors reached the door at the end of the dark hallway. The heat outside hit them like a wall.

"Come back to see me," Captain John Bosco called, watching them dissolve in the sunlight.

IT WAS LATE AFTERNOON by the time Osman pulled up in front of a small café. As usual there had been no time to eat, and Gladys was worried about the children. Junior had taken breakfast at school, but it was likely that his mother and her two daughters had not eaten anything that day.

Osman took a seat facing the street in order to keep an eye on the Volvo and its three temptingly broken windows. The older kids plunged into the piles of rice and chips on their plates, and Rebecca shared a mound of rice and gravy with little Mary Faith. Loud, pulsing dancehall music bounced off the café's red walls.

Gladys was keen to restart the interview. The conduct of mother and daughter at the military barracks, the silence and the crying, had surprised her. To get to the bottom of the matter, she had to trace the family threads to a point much further back than the separation between mother and son. A story like that of Mugerwa Junior Godfrey Victor Mananga Adams did not spin out from one bad break or one poor decision. No way. Many factors must have conspired to create this tangle.

After getting some food into their stomachs, the women pulled their chairs closer together and began to talk. Rebecca's voice was clear, her gaze direct. Away from the tense atmosphere of the barracks, she was a different person. Her fragility now fell away, revealing the stone inside the bruised fruit. It quickly became apparent that someone born into her kind of misery could not have survived on mere luck.

WHEN REBECCA WAS a baby of crawling age and her brother a newborn, her mother had tied both infants into a bag and tossed it into the river. Some fishermen retrieved the bag and saved the children. But the mother was gone.

Unfortunately, Rebecca's father proved unwilling to provide for his stranded children. These babies would simply have to depend on the mercy of his other wives, of which he had many.

"How many women?" Gladys inquired. "Like four?"

"No, more than that," Rebecca corrected. She named a fifth, a sixth, then a —

"Okay, please stop counting. I fear you will get up to ten." Gladys snorted. "And how many children?"

Rebecca counted nearly twenty before Gladys cut her off. It was clear that the welfare of two babies whose mother was not even around would not rank high on this man's list of priorities.

"Your father never catered for you?"

"Not even to buy a pencil," Rebecca said with emphasis.

Like weeds yanked from a garden, Rebecca and her brother were not allowed to take root anywhere again. As she grew up, she stayed with various stepmothers until the mistreatment became unbearable or until they chased her out. Food was scrounged from friends. She cut firewood to pay her own school fees.

Mary Faith began to whine. Her mother had been parceling out her portion of rice on one side of the plate, but the toddler was determined to take possession of the whole dish. She reached across the tabletop with sticky, insistent hands.

"The baby wants her own plate," Gladys noted with amusement. "It seems she feels cheated to get something from someone else's plate."

Osman flagged down the waitress. Once the baby had her own bowl and her own pile of rice, she began stabbing it contentedly with a fork. They chuckled at her satisfaction. All kids liked the feeling of owning something. For many, it was not a feeling they enjoyed very often.

Gladys drummed her pen on the table. "I would like to know how you met John Bosco."

Rebecca nodded and resumed her tale. After living like a beggar in a series of homes, she had again found herself chased away by an abusive stepmother. "And that is when I met this man John. I had nowhere to go, so I just decided to marry him and run away to Kampala."

"I understand now," Gladys murmured, addressing her notepad as she wrote. "Because she was suffering, she would want to run away with someone who promised her heaven and earth."

From Rebecca's abject perspective, John Bosco must have seemed like a man who could deliver on such a promise. At twenty, he was educated, having completed secondary school, and he had a job in Kampala as a guard at Pioneer Mall.

"How old were you then?"

"Thirteen." Marcy's age.

"Did anyone know that you had come here?"

"No one was even looking."

"Eh! No one even bothered to look for you. Can you imagine?" Gladys sighed.

By the time she was fifteen, Rebecca had given birth to two children, born just a year apart: Junior—or rather, Adams—and Marcy. Her husband blamed her when she became pregnant a third time. "He said, 'Now you have conceived again. I don't want another child to come and shout around here.'"

"Why didn't he invite you to use the pill?" Gladys asked. "Or why didn't he use a condom?"

"I don't know." Rebecca shrugged.

He began beating her. He beat her until she became unconscious. He stepped on her until blood flowed from her private parts. The bleeding would not stop, and neighbors took her to the hospital. Fearing what would happen if a third child joined this earthly nightmare, she prayed for her pregnancy to end. Unsentimental in his mercy, her God listened. She miscarried in the hospital.

It was a dreadful story. Fortunately, the room was noisy, and Junior and Marcy were comfortably engrossed in the small coloring books they had been given. Elbow to elbow with her brother, Marcy appeared free of her earlier distress.

Mary Faith, bored of ruling her kingdom of rice, sidled up to her new half-brother, gaping curiously at the pink discoloration at the back of his hand. He mugged at her, sending her away, squealing.

Even after the miscarriage, Rebecca went on, she returned to John Bosco's home. It was the same song: she had nowhere else to go. From the moment she had been cast into the river, she had been forced to eat whatever life served to her. When her husband expressed regret over his behavior, she had no choice but to hope that things would improve.

They did not. She discovered that her husband had taken another woman. Sometimes he was away for weeks, even months. On the rare occasions that he came home, Rebecca could sense that he was not fully present.

"Oh yeah," Gladys commented. "When a man gets a new catch, there is a way they change."

"Even in bed, he's like this." The young woman brushed her

skinny arm against the reporter's substantial one. Then she flinched, as though touching a hot stove. "'Eh! Why are you being so close?'" she growled angrily, pushing Gladys away.

As he moved on to other women, John Bosco wanted to take his children with him, particularly his firstborn son. Rebecca resisted.

Her stubbornness surprised those around her. After all, children were traditionally considered the property of the father. And John Bosco had a good salary as an officer. He could provide for his son in a way that Rebecca could not. Even Rebecca's brother, who had been flung into the river with her, questioned her thinking. "He asked me, 'Why do you want to carry all the burdens? You don't have money, you are struggling. Why don't you leave one child with him?'"

"Don't you think that was also a point?" Gladys asked.

Rebecca shook her head. "I said I would rather suffer with my children than leave them."

Her husband took Junior anyway. Her many requests to visit were routinely deflected. One day she resolved to see her son, invited or not. It was evening when she arrived at the military quarters where John Bosco and his cowife lived.

When the couple strolled in drinking beer, Rebecca sensed that it would be unwise to provoke trouble. "I told him, 'I did not come here to quarrel. My coming here is just to see my boy.' He said to me, 'I am not happy with you. And I will never be happy with you.' When the other woman left to get water, he caught me there, where I was sitting, and started beating me."

"What was he beating you with?"

"Hands! Kicks, what-what." The children and the other woman fled from the house. "And then he started caning me at the table like this: *pop pop pop!*" Rebecca raised her fist and began whipping her arm down toward the table.

"Didn't you scream for help?"

"I couldn't," Rebecca said, holding clawed fingers up to her neck. "He started to pinch me here like he wanted to take my throat out."

"Is it so?" Gladys gasped.

"It's true! He was pinching my throat and I could only make a sound like — *ehhhhhh*. And then he went and got a pistol and pointed it into my face." She made her fingers into a gun shape, her small hand like a child's, and aimed it at her mouth.

She pantomimed their fight over the gun. Somehow Rebecca succeeded in flinging it into the bedroom. "Now, he caught my leg and pulled like it was a rope. He dragged me out of the house like a sack, shouting, 'Go out of my house!'"

The next morning the quarter guards found Captain John Bosco washing his car. "This woman, she has run mad," he claimed, brushing off the incident.

"The man just looked at me like I was rubbish." Rebecca's nostrils flared as she glanced away, an expression both defiant and wounded.

A pop song on the tinny café speaker pulsed into the lull.

> *Every man want a fine girl*
> *Mine she's a super diva*

"Men can really be bad," Gladys muttered.

THROUGH THE OPEN front of the café, Gladys could see Osman leaning against the car with the absent absorption of a young man using his mobile phone as a boredom shield. The day was growing amber, the shadows lengthening. Traffic would be heavy soon.

"It is getting late," she said. "Okay, Rebecca. Just share with me your comment now. How do you feel, seeing your son?"

The young woman drew herself up in her chair, inhaling deeply as she did so. "I was not believing that this boy was alive. Since the father said he had lost him, I thought he was dead. I used to sit alone and cry. But now I am so happy. As soon as I saw him, my heart just calmed."

She looked down the table at Junior, and her eyes softened. He was picking at the splintered tip of his pencil, his lips pursed into a perfect circle.

"I know he doesn't remember me. It has been so long, he forgot me." Rebecca directed the words to her son, although he did not hear her. "But I never forgot him. That's why when he disappeared, I could not settle. I said, 'God, I never abandoned this boy. It is you who knows.'"

"I always feel bad for women," Gladys said. "It seems a lot of women abandon their children. But I really want to hear it from the mother herself." She rapped her pen on the table with each word. "To know. What. Happened."

"I never abandoned him."

"You didn't abandon him," she affirmed. "You were ready to suffer with your children."

"Yes, I would have suffered with him." Her own mother had not fought for her, had not even tried. She would not impose the same punishment on her own children. "Maybe another woman would not manage; maybe she would go to the street to sell her body. But for me, I said no. If someone says, 'You wash my clothes,' I wash. 'Come and cook for me,' I go. Because if I don't go, what will my kids eat? The boy's father left us with nothing."

A high-pitched clamor rose up from the end of the table. Mary Faith was running in circles behind her brother's chair. Giggling, she darted up to one side of his chair, and Junior whipped around, grinning, trying to tag her with his glance. Again and again the toddler whirled away in her lacy white dress, like a moth circling a candle.

Their mother's smile was slightly remote, but more sweet than bitter. "I'll pray that you can continue this work. It is through you that I have my son back. Not through that man."

Gladys absorbed this. To this woman, abandonment was a sin of the highest order. It was apparent now that her silence at the military barracks had not been a protest against her son being kept in school. It had been a statement on John Bosco's crime of tearing the family apart. He had thrown them all in the river.

"I think we are done with the interview," Gladys declared with a sigh. "Let's go back into the jam."

ON THE WAY back to Entebbe, they dropped Rebecca and the girls by the place where they would spend the night before the journey back to Karamoja, sending them off with phone numbers and invitations to visit. Junior poked his shining face through his half-lowered window, calling his goodbyes. His mother and sisters stood at the side of the road, waving with all their hands, the breeze from passing cars fluttering their frilly skirts. It was a touching sight. Had Rebecca borrowed money to buy those dresses, hoping to cloak the family's hardship from her long-lost son?

Gladys lowered her hand as the Volvo pulled back into traffic. "Life," she declared, her blunt voice a gavel.

Osman nodded. "It is not easy."

Mugerwa Junior Godfrey Victor Mananga Adams lay down in the back seat. Weighed down by a belly full of food, he soon sank into a deep sleep. He had begun the day with no family, and now he had a mother, a father, a sister, and a half-sister. Little wonder he was exhausted.

As they drove, Gladys and Osman tried to reconcile the amenable, affectionate father they had encountered at the barracks with the cruel villain of his ex-wife's tale. Had John Bosco reformed? Or did his gentle demeanor spring from his compromising circumstances?

Gladys's opinion was firm. "He was only doing that sweet talking because of the problems. I know men. It's just because he's in problems."

"It's very hard to change," Osman concurred.

"Did you see how he was now pleading with us? 'Please don't forget me, come to see me.' You know, when you are in prison, you feel lost."

"That's why they call it the University of Understanding."

She laughed. "You mean when they put you in detention?"

"Yes. When you come out, you have understood." Osman grinned, warming to his theme. "The myth is like this: if they put you in Luzira Prison and you're a Muslim, when you come out you are either Catholic or Protestant. And if you go in Catholic or Protestant, when you come out you are Muslim or saved."

"So has this man reformed?"

"You mean, is he saved? Do you think so?"

"If you want to hear what I think," Gladys said, narrowing her eyes at the windshield, "I don't give a *damn*. Whether or not he has reformed, which I doubt, he will have to bring some money to support his family. We know he's a captain. Someone of that high rank can afford to pay for his family." The captain owned a car! How could he fail to produce school fees for his children? "This man must face his responsibilities once he comes out," she declared. "Me and Effendi Rebecca, we will not tolerate this child negligence. If we get hold of him, he will not like it! There is no way this John Bosco can run away from us."

Osman disagreed. The man was accused of treason. He would likely be demoted, if not stripped of rank entirely.

Gladys measured out a sigh, a long, slow deflation. Osman was probably right. "Well, he loves his son. I think we saw that. And I know he was not lying when he said he saw the boy's picture in the paper and he knelt in his room and prayed." She stabbed a finger in the air, as though she were pointing to the place on a map. "I believe him. And the son even loves his father. However much he may know that his father mistreated his mother, the boy feels love for both of his parents. So it has been good for them to reunite."

The father of this lost boy was deeply flawed. Was that so shocking? Kids with stable parents were not the ones who ended up on the street. But was there a child on earth who did not benefit from knowing that he or she had the love of a parent, however imperfect that parent might be? Even a leaky roof provided some shelter.

She would never forget the image of the son and the father embracing, each having long given up the other for dead. It was a miracle. A miracle was not a permanent state of perfection; it was a moment of transcendence. A fleeting glimpse of beauty. That is what she had witnessed, and she was humbled by it.

A siren razored its way through the air, slicing a path through the traffic jam. Osman steered to the right just as a caravan of SUVs tore past. The escorted VIP could have been a cabinet minister racing to catch a flight or an official's maid retrieving well-dressed children from school. The ordinary people in ordinary cars idled, the smoky plastic smell of burning garbage wafting through open windows.

As the siren faded, the traffic loosened. Driving toward the descending sun, Osman risked pressing on his window button. The glass obediently lowered. He pressed on the gas, and cool wind flowed into the car like a bath.

"I've never seen people cry like that before," the young man said, his voice full of wonder. "Tears of joy. I thought that was just something in the movies. I didn't think that people did that in real life. But now I have seen it with my own eyes."

The Boy with Seven Names, Part Seven

MUGERWA JUNIOR GODFREY VICTOR MANANGA ADAMS
MUWANGUZI

Out of habit, Gladys surveyed the policewomen as they emerged from the vehicle parked on the driveway of Early Learning School. Three of the five were not in uniform. Arguably their skirts and sandals were acceptable, given that the occasion was a party. But it pleased Gladys to see her colleagues from Kawempe Police, Officer Carol Kushemererwa, head of the Child and Family Protection Unit, and Officer Harriet, dressed in proper attire, from their military-style caps to their shiny black shoes.

Gladys pointed her chin at the colorful flats worn by one of the nonuniformed officers. "Today we have designer police," she teased. In truth she would have been satisfied if they were all wearing *gomesi* and high heels.

All five of the women were CPS officers who had worked with her on her children's cases. Awaiting resettlement, some of Gladys's children had lived at police stations for weeks or months. Douglas, Deborah, Rose, Trevor, Ezra — all had depended on the kindness of these officers for many of their basic needs. These women had offered them food, found them clothing, given them baths, and greeted them in the mornings.

Even after settling at the school, the children often inquired about the officers they had gotten to know. Tiny Rose had grown attached to her "aunties" at Kawempe Police, particularly Officer Carol, whose easy manner belied her high rank. But the officers were busy and transportation was expensive, so they had not visited the children. Until today.

Gladys had called each officer to coax and cajole, invoking the children's long-awaited birthday celebration as a reason to reunite. After all, who did not enjoy a party?

THE CHILDREN SLOWLY approached the cluster of visitors. Some of their smiles were hesitant, the glances sidelong, as though they feared the officers would not remember them.

"Deborah! Rose!" The women began singing out names, allotting some of them extra syllables. "Faith-ee! Doug-a-las!"

Rose grabbed Officer Carol's hand. Deborah slipped under Harriet's arm, winning the officer's gap-toothed smile. It seemed every child was searching for a handhold, trying to board the moving train. Only Trevor stood back on the veranda, a distracted frown on his face, as though the noise of the party were interfering with his recollection of a lost tune.

"Come, Agnes, I want a pho-to!" Gladys called.

Director Agnes's arrival sparked a flurry of introductions. Although the police were partners in assisting the children, not all of them had actually met the school director. It was important to Gladys that these officers shake the hand of the one for whom those "temporary placements" became permanent.

Gladys pointed out Ezra, Deborah, Douglas, Rose, and Trevor. "All these are Kawempe products."

"Kawempe Police is the winner!" quipped Agnes. "They have the most!"

Within moments everyone was joking and talking so animatedly that photographing the group proved about as easy as catching butterflies with a spoon.

Someone tugged on Gladys's arm. She looked down to see the pink-spotted hand of her boy with many names—Mugerwa Junior

Godfrey Victor Mananga Adams. After Agnes had given him his seventh name, Muwanguzi, or "victory," he was now Muwanguzi Victor, or as Agnes and Gladys joked, Winner Winner.

Victor was grinning at her. She had seen that round face hardened by pain, or at other times submerged in emotion like a stone dropped into deep water. But today the face was open and present, like that of a much younger child.

"How are you?" Gladys asked, her hands on his shoulders.

"I am good," he said. "I slept so well, Auntie."

"Eh! Yes?"

"Yes. I dreamed that my mother came for me and took me home."

"Ahhh!" Her cry was as sharp and triumphant as the blast of a trumpet. "He had a dream that the mother took him home!"

FUNDS DONATED FOR the party allowed for some transportation costs, a few modest party favors for the kids, and a proper feast for lunch: *matoke*, groundnut sauce, rice, *posho*, greens, and enough goat for even the last person in the line. The children served the police officers, who oohed and aahed as they accepted the heaping plates and balanced them carefully on their laps as one would a baby.

Afterward the students, staff, and visitors filed into a classroom that had been prepared specially for the birthday celebration of Gladys's ten children. The students sat at the desks, three or four to a bench. The officers and teachers sat against the chalkboard. In between stretched a long wooden table upon which had been arranged a white cloth, a vase of fatigued yellow daisies, a few bottles of water and soda, and a rectangular metal pan containing a round cake. Although the children had just eaten lunch, they found it hard not to stare at it: two thick disks covered with chocolate, each layer as solid as a grindstone.

After an opening prayer and a few songs, Agnes announced, "We are here to celebrate the birthdays of Masembe Trevor, Faith, Rose, Deborah, Ezra, Evelyn, Victor, Katamba, Jeremiah, and Douglas. They are celebrating on this day all of their birthdays. Maybe someone wants to say something. Stand up, you can say something." There was a shy pause.

"Eh, Deborah is standing," Gladys said, pointing.

All eyes turned to the compact figure in the pink plaid sundress. "I want to thank God for Aunt Gladys and all the members who are sitting in front," Deborah said in her clear, sweet voice. "Because if they were not there, I couldn't be where I am now."

One by one the birthday children said a few words, most speaking so quietly the crowd did not know when they had finished.

"Who has not said anything?" Agnes asked, walking among the desks.

"Trevor? Can you say anything?" The boy had trouble communicating, but Gladys did not want to ignore him.

There was a long silence as Trevor examined his desk. His mind seemed more remote than ever. These days it seemed that when he was not fighting, he was wandering off. Even the cook at the school was no longer willing to take him into her house. Several times her whole family had been forced to roam the streets, asking the local chairmen of various villages, "Have you seen this boy?" only to find Trevor kicking his football around somewhere, without a care in the world.

Agnes broke the awkward moment by rubbing the boy's head and speaking for him. "He says, 'Thank you so much for coming. He is happy. His favorite game is football!'"

Who was left? Gladys scanned the group, her gaze landing on Victor. "What happened to the policeman? There was one who wanted to be a policeman. Can he say something here?"

Victor smiled and rose to his feet as though he had been waiting to be asked. He shifted slightly from side to side as he spoke, but his voice was surprisingly strong and confident. "My name is Muwanguzi Victor. I thank God, I am very happy. I joined my rela—, my rela—"

"Relatives," Agnes prompted.

"—my relatives. My father and my mother who had abandoned me. I thank God for that, that—that Aunt Gladys took me there. And changed my life." He wagged his head as though struck by the truth of these last four words. A hint of a smile crossed his face, then he sat abruptly and covered his eyes with a scarred pink hand.

Gentle applause filled the room. "So humble," Gladys murmured.

Victor tilted his red, brimming eyes to the ceiling. But when Agnes put an arm around him, he gave up and let the tears spill.

The five policewomen sighed and clucked and smiled. This was why Gladys had wanted them to come to the party. To witness how these children appreciated what had been done on their behalf. Nothing that was given to them—not even a word of greeting—went to waste.

IN THE END there were no candles on the cake. The logistics of designated candle extinguishment aside, the expense seemed unnecessary. After everyone sang "Happy Birthday," Ezra held the handle of a long kitchen knife, and the other nine children placed a hand somewhere on top of his or on his wrist. Ten hands pressed the blade into the formidable cake, which was nearly as tall as it was wide.

The cake disappeared within minutes, leaving only chocolatey traces on the children's lips and cheeks to indicate that it had ever existed. Agnes, who had baked it, received compliments on her creation with ironic pride. Who said that a dentist could not also bake a deliciously sweet cake?

"Aunt Gladys has done for us a birthday!" Agnes announced, and everyone cheered.

Gladys cheered too, with relief. The birthdays were taken care of for the year.

But how many children would stand around the cake next year? Twelve? Fifteen? How thin could one cut the slices? She needed the garden project to start producing. This cake would not be getting any larger.

It was on this point that her thoughts pivoted to Zam. Given the young woman's dynamic commitment to the project, she had expected things to take off. Instead, after those first industrious days, progress had stalled. Thefts continued unabated. Bush went uncleared. The foundation of the house was found to have been filled with tree trunks, not the compacted gravel Gladys had paid for.

Zam was quick to point the finger at Kiviri, an easy scapegoat.

Sure, the landlord often spoke in a voice calibrated for maximum speed and volume, like a born-again preacher recording a mobile-money ad. But he was a businessman, and he had been fairer than expected in his dealings with Gladys and Esther.

Anyway, how could Zam hold anyone else responsible for duties that belonged to her? Trees went unplanted. Seedlings dried up for lack of water. Fertilizer was purchased but not applied. There was no yield to sell.

Perhaps the girl was in over her head. Or perhaps she was not taking the job seriously. "You have the right person," Mike had declared, and Gladys had agreed. But something was wrong, and soon she would have to deal with it.

Not today, though. Not with this room filled with darting children and dancing balloons. An occasion like this was all too rare, and she wanted to enjoy it.

SOMETIMES SHE OPENED her computer and scrolled through her photo library. It contained photos of all her children, marking the day she found this one, the place where she picked up that one. This boy had been hungry for a week; that girl had needed urgent medical care. What miserable expressions they had presented to her camera.

Seeing them pose for pictures today, it was a different story. These ones were happy, healthy, safe. Some she had known for years, like Ezra, and some were new, like Victor. They had come from all over, from Fort Portal to Kibuku. Now there was even one from Karamoja. *You never know,* she thought, chuckling to herself. *Maybe one day I will come across a Dinka!*

Gladys watched Victor, her Karamojong son, marveling at his transformation. It brought to mind the way a fish, dazed and inert at the bottom of a bucket, could spring back to life in the water. That was Victor, swimming along as though nothing had happened. He batted a green balloon at Douglas; he giggled with Faith when the balloon popped. Now he sat looking at nothing, moving a candy from one side of his mouth to the other. The look itself was a triumph. It was a look of simple distraction, not suppressed anxiety or stoicism. No longer was that face the battlefield upon which he fought to control his emotions. It was open land.

The boy had recovered his family. He had friends, a school, and a safe place to live. The name he had arrived at was exactly right. Winner Winner.

A Day at the Beach

WHERE ARE MY RELATIVES?
Since Kawempe Police Station received Rose Nabulime about three years ago, her relatives have not shown up. Information obtained by the Police indicates that her mother died when the girl was only one year old . . . Police appeal to her relatives to call to enable her to re-unite with her family.

Though disconnected from their parents, many of Gladys's kids at Early Learning School had relatives who knew where they were: an auntie or uncle, a grandparent, a stepmother. If a child had any connections to family, she also had a link to a village somewhere. A place to which she could return.

Little Rose had no such family ties — save one. "When are you going to take me to see my father? I want to see him," she would ask, pestering Gladys, after putting in her requests for sugar and soap and clothes and toothpaste and pencils and notebooks. "And pocket money. And some eats. Please, Auntie Gladys?"

If the dik-dik was the most delicate of antelopes, Rose was the human dik-dik: tiny, fragile, wide-eyed. Her limbs were thin, like young bamboo stalks, her forearms and calves no thicker than her wrists and ankles. Her impish smile popped up at the slightest prompt, a reflex response to eye contact or the sounds of others' greetings.

Rose's age was a topic of some debate. In Agnes's professional opinion as a dentist, the girl's teeth marked her age at around eleven. Rose claimed she was nine. To visitors, she looked six.

It was not just her size that made Rose appear so young. Gladys's observation was that Rose was intellectually underdeveloped. Her thinking was often illogical, and touched with a whimsy more appropriate to a toddler. For instance, well before the joint birthday party, Rose had a tendency to announce her birthday. The first time there were no gifts for her, only congratulations and a bit of fuss. But the girl enjoyed it so much that she declared her birthday would occur again the next week. This imaginary calendar had amused Gladys and Agnes. At such a rate, Rose would out-age them before year's end.

The child craved attention and demanded her share. If Faith or Deborah held Gladys's right hand, Rose would hurry to grab her left. She kept an accountant's tally of hugs and treats and favors given to others. "I saw you gave Ezra two thousand shillings, but you gave me only five hundred," she would report to Gladys in her playful, singsong voice. "And you brought a hankie for Faith. Can you bring me a hankie too?"

And so, after Deborah's successful reunion with her family, there was no ducking Rose's pleas to see her father.

"Okay, Rose," Gladys said, relenting. "We will try."

ON THE MORNING of the journey, Rose bathed before donning her school uniform, a cotton jumper with red pinstripes and a sailor collar. She ran to take Gladys's hand, trailed by an untied sash, her rail-thin body a clapper in the bell of her loose dress. Her clean, shiny face glowed with excitement.

As the taxi puttered its way out of Entebbe, Rose gazed at Lake Victoria through the window. How free and open it was, the water stretching out as far as the eye could see.

Rose loved the beach. It was the one place on earth that was only for fun. Aunt Agnes had taken them there. How she and her friends had played and kicked up the water! But she did not want to stop at the lake. Today was her turn to go on an adventure that was all her own.

Gladys's view of the day was more clouded. She could not refuse Rose's request, but did the child have any grasp of what might be in store? In most cases, reunion with family members brought a measure of closure. In Rose's case, it might be a painful reopening.

Gladys had met Rose almost two years before, at Kawempe Police Station. The year before that the child had been living with her father after her mother's death from AIDS. One day a neighbor noticed that Rose was limping, evidently in pain. After she was found to be bleeding between her legs, the police arrested her father for rape.

Since then Rose's father had been in Luzira Prison, waiting for the High Court to hear his case. Gladys's intention in taking the girl to Luzira was not so much to reunite her with her father as to find other family connections through him. The girl did not have a single known relative aside from her father. Surely there was someone out there who would want to know of her existence. And a child had a right to know her family.

Gladys did not know if they would be allowed to see Rose's father at Luzira. They could easily be made to wait for hours or turned away altogether. And there was no guarantee that the father would offer any assistance. After his arrest, he reportedly claimed to know nothing of Rose's mother's family and could give no information about his own kin.

Gladys did not believe it. An African man with no relatives? No way. He had to know someone. If she could look the man in the eye and ask him herself, maybe he would speak. After this time of being alone in prison, could he not understand that his child was alone as well?

There were no relatives to take Rose in after her father's arrest, so the girl had spent weeks living in the shipping container at Kawempe Police Station before being shifted to a crowded juvenile facility. After she had languished there for an entire year, Gladys had decided that enough was enough. Again she had begged Agnes to take in one more child at Early Learning School.

Early Learning was the first school Rose had attended. She reveled in the place, in the belonging. She had friends, teachers, and her beloved Auntie Agnes. Her friends had their own beds, and so did Rose. When they ate, Rose ate. When they bathed, Rose bathed. And when her friends went off with Gladys to see their relatives, she wanted that too.

IN KAMPALA, MIKE met them with his Volvo. "Today Auntie Gladys is taking me to see my father," Rose announced, settling into the back seat. "And I will see my friends at Kawempe Police. I will see Auntie Carol and Auntie Florence and Auntie Harriet. I will see all the friends . . ."

Rose's merry prattle was interrupted by her discovery of a bag of orange hard candies by her feet. Mike had picked it up for the children at Early Learning School, but Rose was given permission to take some for the day's journey. She piled some onto the skirt of her school dress. Loud crunching sounds soon filled the car. Rose was clearly not one to savor a sweet, especially when she had a lapful!

"Don't eat all the candy," Gladys called over the seat. "Save some for tomorrow." She suspected that such self-control was out of reach for sugar-obsessed Rose, but she voiced the warning out of respect for Agnes. As a trained dentist, Agnes would surely object to molars being used as grindstones for hard candy.

Rose merely laughed, offering a glimpse of an orange-streaked tongue. The day was starting out well. *Crunch crunch crunch.*

LUCKILY, GLADYS AND Rose would be accompanied at Luzira Prison by a powerful escort: Kawempe CPU head officer Carol Kushemererwa. Many officers of her rank would not take the time to assist in such a tangential matter as a parental visit, but Carol valued Gladys's efforts, and she was fond of Rose. A bond had formed between the little girl and the "big boss" during the weeks that Rose had stayed at the station.

"Auntie!" Rose had squealed when they picked Carol up at her office. It was fortunate that the girl weighed only about forty-five pounds, or her wild hug might have toppled the woman.

Officer Carol had laughed, feeling the familiar warm push of

Rose's tiny fingers into her palm. It was as though the girl had to grab her hand before someone else took it.

Prisons were intimidating, capricious bureaucracies, and Luzira was Uganda's largest. Originally built in the 1950s for six hundred inmates, it now housed more than six thousand. A sprawling, hilly complex outlined by miles of razor wire, it included several prison facilities, a training academy, schools, shops, housing, a chapel, a mosque, and a tantalizing view of Murchison Bay. It was hard to gauge whether the last served as salve or torture for Luzira's inmates.

As the Volvo began the journey from the main gate to the lower prison and then to the upper prison, Officer Carol's presence proved invaluable. One glimpse of her uniform and Carol's party was greeted collegially at each gate and station and office and waved to the front of the line. How different the journey might have been if Carol had not been with them. At the lower prison, Gladys, Rose, Carol, and Mike were given prime space on a shady bench as they awaited confirmation of their prisoner's location; across from them, in the open sun, an endless procession of visitors waited with supplies for loved ones. Guards rifled through loaves of bread and packages of soap and sacks of beans and rice and *matoke,* probing for contraband. A man carrying a live chicken was pulled out of the line and handed a short knife. Moments later, returning with the headless dead chicken, the man was allowed to rejoin the queue. In twenty minutes the line barely moved.

Even with Carol's assistance, the journey to the upper prison took well over an hour. Finally their group was led into a narrow office, with two long benches facing two desks. Carol handed over the paper with Rose's father's name on it. "Samuel Bwanika. Aggravated defilement," it read. The charge, a capital offense, could carry a sentence of twenty years.

Officers shuffled papers and tapped on keyboards as inmates filed in and out of the space, performing errands. At the end of the room the grated windows were closed, but every pane was broken, allowing an occasional breeze to drift through the crowded room.

Outside, Gladys could see prisoners milling about, a glum lot in their incongruously bright yellow uniforms.

As they waited, Rose nestled between Carol and Gladys, swinging her skinny legs above the floor. It was already midafternoon. *The girl must be hungry,* Gladys thought, with so little meat on her bones and nothing to eat since breakfast except a few candies.

An inmate was escorted to the desk officer closest to Gladys and Carol. The new arrival was a slight, dark-skinned man in his thirties, with stick-thin calves poking out of his short yellow pants. He glanced around the room, his eyes landing on Rose's tiny figure in the corner. His head jerked backward as the rest of his body froze, like he'd walked into a wall.

The officer beckoned the prisoner to approach. Carol and Gladys introduced themselves, but the man's eyes stayed fixed on the girl. "It is you?" he said.

Rose slid off the bench to stand in front of him, a shy smile on her face.

The man knelt nervously by the window, lowering himself to look directly at his daughter. As his face came closer to hers, Rose's smile faded, then disappeared. He reached for both of her hands, but she kept one to herself, a finger held to her mouth.

"I did not think I would see her again," her father said in a trembling voice.

As he spoke softly to her, Rose began to cry. She pulled up the collar of her school dress to cover her eyes but seemed unable to remove her hand from her father's grasp. A thin whimper rose from her, a mosquito whine of distress.

Officer Carol turned her around, whispering and pointing to a chair at an empty desk in the office's opposite corner. Rose moved away without a word.

At his daughter's departure, the prisoner now absorbed the presence of his other visitors. He held Carol's gaze, then Gladys's. Looking into his wary eyes, it was impossible not to think of the crime with which he was charged. At nine, Rose was a wisp of a girl; at six she would have been a mere toddler. That a man — her father! — could have hurt her in that terrible way . . .

Gladys opened her notebook. To get what she wanted from this man, she could not let the poisonous image take root. She began confirming the man's basic information: Samuel Bwanika. Casual laborer. Worked unloading trucks. Confined to Luzira Prison for over a year.

"Now," said Gladys, "I don't know when you are coming out of this place. But what are you planning for this child?"

"I am in here. How can I plan for outside?" Samuel gestured with upturned palms.

"What about family? You must have some family."

His headshake was more a dismissal than a denial.

"Do you have any relatives I can reach?" Gladys pressed matter-of-factly. "Because I would like to let them know about this child."

Samuel rubbed his nose and looked out the windows. Gladys waited, pen poised, eyes unblinking. Maybe the man was trying to decide how to win some concession. Maybe he was trying to remember. Behind him, two officers laughed, pointing at something on a computer screen.

Whatever the prisoner's thoughts, he eventually released them out the window. Turning back to the women, he mumbled something about some siblings who lived outside Kampala.

"Okay, I will try to locate them." Gladys kept her tone neutral, as though her insides were not twitching with excitement at this information. "What message do you want me to take to them?"

"I need to get out of prison before anything else."

Gladys gave a nod of acknowledgment. "I understand, you want to be free of this place. But what I want is for Rose to have some connection to her family. You say you have relatives . . . which ones?"

His offerings were slim: the names of two sisters, whose phone numbers he did not know. "They have not visited me," he complained. "Tell them to help me get out of here."

On the other side of the room, Rose was dwarfed by the desk at which she sat. Too far away to hear anything, she watched the conversation absently, like a student hiding in the last row of the classroom. Her tongue, which protruded slightly from her slack mouth, was still stained orange.

After Rose's mother died from AIDS, Samuel said, "I was taking care of the child by myself."

Gladys registered the man's sallow skin, patchy lips, and reddened, cloudy eyes. The room was still crowded with people, so she leaned in to ask, "Have you been tested? And your daughter?"

He was HIV-positive, Samuel replied. At the time of his arrest, Rose had tested negative.

Gladys filed away a note of worry; she did not trust that the girl was safe.

He had been sick a long time, Samuel lamented. Too sick to commit any crime. "When police came to arrest me, I was laid up in bed. I could barely stand; I felt like I was dying." His words brought tears to his own eyes. As he dabbed at them with a hankie of yellow prison cloth, he stole glances at his audience. The women's expressions were attentive, if impassive.

"I kept asking the police, 'What have I done?'" Samuel went on. "I had no knowledge at all of what was happening."

While it was not Gladys's role to determine the father's guilt or innocence, she had come a long way to have this meeting. It cost her nothing to hear him out. "So you are saying that you did not commit this offense."

"How could I sleep on such a young child?" he protested, chin raised in wounded defiance. "A child that is my own? How could I do such a thing?"

His theories came tumbling out, loose change that he hoped would add up to the bill. There were other men living close by. There was the landlord. What about that neighbor who had quarreled with him? Many kids running around, too. And there was the time Rose had reported that a playmate had kicked her. Who knows what might have happened?"

None of the father's theories explained one crucial fact. "Isn't it true," Gladys cut in, "that Rose told the police that you were the one who defiled her?"

Samuel admitted that when he was arrested, the police put him on the phone so he could hear Rose accuse him. "Maybe a neighbor woman gave her that idea," he said, sounding aggrieved.

The yellow hankie reemerged. As Samuel leaned forward to blow his nose, light from the window entered his breast pocket, revealing the silhouette of a razor blade.

"I think we are finished here," Gladys announced, closing her notebook.

Rose's father glanced up, eyes moist and expectant.

Gladys said only, "Pray for us, that we can find your relatives."

As they exited the office, Rose held tightly to Carol's hand. Samuel stood by the door, staring down at his yellow prison slippers.

"Do you want to say goodbye?" Gladys asked quietly. The girl had asked so many times to see her father.

Rose shook her head stiffly and pressed her face to Carol's side. She began to wail again as the women led her down the hallway, a soft keening like a distant siren.

Her father did not look up.

"SOME PEOPLE HAVE a hard time telling the truth," Officer Carol commented as they made their way down the dusty path to the car.

Gladys agreed. While she was not there to wear a white wig and sit in the high judge's chair, she believed the child more than the man. Why would a girl accuse her own father of a crime as monstrous as rape if he was not the one who had done it?

The car was oven-hot, but Rose hopped in eagerly. She unwrapped another orange candy and began crunching noisily on it. No one scolded her.

As the Volvo trundled back down the hill, past guard stations and checkpoints and the final perimeter of razor wire, Gladys considered the day's mission. In a way it had been a success. She had gotten what she had come for: some names of Rose's relatives. These leads could connect the child with her family.

On the other hand, the encounter with Rose's father had obviously distressed the child. Gladys hated to see kids cry. Adults might shed tears over nothing — sentiment, or slights that they should be able to handle as mature beings — but children lacked both autonomy and armor. They cried because they could do nothing else.

In the back seat with Carol, Rose explained her reaction to seeing her father. "I remembered when I was little," the girl said simply. "I remembered what he did to me and I cried." She played with the empty candy wrapper in her lap. "One day Aunt Agnes asked me, 'Have you forgiven your father? Even bad sinners are forgiven.' Now I love him," she said, twirling the wrapper between her fingers. "When I grow up, I will buy him a car."

Could a child understand what it meant to forgive so big a sin? Especially a child like Rose, who displayed the maturity of a six-year-old?

"We will come back again tomorrow?" Rose asked. "I want to see my friends at police."

Gladys shook her head. "It's time to return to school. We will get you something to eat, and then Uncle Mike will take you back."

"What food do you like?" Mike inquired.

This question instantly silenced the girl; she stared out the window at the storefront for Martyrs' Supermarket, her expression almost dreamy. "When Deborah came back from visiting her family, she had chicken and chips," she said finally. "She brought some to school, but I did not get any. I would like to eat chicken and chips too."

"Will you bring some back to your friends?" Officer Carol asked.

"No! I will eat it all!"

"How about the candy?"

Rose grinned and popped another piece into her mouth.

Carol laughed. "And what will you tell your friends about today?"

"Nothing."

"Nothing?"

Rose's voice fell to a level just above the noise of the traffic. "I don't want you to tell the other kids that I saw my father," she said.

"You don't want anyone to know."

The small head shook firmly.

"She doesn't want the others to know that she saw her dad," Carol relayed to Gladys. "Did you get that?"

"Yes, I get it," said Gladys.

Carol patted Rose's hand. "We will keep it a secret."

"You will tell only Aunt Agnes!" Rose announced with sudden authority.

"Okay." Carol looked at her. "What will you tell your friends about where you went today?"

The girl's brow knitted and her mouth puckered, the lump of candy tenting her slender cheek. Then her expression relaxed. "I will tell them that I went to the beach."

"The beach!"

"Yes," the girl said, giggling.

Carol and Gladys laughed. "Who took you to the beach?"

"Aunt Agnes took me to the beach. And she gave me candy and I played all day." She leaned her head against the window as the car turned north. Sunlight rippled across her face in waves. "It was a fun time."

House with No Roof

They could see it even before they turned down the driveway: a clean rectangle of red against green. For so long the foundation's brick outline had only suggested a building. Now the idea lived in three dimensions. The walls were going up.

Some Americans had sent a donation to the garden project, which Gladys decided to apply to construction. It was not enough to complete the house, but after three months of setbacks and no harvests, she felt the urge to see progress in tangible form. She strolled from the car, savoring the view. A crew of four men was bustling around the structure, ferrying bricks here and there.

"It is going up!" Gladys sang, aiming the beam of her smile up at the workers on the scaffolding. "Now there is something to show."

Esther looked almost merry on her friend's behalf. "The house is looking so nice already, even without the roof."

"You workers are doing a good job," Gladys declared, her gaze sweeping up and down to include all the men. Their skin glistened, almost metallic with sweat. "When it is finished, it will be a fantastic house."

A fellow on the scaffolding called down, "We want it to be an eye-catcher!"

Gladys turned at the sound of a rattling wheelbarrow. Two men began to shovel dirt into the tray, each deposit shooting a puff of dust into the air.

"Hey!" Gladys put her hands up to her glossy new bob. "Do you know how much I spent on my hair?"

"We are used to this kind of dust!"

"So you are going to wash my hair again, boy?" The men joined the women's laughter. "Eeee!"

Gladys and Esther wandered through the half-built structure, looking at the layout of the rooms. Ezra and a couple of the other boys had recently visited the garden. Next time they would be able to stay in the room on the left, which was a decent size for two, a manageable squeeze for three. There was a middle room for storage or additional beds. On the far right, Gladys's room would have its own door. She wanted to make sure that she could check on those young ones while maintaining her privacy.

She and the builder chatted about the next stages: the plaster, the roof, the ceiling, the veranda. There was no money yet for any of it, but she wanted to be prepared. If the projected costs made her knees wobble, the surrounding progress kept her upright.

She looked up at the walls again. "Okay, so I don't know when we can afford a roof. But at least we have reached somewhere."

IN THE GARDEN, however, progress was less evident. There were bright spots, like the passionfruit vines, whose white-and-purple flowers now intermingled with young green fruit, speckled like weavers' eggs. The rows of cassava plants were waist-high, with a fair portion of tubers ready for harvest. But there were many shortcomings to point out: the bananas still tangled in overgrown bushes, out of reach; gouges along the edges of the cassava field where tubers had been pulled up and spirited away.

Zam appeared, wearing a soiled yellow skirt and a pink tank top with cracked lettering down the front reading LOVE YOU. Her hair was uncovered. Her loosened plaits and solemn expression gave her an air of dazed alertness, like someone startled out of sleep. She looked not unlike baby Maria, who clung to her mother's shirt, judging the world with her usual stern befuddlement.

For a moment Zam lurked on the periphery of the group, in

apparent anticipation of disapproval. With good reason, thought Gladys. It was high time they had a talk, and not just about the gardens.

"How are you doing here?" she asked.

The girl laughed uneasily. "Okay."

As the party moved to the planted areas beyond the house, Gladys stopped to point. "Why are those trees not yet made into charcoal?"

As Zam had suggested, Gladys had paid a man to cut down the cluster of "unuseful" trees. Two months later the stumps and branches still lay in an enormous pile on the very spot where they had fallen, forgotten corpses on a battlefield.

"I am not the one who is supposed to make the charcoal," Zam said. "There is a man who is supposed to do it."

"Last time the excuse was that it was the rainy season, so we should wait till it's dry. Now it's the dry season and the wood is still just sitting there."

"The man is somebody that Kiviri knows. I don't know him personally."

Looking around, Gladys saw tangled branches that had been hacked away to make room for planting, tossed here and there like dirty laundry. "And that loose wood. You have not collected it yet?"

"If we are burning all this for charcoal, I need to collect everything at one time," Zam said, shifting Maria from her left hip to her right. The excuse was halfhearted, and they both knew it.

"When you told me, 'Mommy, I haven't got any money,' I said, 'Get the money by selling the charcoal.'"

Zam did not reply. Gladys sighed. She had expected the girl to follow up on such matters, to take charge and get things done. But Kiviri's help was again required.

"Where are my avocados?" Gladys continued.

"You mean those things that you gave me? They're down over there. Near the potatoes."

"Did you plant them?"

"Not yet," Zam replied. "I'm just keeping them moist for the time being."

"Other people around here are digging, but you are not digging at all."

"The sun is too hot," Zam protested. "It is not good to plant trees in this heat."

Gladys informed her that there was a costly load of additional saplings in the boot of Mike's car. "They must not go to waste. You must plant them and water them every day. If I come and I find these trees dried out and dead, I'll eat you up!"

Zam mumbled assent. The sun was high and hot, but the baby's whimpering elicited only a perfunctory jostle from her mother.

AFTER THE UNSATISFACTORY evaluation of Gladys's gardens, the party drove to Esther's plot, where they took some bread, sugar, and soap out of the boot for Zam to take to her room. As they handed her the goods, Gladys glanced around. She was looking for someone, and there he was.

That man. The one she had seen here before. The one Zam called her brother.

"Come over here," she called, waving to him.

The man approached, head slightly lowered, eyes hooded and cautious. He was a slight fellow, no taller than Esther, with small features. Even his teeth were small, like kernels of corn at the thin end of the ear. He wore a brown striped shirt and jeans that pooled around his ankles.

Gladys asked his name.

"Robert."

"What relationship do you have with this one?" She pointed at Zam, standing a few feet away, with bags of provisions dangling from each hand. "How do you address her?"

"That is Zam," Robert answered.

"I know her name," Gladys said impatiently. "I want to know her relationship to you."

The man's eyes darted toward Zam, but the big woman blocked his view. He blurted, "She's my wife."

Gladys swiveled around to face Zam. "That is not what you told me before."

Zam did not reply.

Esther's lips pursed in satisfaction. At last it would all come out.

IT HAD BEEN over a year ago now since Zam had called Gladys to plead for assistance, claiming that the man who had gotten her pregnant had abandoned her. As the young mother had had no other means of support, Gladys had helped her with the startup money for the food kiosk business and then with the job at the gardens.

After some months in Luwero, Zam had mentioned that she had run into a brother who happened to be working nearby. It was a happy coincidence that the siblings found themselves living in the same village.

Strange, then, when Gladys had received a phone call a few weeks ago. A man introduced himself as "the husband of your daughter." Had Gladys seen Zam? She had been absent from the gardens for several days, and he could not reach her.

On Gladys's next visit to Luwero, she had noticed a man — this man — outside Zam's place, roasting corn over a small fire. "Is that your husband, Zam?" she had asked.

"No, that is my brother."

"So it is not true you have a husband here?"

"No, Mommy!" Zam had laughed prettily. "By the way, I love you, Mommy!"

Gladys may have been willing to wait and watch, but Esther had seen enough. Too many signals had tweaked her antennas: Zam's constant excuses for unfinished work, her quickness to blame Kiviri, the way she flitted around Gladys with her complaints like a nightjar feigning a broken wing. Once Zam claimed that the landlord had planted only forty-six banana plants instead of the seventy Gladys had paid for. Esther went to the garden to count the plants for herself and discovered that there were actually seventy-two!

It was high time this shifty girl answered for her deceptions.

Fortunately, this Robert fellow seemed incapable of deception, not out of principle but out of slow-wittedness. Stunned by his own confession, he followed the trio of visitors to the side of the building where Zam stayed, where he could be interrogated separately from his wife. The precaution proved unnecessary, as Zam had retreated out of sight the moment Robert uttered the word *wife*.

Standing before Gladys, Esther, and Mike, Robert winced like a child listening for the crack of the switch. But the big woman spoke calmly.

"Zam told me that you were her brother. Now that I know you are her husband, I feel really insulted. She tells me a man has made her pregnant and then abandoned her. Then she brings the man back here. I find that a problem. Why should I pay your rent? Why should I bring fuel, food, a mattress, and supplies like that? When the child was sick, I paid the hospital bills. While you are just sitting here eating samosas. That is not fair."

Robert found it hard to meet her gaze. His eyes floated from face to face, searching for a soft place to land and finding only stone. Behind Mike and Esther, two kids yanked on the branch of a tree, trying to shake out some fruit that was not ready to fall.

"I don't object to you and your wife being together. I object to you asking me to provide for you."

"I would like to say something," Robert interjected. As he spoke, his hands formed a cage, the fingertips pressing together as if to keep a bird inside. "With everything you've said, I agree. You are our elder, our mother. But if you come here in the morning, you will see that I don't do anything but get up and go digging on your land. I have told my wife that I will not work anywhere else unless our mother tells us to go away. Because she buys us fuel, she buys us —"

"I've never been your mother," Gladys interrupted calmly, daubing at her face with her handkerchief square. "You've never come to properly introduce yourself to me. Your wife let me think you were her brother."

"This is where the problem comes in," Robert said, nodding, grasping for some point of agreement. "Because there is a misconception somewhere here. Your daughter made a mistake, because she did not tell you the truth."

Gladys chuckled dryly, noting that Zam was no longer his wife but rather her daughter.

"Today's my first day to stand before you and speak to you," Robert went on, no doubt emboldened by Zam's absence. "Your daughter did not tell you the truth, and I ask for your forgiveness."

"My forgiveness is no guarantee that I will continue to look after your family for you. You cannot get up in the morning and tell me that your child is sick and ask me for money for upkeep. I won't allow that."

"I would just ask you to help us with small, small things," Robert proposed, as though this were a significant concession on his part.

"I will no longer bring things like rice and food, because you are the man of the home. You should provide for your own family instead of waiting for me. It is very silly."

"Old woman, we are very grateful, but—"

"How old are you?"

"I am thirty-four years old."

Gladys gave him a withering look. "No man of thirty-four can sit there and ask another person to look after his wife and his child."

Robert's mouth slackened, tightening on one side and drooping on the other, as though he were about to be sick.

"Me, I hate when people lie to me." Gladys turned to Mike and Esther, speaking of the man before them as a hypothesis, an abstraction. "And when you are a man of thirty-four and you can't mind your own life? You are not a boy at thirty-four years. Boys of twenty years are paying their own rent."

She listed off all the ways she had provided for Robert's family, from the salt in their food to the lamp on their wall, still without raising her voice. Robert's expression suggested that it would have been easier for him if she had screamed in his face and stormed away—anything but this meticulous dissection: slow and painful, like plucking a live chicken, one feather at a time.

Gladys finished, turning her gaze back to Robert. "I don't see how you can expect me to be funding your lives. As a *man*."

Denuded now, he shriveled. Nearby there was a small snap as

the kids broke a branch of an orange tree. Green fruit pelted the ground.

"You should find other work for your income. You must not just sit there with your woman and wait to be fed. It's like you marry a girl and your mother-in-law buys you fuel!" This drew peals of laughter from the two women. For the first time in the conversation, Gladys's voice grew loud. "Ehhhh! Shame on you!"

"That's not the way, Madam," Robert managed.

Esther asked dryly, "What plan do you have, as a man?"

Robert's mouth opened a half inch and froze, like one of the stuck windows on the Volvo. Gladys was quite certain that this fellow had never had a plan. Zam had her hands on the wheel of this scheme; Robert was just the manual labor, loading the goods in the back.

"Get out of your box," Gladys advised, throwing metaphors his way. "You're packed in such a small box. Your brain is iced up. Your woman has put you in a bottle. You're just locked up in a bottle. That's how you are existing right now. Wrapped up on her hip." She spoke in a child's voice. "'Zam, has Mommy has brought sugar? Has Mommy brought rice? Tell Mommy we don't have fuel.' A man of more than thirty years?"

Robert hung his head. "Old woman, I ask for your forgiveness."

Gladys sighed. Was this one incapable of any response except to ask for things? "We are forgiving, but we are telling you to grow up. Don't just depend on me. You seem to think I'm made of money. Most months I earn only three hundred thousand shillings. Don't you think I would love to dress up and look smart like other women? I don't buy clothes because I've got so many obligations and people to take care of. It is not just Zam I am helping."

"Thank you so much for your advice. You're my mom."

"You're joking with me, calling me your mother. As if I have not had kids whom I've mothered?" Gladys shook her head, dismissing him. "If you don't start being creative, you will be in problems. Sort your brain out."

"Mom—"
But Gladys was already walking away.

NOW IT WAS Zam's turn.

The girl was watching her from the veranda, rubbing a knuckle absently back and forth across her mouth as though trying to erase it. On the mat behind her, baby Maria slept sprawled like a spilled load of firewood.

Gladys headed for the car, opened the door, and stood with one hand on the frame, signaling her eagerness to leave this place. "Come here."

Zam approached.

"You must stop this low-class behavior," Gladys said, steadfastly refusing to look at her. "You are telling me you are going to the garden, but you are not digging. When Ezra and the other boys were here, they said, 'Zam never goes to the garden. And sometimes she would not cook for us. We just ate jackfruit.'"

"I was cooking for them," Zam insisted, without conviction. The lack of eye contact seemed to unsettle her; she could not get a clear view of her target. "But sometimes they would refuse to eat."

"I've told you, change your ways."

The confrontation was shorter than the one with Robert, but the points were the same. The sister-and-brother charade had been uncovered. "Mommy" could no longer be manipulated. Zam must reform or face drastic, albeit unspecified, consequences.

The young woman was standing barefoot on some cold, cold ice. But her feet were also ice. She did not flee, she did not fight back, she did not cry. And unlike her husband, she did not apologize. She withstood Gladys's castigation, not stepping back until the car pulled away.

"I AM VERY pleased with the progress on the building," Gladys announced as they headed back toward the main road. "I did not expect the walls to be that high already!"

It was like that for Gladys. Her temper might burn as hot as a string of firecrackers, but it was just as quickly spent. Anger was a purgative, not a fuel.

Esther, however, was not so eager to move onto sunnier topics. "Zam and Robert have been together, you know," she said. "All along. For five years."

"That's what Robert said?"

"Yes. When I remained there talking with him, that is what he said."

"So he never abandoned her."

"He never abandoned her. They have never been separated." He had even been living with Zam in Kampala, Robert claimed, when Gladys had met her.

"What I really feel," Gladys said, sighing, "is that I would have been happy if Zam had said, 'You see, Mommy? The dad of my girl is finally here.' I mean, if I'm helping you, why would you hide that from me? That annoys me."

"For me, I'm not annoyed. I'm disappointed. It's deeper than annoying," said Mike. It was rare for him to be deceived by a person's nature, and he was rattled. "I've just been shocked out of my skin," he confessed. "The girl disappointed me. So disappointed me. I want to take the bread and sugar back!"

"Hah!" Gladys's laugh was sharp, a stone pinging off the windshield. "Do you remember, I was so happy when Zam came here!"

What should be the consequences of such a betrayal? Most people would label Zam's actions inexcusable. *Dump her on the side of the road!* they would shout. But Gladys could not kick Zam out. She knew this. She knew Zam's family, knew where she came from. She had called the girl daughter; the girl had called her mother. It was not easy for Gladys to break the relationship. She had invested something of herself in this bond, even if the girl's reciprocity was insincere.

And of course there was an innocent bystander at this traffic wreck: baby Maria. Gladys would be doing the child no favors if she threw Zam out. Zam was the mother and Robert was the father. They needed to stay together.

Even Esther, satisfied as she was to have her suspicions validated, was inclined to mercy. "You give her a second chance."

"I want to keep her," Gladys agreed. "But I am now concluding that she may be a person who cannot reform."

She would not banish Zam, but from now on she would pay the salary to the husband, not the wife. If Robert had truly performed the work—as inadequate as it was—while Zam collected the salary, he had earned an opportunity to prove himself. Through him they would get their second chance.

They had lost one chance forever, though, this unreliable couple: they would never live in the house at the gardens. After all that had transpired, it would be folly to let them sleep there when it was finished, even for one night. Gladys knew those two would burrow in like porcupines, ready to flare their quills when roused.

AS THE VOLVO rolled down Masindi-Kampala Road, it began to chug.

The engine's hesitation was subtle, but Mike knew his vehicle well. He pulled over to check under the hood. Esther, who worked with engines at the airport, joined him. Soon they were scowling at the air filter, which was caked in what looked like red powder. For drivers in Uganda, dust proved an inescapable nuisance, clogging filters and valves, obscuring mirrors, and seeping into window seals and upholstery seams.

While she waited, Gladys tucked her well-used handkerchief into her purse and came upon a note. It was from some of her girls at Early Learning School. Sometimes the children slipped her little messages, enjoying the fuss she made over their writing. This one was a folded piece of lined notebook paper, on one side of which was written "From your girls to you." Three stick figures with triangle skirts, labeled "Faith," "Esther," and "Rose," were drawn in descending size. On the other side, the words "We love you" were surrounded by colorful stars, hearts, and trees.

Her sweet girls. It was just like them to give her a thank-you note just when she needed it. Unfolding the paper, she discovered three neat columns running down the length of the page.

Shopping List

Evelyn	*Rose*	*Faith*
soap	socks	Bags
Bag	Backets	soap
Shoes	Pencils	Backets
nickers	container	Pencils
colours	bottle	Pens
Backets	Net	Books
Pencils	bathing soap	note book
Socks	washing soap	Shoes (sundles)
books	Eats	Eats.
Eats		

Thank you for caring for us.

"A shopping list! Oh my Godddd . . ." Gladys laughed and laughed.

It was not solace her girls had sent her way but motivation. They had their needs. Her boys had their needs. Douglas needed secondary-school tuition. Ezra needed money for exams and for transport to visit his village.

And what of Trevor? The boy needed everything. He lost clothing constantly, or perhaps other children stole it from him. He was always hungry. Recently he had walked off with a sack of pounded groundnut flour from the school kitchen, hunkered down behind a classroom, and eaten the whole thing. An entire kilo! From what she had been told, the boy would eat anything, even plastic bags. How could she possibly let herself become discouraged when one of her children was found chewing on *kavera*?

Chunk. The hood shut. Mike turned the ignition over, and the car puttered back onto the tarmac.

Theft, deception, pilferage — they were a nuisance. Dust in the air filter. In Uganda, what person moved forward without running into a few crooks? One had to sift out the corruption and press on. What mattered was down the road.

Passed Along

"Where is the girl?"

Gladys surveyed the patch of muddy ground: a sewage canal on one side, on the other a large tree with plastic sheeting hanging from its branches, an array of cooking utensils and frayed sackcloth spread around its trunk. Nearby, tarps spread with millet dried in the sun, the seed to be distilled into strong, low-cost *waragi*. A couple dozen children of the slum wandered over to scrutinize the visitors. None of them was the one Gladys was meant to meet.

Two officers from Kampala's Kitintale Police Station, one male and one female, had led Gladys, Esther, and Mike there to review the case of a poor old man and a mysterious disabled child who had been dumped at his door.

"Madame, where is the girl?" Gladys asked again.

"She is inside there." The policewoman pointed at a shack to the right of the tree. It was a perilously ramshackle structure, with some walls of brick, others of wood, and some of mud, the long cracks between the sections stuffed with old clothing, cardboard, and wadded-up plastic bags: a standing chronicle of its owner's declining fortunes. A sheet hung over the doorway in lieu of a door; Gladys pushed it aside and peered in.

The room had no windows, and it took a good ten seconds for her eyes to adjust. Eventually she discerned a tight space lined with cardboard, scattered bedding, a dusty bicycle, and the tiny, spindly figure of a girl. She was hunched on the ground, legs folded up so compactly that her head was framed by bony knees.

"Ehh . . ." breathed Gladys. "She is here."

For a moment the girl lifted her face, her huge pupils contracting in the encroaching light. The beam of a cell phone seared the darkness, and she quickly pulled herself into a tight ball, as though she were a knot in a rope that had been yanked at both ends.

It felt bad to stare down at the child. It was like witnessing some secret shame. Not the shame of the blameless girl but the shame of the people who had allowed her to descend into this wretched state: helpless and cowering in the dark. The image could have been a child abuse prevention poster on a police station wall.

"Hello." Gladys's voice was loud but gentle.

The girl did not respond.

How old was she? Ten? Thirteen? It was hard to tell. "Is she squatting?" Gladys murmured. "Can she stand?"

The old man explained that the child could not stand or walk or speak or feed herself. *Could she have cerebral palsy?* Gladys wondered, having written about the disorder before. *Or polio?*

"Can't we bring her outside? Into the light."

"Yes," said one of the officers. "But she has soiled herself. Let them clean her up first."

AFTER A FEW minutes the girl was carried from the shack. Her whimpers culminated in a low squeal when she was placed on the ground. She stayed crouched in the loose woman's dress they had put her in, her body like a fist wrapped in a handkerchief.

"Mm-mm-mm," uttered the girl, blinking at the sunlight.

The *mzee,* the old man, sat on a stool behind her. When he removed his cloth cap, his head glowed with its halo of receding white hair. Two white tufts of mustache framed his mouth, giving him the look of a mournful walrus. His name was James Opoki.

"The child appeared at midnight," he said. "A neighbor woman found her lying on a bedsheet under that tree and called me outside. That was the first time I ever saw her."

Several neighbors nodded in confirmation of his account. They suspected that the mother of the child had targeted the old man, who often cared for his six grandchildren during the day.

After three weeks with no one coming for the girl, the old man went to the police station for assistance. For a week he waited from morning till afternoon. When the officers offered him lunch, he politely declined. James Opoki was a principled man. He was not seeking charity, only a solution.

The old man's dignity spurred the police into what little action they could take. They contacted the Probation Department, only to be told there was nowhere to place the girl. Even Naguru Reception Center refused to take her. So the police called Gladys.

"*Mzee*," Gladys asked, "what do you want to be done for you?"

"I have finished one month with this child. I don't have any assistance at all." Opoki cradled the blue cap in his hands like an empty bowl. "I used to be a mechanic. But I'm seventy-eight years old now, and I don't even have money for food. Yesterday I only had two pieces of fried cassava to share with this child. And you can see, every day she must be cleaned, because she has constant running tummy. She cannot clean up after herself."

Gladys glanced down at the girl, at the circle of flies around her head, the running mucus under her nose. She turned to Esther. "These people need some Pampers. They can't keep cleaning such a big girl all the time."

Pampers, soap, panties. All those things were expensive. How to get them? Rifling through her mental files, she began to compile a short list of places to approach.

"I am grateful to the police for trying to help with the situation." The old man's voice quavered with apology. "But the government needs to find a place for this child. Because me, at my age, I can't do it."

HALF THE SLUM stood by to watch Mike turn the car around. The Volvo worked back and forth on the thin strip of land by the sewage canal, making incremental shifts like a spider at the nexus of a web.

"Now that I have seen the situation, let's team up and see what we can do about it," Gladys said, bidding farewell to her police colleagues. "*Effendi*, if you do locate the girl's mother, do not beg her to take care of her child. It is the child's right. The girl did not ask to be born. She did not fill out an application for birth."

They drove on to their next appointment, Gladys fuming. A mother dumping her own daughter under a tree. What was she supposed to eat? Leaves and bark? Of course life was not easy. It was hard for a poor woman to raise a disabled child. But how much harder was it for the disabled child, once abandoned?

Gladys found her thoughts turning to Trevor. These days she was always thinking about Trevor. Smiling, limping, quiet Trevor.

"After seeing this disabled girl in Kitintale," she remarked to Esther and Mike, "what it shows me is that Trevor's parents were aware of his state when they separated from him. And they felt relief."

Gladys had never run a child's profile in her column so many times. Was it twelve? Fifteen? While Trevor may have grown over the past two years, his face looked much the same: there was either the detached half-frown or the carefree smile. Trevor's photo had been seen by millions of readers; Gladys had been praying that his family members would be among them.

Now, she realized, maybe they had been. Maybe the parents had seen their boy in the paper hugging Director Agnes, and that was fine with them. Maybe they had wanted to be rid of that troublesome one who would not listen to orders or clean himself or fetch water or show proper respect. Wasn't their impatience imprinted in Trevor's harsh utterances? *I will beat you! I will whip you!* One had to conclude that parents who taught their son these words might well have thrown up their hands. Like the mother of this Kitintale girl, they had passed their child along.

And now Trevor was being passed along again.

"YOU KNOW, GLADYS, we have a problem with Trevor."

"Again?"

These days every conversation with Director Agnes began this way: it was always trouble, and it was always Trevor. Smiling, limping, confounding Trevor.

"Now what has Trevor done?" Gladys asked.

Agnes sighed. "You need to look for a place to take him."

"Agnes." Gladys's voice dropped placatingly. "Where can I take Trevor? What has he done now?"

The child's exploits at Early Learning had been escalating to the point where every time the school director mentioned his name, Gladys winced. Recently, when Trevor had spotted his football in a locked classroom, he had taken a rock, thrown it through the window, reached through the broken glass to retrieve his ball, then skipped off as though nothing had happened.

Another time he had thrown a heavy stone at one of the younger boys, knocking him almost unconscious. Agnes called Gladys from the hospital, blasting her: "Look now at what your boy has done!"

The list of crimes grew longer and longer. Even with all their years of experience, the two women did not know what to do. Agnes still eschewed the traditional punishment; she would not beat him. "That's not the way to treat children," she would say. "The way to treat them is to talk to them."

But no matter how much she talked to Trevor, his behavior did not change. "You stupid woman!" he would bark at Agnes. "I will beat you!"

Early Learning School had given the boy space to recover from childhood trauma. But the tactic had backfired. He did not learn to swim at his own pace; he merely drifted further and further away. After two years the teachers had given up any hope of Trevor studying at a desk. The boy entered and exited from classes with impunity, stepping out to play with his ball whenever he felt like it. And now he was roaming off the grounds all the time. The school lacked a fence, so it was easy for him to wander.

Gladys wished Trevor could explain his motivations. If he could tell her, *You see, Auntie, I went away because of such and such,* then Gladys could suggest some changes. Improve the situation. But this was a boy who could not even tell you where he had gone. He would only offer that distant smile, saying, "I've been somewhere there."

This latest time, Agnes gravely informed Gladys, it was bad. How and when he had slipped away from school, they didn't know. But somehow he got all the way down to the Nakumatt market on Berkeley Road. According to the boda-boda man, the one who saved Trevor's life, the boy was in the middle of the road, that busy intersection in front of the shopping center, playing with his ball! All the cars in both directions were skidding and honking and stopping in a traffic jam while the boy ran blithely across the lanes, pretending to be Ronaldo or whoever. The boda man had jumped off his motorcycle, run into the road, and pulled the boy to safety.

After such an incident, Agnes would not entertain talk of giving the boy more time to adjust or of renewing efforts to find his people. The closeness of the disaster had wicked away such palliatives. Both women knew it was only by sheer luck that the boy had not been injured or caused an accident. What if the blame for such a tragedy fell on the school?

Trevor's banishment from Early Learning was not an easy decision for Agnes. While she was undoubtedly weary of his wandering, his bed-wetting, and his shouts of "I will kick you! I will stone you!" her soft heart did not easily give up on a child.

Gladys did not beg for Trevor to be given another chance, but she asked for more time. It was no minor task to find placement for any child, but doors swung open more swiftly for the newborn abandoned in a bin, the housemaid burned for breaking a dish, or the helpless Kitintale girl shut away in a stranger's hut. That one had been welcomed into an NGO for special-needs children with medical issues. But a boy who cursed, threw rocks, and chewed on plastic bags?

GLADYS OUTLINED her dilemma to Mike and Esther. "Agnes tells me, 'You know, Trevor needs a place where they can care for those mentally retarded children.'"

"Yes, he can't be in a mainstream school," Mike said. It was no glib comment; one of Mike's grown daughters lived in a private facility for people with cognitive disabilities. She had been deprived of oxygen at birth because of a medically botched delivery.

"But he doesn't really have mental retardation. Don't you think he can get worse in such a place?" Gladys protested. She had visited several facilities where the children were very badly off; many had severe physical problems as well as mental ones. One could not coop up Trevor with such vulnerable types. What if he were to take out his frustration on those around him?

Some considered the boy mad. Gladys was not sure what they meant by madness, but she did not think that Trevor was acting senselessly. His behavior reflected some disarranged internal logic. They needed to figure out what was disarranging him.

But how? Right now she could not even figure out where the boy should sleep. She only knew that she did not want him to end up in the one place that would take him.

"If he is sent away from school, Probation will have no alternative. They will dump him in Naguru. And what will happen to him in Naguru?" Gladys shook her head. Allowing the boy to be sent to that overcrowded warehouse was tantamount to giving up. "I'm disturbed."

Esther and Mike said nothing. Gladys gazed out the window at a procession of marabou storks on a rubbish pile, as downcast as mourners at a burial.

"Just give me some time and I'll sit down and see what I can do about it."

SHE DID NOT get the chance. Agnes called Gladys to report that she was pushing the unruly fledgling out of the nest. The school could not accommodate Trevor for a single day longer. He would be taken to Entebbe Police Station.

Gladys begged for leniency. Entebbe Police had nowhere to keep a child, and Gladys could not safely keep him in her own tiny place, as she and Esther were always out.

Agnes would not budge. The boy had mental problems. He had to go.

If only the garden project were further along in its development, she lamented. Maybe someday Trevor could be looked after in that place. But this was no time to indulge in "somedays" and "if onlys."

Gladys reached out to Bright Kids, a home in Entebbe that had previously accepted some of her charges. The director regretted that the home's finances were far too tight already. Gladys called Officer Carol at Kawempe Police, who confirmed that the only option for the boy was Naguru Reception Center. In desperation, Gladys emptied every pocket of her memory. There had to be a name tucked away somewhere, the name of someone who could help her with Trevor.

It was then that she remembered a doctor, Robert Kironde, whom she had written about in *New Vision* seven years before. They had become friends, and although she had not seen him for a long, long time, she felt she could call on him.

Unfortunately, Dr. Kironde did not specialize in behavioral matters. Nor was he a pediatrician. So okay, he was a dentist. She had quoted him in an article titled "Do Not Let the Dentist Remove Your Teeth." But he had been kind enough to give her advice on the frequency of her malaria, and she recalled his mentioning to her that before choosing a specialization, he had had to learn general medicine. Perhaps, she thought, he could provide some insight into Trevor's case.

"Can I see this boy?" Dr. Kironde asked after they discussed taking him to the national mental hospital. "Can you bring him around?"

Gladys hastily arranged for Trevor to travel with her from Entebbe to Kampala. The day taxed her severely. She was recovering from typhoid, and delays forced her to wait in the rain for two hours. The scheduled eight a.m. meeting finally took place at one in the afternoon. Gladys watched anxiously as Dr. Kironde attempted to engage the shy boy in conversation, Trevor surrendering words like they were 10,000-shilling notes.

After a few minutes, Dr. Kironde smiled at Trevor and stood up. "All right. Let us go."

"To the mental hospital?"

The doctor shook his head. "No, this boy does not need to go to a mental hospital. I know where we need to go."

THE NAME OF the place was unpronounceable, like the sound someone might make in trying to suppress a loud yawn: L'Arche. It was a faith-based NGO founded by French people. The staff there described it as "a community of hope for people with and without learning disabilities."

The doctor and a counselor listened as Gladys related Trevor's traumatic history and his problematic behavior. The abusive language, the rock-throwing, the running away — she left out nothing. After some time observing the boy, the L'Arche staff came to a conclusion. Trevor had a developmental disorder, and they had a name for it: autism.

Gladys knew nothing about this autism. The term was new to her.

The doctor tried to explain. Gladys was right — Trevor was not mad, but he was not able to understand things or communicate the way other children did. One should not expect someone with autism to do what he was ordered to do. If one said, "Go in this classroom and do this exercise," a person with autism might not respond. He might stay focused on one particular thing.

The staff showed Gladys a resident with autism whose sole concentration was the care of poultry. The chickens and their eggs. How many eggs were there? Where were they laid? And so on. Another resident was concerned only with the care of the pigs. He had to rush to see that the pigs were fed, otherwise he would become agitated. Once at the piggery, he could monitor the animals for hours.

For Trevor, Gladys knew, the "one particular thing" was his ball. If the boy had a ball that was his own to kick and chase, he could be content all day.

"Eh!" Gladys found herself saying again and again, and "Ah-*hahhh!*" She was fascinated by this new knowledge. It was as if she had been struggling to decipher an unknown language and she had finally found an interpreter.

Trevor, however, was unhappy. When Gladys tried to get the boy to pose with the staff for a picture, he started to cry. He apparently feared that his auntie was trying to pass him along to these strangers. And when the staff arranged for Trevor to have lunch with some of the other residents, he ran away from the dining area. They had to bring him back into the office with his food. While Gladys could not help but laugh at the boy's stubbornness, she wondered, *What am I supposed to do now? I can't take this boy back to Entebbe, but it seems he is stuck on me.*

Observing the boy's distress, one of the staff directors commented, "You know, we must keep in mind that Trevor has been in many places."

It was true. The boy was only about nine, but he had already been through very tough times. His life could not have been easy before he had been dumped at the clinic at Katalemwa. And in the two years since, he had been kicked down the road like his well-worn football: housed at the shipping container at the Kawempe Police Station, sent off to the ironically named Good Samaritan School, stranded after the police raid in Rakai, then settled at Early Learning for over a year before being kicked out. In Trevor's world, change often meant bad things.

It was important, the staff told Gladys, that the boy acclimate to a new environment. Although the facility could not accept a resident as young as Trevor, the staff invited him to make weekly visits. Gladys agreed to deliver Trevor to L'Arche on Saturdays, and during the week she would contribute a small sum for the maid at Dr. Kironde's residence to look after the boy.

The staff took Gladys and Trevor on a tour of the grounds and living areas, briefing Gladys on the routines of the community and what the boy would need while there. With Gladys and Dr. Kironde combining resources, Trevor might finally visit a place where he was understood.

Trevor seemed to sense that he was in safe company. At some point during the tour, Gladys noticed that he had taken the doctor's hand. Then the doctor found a ball, and the two began to dribble it back and forth.

Thup thup. Shuffle shuffle THUP.

It looked so tantalizingly ordinary. If Trevor could laugh and kick a ball to a stranger, might he one day smile and greet a stranger? Might he one day sit in a classroom and ask a question? Or speak the name of his mother?

The Meat Market

ORPHANED SIBLINGS FIND CARE

Two years ago, just days before she died, Susan Nabugwere came to Saturday Vision *for help in finding a Good Samaritan to cater for her children and their education. The father of her three children died earlier, leaving Alex, 9, Annet, 6, and Mercy, 5, with no parent.*

Pastor Fred Shimanya of Young Hearts Orphanage read about the children in Saturday Vision *and offered to take them in. Shimanya reports that the children have adjusted to the home and are studying well.*

It was a nice photo, Gladys thought: the girls' beaming faces bordering Pastor Fred's stomach like taillights flanking the boot of a car and, if one did not look too closely, Alex's lips pressed into something approximating a smile. As Gladys had insisted, Freddy was keeping the three siblings together at the orphanage, and she was pleased to be able to highlight his service. Press like this could benefit Young Hearts.

Perhaps it already had. When Gladys had informed Pastor Fred that she would be visiting the home again, he had sent her a message saying that he had found sponsors for Alex and his sisters. The sponsors were in town, and Gladys might even be able to meet them. This was exciting news, as sponsors could provide the children with supplies, clothing, school fees—all the things that their dying mother had hoped for them.

The day was bright and brilliant, with white clouds stretching in rows across the horizon. As Gladys, Esther, and Mike headed east on Jinja Road, the lush green hills ran with them, clusters of red roofs popping out here and there like flowers.

Before traversing the last bit of road to Young Hearts, Mike stopped at a steppingstone of a village where Gladys could buy bread. Although Pastor Fred's enterprise did not seem to be struggling, she did not like to arrive empty-handed.

"Eh! Look at that," she exclaimed.

Mike had parked by a butcher's kiosk. Esther looked over to see a purplish slab of meat draped over the counter and down the front of the stand. The two women clucked their tongues in disapproval.

Gladys had once worked on an article about the Livestock and Meat Commission; she knew how meat should be kept. Behind glass, safe from flies. At the very least it should be kept hanging, not resting on a dirty surface.

Two dogs hovered nearby, noses quivering, ready for a round of snatch-and-run. "Don't you think the meat will be put away at night, but the counter will not be cleaned, and the dogs will come and lick it?"

"Of course," said Esther.

"And you see that stump? Where they cut the meat?" A rooster had hopped onto the makeshift butcher's block and stood pecking at a scrap of flesh embedded in the cleaver marks. "Eh-yehh!"

Gladys wanted to get a photo, but before she could produce her camera, the chicken hopped off with his rubbery prize. Maybe she should write a follow-up article about roadside butchers and sanitation. To think that people would bring their hard-earned money to a kiosk like this one, not realizing that the meat they bought had been contaminated by flies and dogs' tongues and chicken's feet and God knew what else. This butcher was not bothered that a customer might end up curled into a ball of pain, or that a child might die from diarrhea.

It was the lack of caring as much as the lack of sanitation that turned Gladys's stomach. Daily, one witnessed small offenses that could cause severe damage. From the boda drivers who dashed between vehicles to the women who used babies to beg to the men who seduced young girls, everywhere you looked there were those who played with the welfare of others in their pursuit of a shortcut or a few shillings or a moment of pleasure.

It was much rarer to find people at the other end of the spectrum, those few souls drawn to clean up the destruction caused by others. People like Pastor Fred. True, she did not agree with his old-fashioned philosophies concerning gender roles and the need for girls to marry, but how many people would pick up the phone after reading an article about three homeless, penniless siblings and offer help?

AS GLADYS, ESTHER, and Mike drove onto the grounds of Young Hearts, they could see progress in the home's construction: the long building across from the office had a roof now, and several smaller structures were under way. Thanks to the recent rains, the green of the yards was as solid as pool-table felt. Younger children washed clothes in a tub while older children worked a patch of garden with hoes. A tethered cow nibbled at the dense grass.

The primary purpose of Gladys's visit to Young Hearts was to see Benjamin, the abused infant of young Sylvia, the girl who had claimed to have been bewitched by a chapati. But Gladys was also eager to check on Alex, Annet, and Mercy, whom she had not been able to visit for a long time.

Pastor Fred was coming from his residence, one of the staff assistants reported. Once he arrived, they would bring out baby Benjamin.

"Where do you keep the babies?" Gladys asked. "I would like to see where they stay."

The assistant explained that the babies' quarters were behind the office, but she needed to check with Pastor Fred before taking visitors back there.

There were other parts of the compound to explore, and Gladys did not feel shy. She had brought children into this home, after all. With the assistant close on her heels, she crossed courtyards and chatted with students and peeked into classrooms and dorm rooms, all the time keeping an eager eye out for Alex and his sisters. She had expected to have seen them by now. Surely Freddy had told them that she would be coming by?

When they circled back to the office, the pastor met them, his broad face gleaming. "You are looking younger these days," he said to Gladys in greeting. "I was telling people that this old woman was looking after these kids, but now you are looking so young."

It was not the most gracious compliment ever delivered, but Gladys accepted it with a good-natured laugh. The only thing that had changed about her appearance was her hair. On her last visit to Young Hearts she had worn a smooth, short cap of a hairstyle. The ladies at the salon had convinced her to switch to a looser style, one with dangling curls all over, the size and shape of peapods. Gladys had worried it might be too youthful a style for a woman her age, but it was nice to try something different.

A matron approached the group with an infant pressed to her shoulder. The baby was rag-doll thin, his face puckered with worry, his body all quivers and jerks. He whimpered in the distressed way of a kitten with matted fur, unable to escape his discomfort.

"This is Benjamin?" Gladys cooed sweetly at the child. He had been at Young Hearts for only a couple of weeks; his limp hair was still the color of sun-dried corn silk, a telltale sign of malnutrition. "Hello, Benjamin. Ah, baby . . ."

Without ceremony, the matron pulled down the back of the baby's blue-striped pants, revealing a long scar across his buttocks, as though his stepmother had branded him with the flat side of a dagger. His backside should have been soft and smooth, a sand dune; instead it was a battleground, marked everywhere with scars and scrapes and shadows that would not fade.

"How can you mistreat a child like this?" Mike murmured.

Gladys said nothing as she snapped pictures of the damage. While Benjamin might be safe for now, the case lacked a clear solution. This child had two parents, but nothing like a mother and a father.

Gladys again inquired about seeing the babies' quarters. Freddy conferred quietly with a matron, who then led the visitors to a small courtyard behind the office. Eight or nine children, mostly infants, sat with a trio of matrons on the cement floor of a walkway. Gladys made her way around, greeting each child with a smile and a pat. There were two that she remembered: Sophie, a toddler who had been locked up with a father dying of AIDS, and Charity, the baby who had been retrieved from the pit latrine. When Gladys had first seen her, Charity's eyes had been crusted shut. Now, at three months, the infant looked round and alert. Then there were new ones: twins conceived through rape, and a newborn fed on cow dung by a mentally ill mother . . . No child here had had a gentle entrance into the world.

For now they had found sanctuary in this tranquil courtyard. But Gladys sensed something odd, like an aftertaste from a cup of water. The matrons, though polite, seemed indifferent. When a little girl started combing her doll's hair with a sharp piece of plastic, no one moved to take it from her. Another girl was walking about wearing only a shirt, no pants, no panties. When a matron noticed the visitors' stares, the child was whisked away.

Looking around, Gladys could see that none of the children had slippers, although many were of walking age. Mike inquired about a toddler with a swollen knee. She had tripped while playing, he was told.

"She must have fallen from a height," he demurred. "A knee doesn't get big like that from tripping."

Gladys asked a matron to hold a baby so that she could snap a picture. "Why do I have to hold the child?" the woman griped, gesturing to a coworker. "You hold it!"

WHEN THE VISITORS returned to the office, Freddy laid out several folders on his desk. Gladys tried to listen as he presented several other children's cases, but she was impatient to see Alex and his sisters.

"Freddy, you've not shown me my children," she scolded. "Where are they?"

"That's the reason why I wanted you to come and sit down. So that I can explain." He leaned back in his chair, his meaty forearms leaving faint prints on his desktop. His tone, though mild, set Gladys's senses on alert. "I sent you the message explaining that your children have got sponsors."

"Yes, that's good."

"You see, these sponsors are a couple. This man and his wife showed interest in the children, so I took them to the probation officer." He explained that he had spoken to Nabukonde, the witch doctor's widow who had given the family temporary shelter when Susan Nabugwere was dying, and to the council chairman of the village. Both had responded positively to the sponsors' involvement. "So this couple will be taking Alex and his sisters. To the U.S."

The words rolled out of the large man's mouth as smoothly as pebbles down a hill, piling onto Gladys and pinning her to her chair. The children were being adopted?

Pastor Fred continued speaking, but Gladys found it hard to listen, let alone respond. What rang in her head was her last directive to Fred about Alex, Annet, and Mercy: *The moment you feel you can't handle these children, please let me know. Let me take them and maybe we will get some other place.*

The sponsors were in Uganda, and the children were already with them. "The couple will be in Kampala this week. You can link up and have a chat with them," Freddy was saying.

"They are from where?" Gladys managed.

Freddy shuffled the files on his desk. "They are from New-Braska."

"From where?"

"New . . . no, *Neh*-braska."

"So are they Ugandan?" asked Esther.

"No, they are Americans. They have also been sponsoring a school in Uganda. The man is an architect, he owns a company. The mother is a teacher. I told him that you were the person who had profiled the children originally. So you can meet with them and ask them some questions."

"Yes, because I would like to know where the kids are going."

"We can meet you in Kampala," Freddy reassured her. "Let's meet on Monday."

"I would love to get the story from them, because I have been following these children for a long time."

"Can I take you for lunch now?" Freddy seemed ready to close the matter. "I would like to give you lunch."

Gladys ignored the offer. Yes, she was heavy like Freddy, but that did not mean that she was so easily distracted by food. "If the sponsors are going to split these kids up, that will be a problem."

Pastor Fred assured her that all three kids were to be taken.

Out of the country. By people whom she had not even met.

"Why did you not tell these sponsors, since they have this sponsorship of a school, to take the kids there instead?"

"No, the sponsors want to take them to their country," Freddy said simply, as if he were discussing someone's preference for *posho* over *matoke*. "The kids will get their education from there, not here."

A silence landed, heavy as sand.

"I think maybe Freddy is tired of the kids," Gladys remarked, her tone teasing but her eyes as cool and still as river stones. "So he's sending them away."

"No, I've never been tired of the kids," Freddy protested quickly. "I wouldn't send them away."

THEY LEFT YOUNG HEARTS on cordial terms, with Pastor Fred vowing to take the three of them out for pizza the next time they visited. He and his wife would soon be taking a vacation to India; might Gladys visit again before they left?

The way back took the Volvo through Njeru, near the streets where the mother of Alex, Annet, and Mercy had slept for a month, searching for some trace of family. Tuberculosis had consumed her by then; Gladys would never forget the violence of her coughing. It was like a panga hacking at gravel.

Remembering this, Gladys's dismay began to pool in her mind. Two years ago Susan Nabugwere had put her trust in Gladys, and

Gladys had been involved in the children's welfare ever since. So why had Freddy failed to communicate with her about giving the kids away?

"I didn't know that Alex and his sisters were going to be adopted. I was just hearing it for the first time," she said to her companions, who had also been startled by the abrupt announcement. "But it seems the matter has already gone through court."

"Freddy has got a good agenda," Mike offered diplomatically. "But now he's talking of sending these kids to New-braska, No-braska, whatever it is . . ."

"These places he's talking of I've never heard of," Gladys said.

They all knew of orphanages with shady practices. There were rumors of homes padding their flocks with "orphans" who still had families. There were cases of neglect. Sexual abuse. Parents who were duped into giving over custody of their kids. Websites that solicited donations using photos of cute children who were not even in the home. Gladys had no evidence that Young Hearts was one of these corrupt places, but Freddy's maneuverings unsettled her.

"At least it is good we're meeting that American couple on Monday."

"Yes — when you talk to them on Monday, you'll be able to judge the situation for yourself."

As they reached Mukono, where the worst traffic funneled into Kampala, they found themselves behind a *matatu* topped with dozens of live chickens. The birds were not in cages or crates; they were strapped down directly on the hot metal roof as if they were being roasted in their feathers. Even from a distance, one could see the birds' open mouths and pulsing throats as they gulped at the air in thirst and distress.

"Disgusting." Mike spat the word. "That is brutality."

"They are not supposed to transport animals like that," Gladys agreed. "By the time they reach Kampala, many of those chickens will be dead."

"Yes, the wind can be hitting them at a hundred and forty kilometers per hour!"

"But they will not dump those dead ones. They will pack them and sell them to the markets as freshly slaughtered."

Street vendors came threading through the traffic lanes, wielding footballs and toilet paper and phone chargers and rainbow-colored feather dusters. Mike rolled up his window. "There is so much impunity in this country, I am telling you."

Staring out at the dying chickens, Gladys acknowledged a festering unease. The miserable cargo recalled the unsanitary butcher's place they had seen that morning: another small, unimpeded circuit of negligence and deception and injury.

Gladys could not shake the sense that she had been roped into such a cycle. Was Pastor Fred involved in shady trade?

Frozen Wings

The next morning Gladys announced to Mike that she had cleared the day's program. A scheduled trip to Ndejje to visit three sisters with HIV would have to wait.

Gladys's mind had been so unsettled by questions over the adoption of Alex, Annet, and Mercy that she had no choice but to seek answers. There were two men she could turn to in this case: Adam Kulubya, a social worker, and Jacob Kaheru, a police officer. Both worked in cases of child welfare, Adam supporting the victims, Jacob pursuing the offenders.

Although she had spoken to Adam several times over the phone, it was Gladys's first time meeting him. Tall and slender, the young man possessed a composure that bordered on elegance. He wore stylish glasses, with frames of clear amber and lenses elongated like miniature windshields; behind them, his eyes took in everything with patient attentiveness. Gladys liked him immediately.

"I realize that I really, really need your assistance," Gladys began once they had settled into the meeting room. "I need to talk to you about a case I've had for some time."

Telling the story of such a case was like cooking a meal. One could not rush. One could not skip a step. Gladys took a full forty-five minutes to walk Adam through the journey of Susan Nabugwere and her three orphaned children. The young man listened thoughtfully, making occasional notes in his book. Not once did he glance at his watch or let his gaze wander to the courtyard.

Gladys ended the tale with her request for Adam to accompany her to meet Pastor Fred and the American couple. "You will be able to tell me whether my fears are warranted. Whether this adoption is proper. I don't want someone saying, 'You wrote about these children in the paper. But where are they now?'"

Adam stood up from the table. "Let me invite this gentleman who can advise us. As you know, Jacob is an officer who specializes in issues of child trafficking. He has been in this field for over fifteen years."

Gladys was eager for the chance to meet Assistant Inspector Jacob Kaheru. Nicknamed "the Hammer," the inspector was an intensely busy man known for his uncompromising nature.

The Hammer turned out to be an unassuming man of average height, with unremarkable features. Dark skin, close-cropped hair, ready smile. It would be difficult to pick him out in a crowd.

"I heard of your work back in 2005," he said to Gladys. "When I was with Child and Family."

Gladys beamed. It was always a good sign when someone in this field knew of her column.

"Gladys has got some kids resettled at Young Hearts," Adam said. "Do you know that pastor?"

"I know him very well," Jacob said casually, placing weight on the word *very*.

Adam produced a page from his folder, on which was taped a newspaper clipping. "I always get these stories from the paper," he explained, passing the page to his colleague. "And I keep them on file."

It was Gladys's follow-up article: "Orphaned Siblings Find Care." Jacob stared down at the smiling faces of Freddy and the three children, then slid the page back without comment.

Though Gladys had cooked a three-course meal out of the story for Adam, she sensed that Inspector Jacob would have time only for a snack. She compressed the case into a few minutes, ending with her consternation at hearing that the children were being taken out of the country without her prior knowledge. She explained that earlier she had blocked the pastor's plan to split up the siblings and put Alex up for adoption. "I told Freddy, 'If you ever get tired of taking care of these three, let me know.' But he never even communicated before arranging this. Is it really proper? You're saying that you know Freddy."

"*Very* well." Again the word *very* was delivered like a too-hard handshake. And then came the punch. "To tell you the truth, I knew Freddy when I was investigating him on trafficking. He's not the best person to—take—care—of—our—children." He rapped his pen sharply on the table, each word driving a nail into Gladys's chest.

Investigating. Trafficking. Children.

"He keeps taking children on 'legal guardianship.' If you went deep to investigate, it's a nasty story. Because I followed him on a case of trafficking. He had the child almost already leaving. I entered in, and I stopped the child. With your case, okay—"

"It's not okay!" Gladys burst out. "It's not okay."

Jacob paused. "Ask yourself. Why did he not involve you?"

A clamor rose up through the window. A flock of pied crows marched through the yard, shrieking accusations. Jacob's voice drowned out the birds, his words breaking over Gladys like a thunderstorm. "You were the one who published this story. You are the one who tried to settle them. And you are the one who stopped him from giving out the boy. So when you see him passing behind you, then you know it is fishy."

Jacob went on to say that in Uganda, he had seen children bought and sold. Children taken from their rightful families. Children trafficked for their kidneys. It was a bigger business than ivory smuggling.

"I am sorry to tell you that most of these children who go abroad, they are just sold. It can be fifty thousand dollars per child."

Gladys sagged in her chair. "I am dead."

"That is why the government is looking at an alternative care framework." Jacob steamed ahead. "As of today we have a national adoption panel. With officers, psychologists, lawyers. Whoever wants to adopt a child must come and face the panel. But people are still doing it illegally. Our children are going out, every day, on legal guardianship. For proper adoption, the couple has to stay in Uganda for three years. But on legal guardianship, you get the order, and you take the child right away. And then people end up finalizing the adoption process in the United States or whatever the other country is."

"How do they get this legal guardianship?"

"Most of it is influenced by how much money you have. You influence this and that, you get the papers, and at the end of the day . . ."

"So the courts are also bought?" Gladys asked.

Jacob snorted. "You, what are you talking about?"

Gladys rolled her eyes. "As if I'm not in Uganda."

So someone with money could obtain a child and circumvent the proper vetting. It didn't matter whether these Americans were suitable parents or not, as long as the right palms were greased.

"A lot of money is changing hands. A lot. Probation officers, the ones who run the homes, lawyers. And then when you tell me this American is an architect . . ."

"Architects in the United States make a lot of money," Adam put in. "Some homes defraud such people. They tell them the court process needs this and this and this. And the ones who want to adopt keep giving out money—they don't know these are lies."

"There are lawyers who buy houses in Kampala every six months out of this business!" Jacob ranted. "It is only me whom you will never compromise in a case. I would rather die than take money."

Jacob told them how he had once chased a suspect through the ceiling of a building. When cornered at gunpoint, the man had offered him 5 million shillings to let him go. "I said, 'I will never eat such a money!' But indeed, the other people ate it."

Jacob's phone buzzed. Raising it to his ear, he listened for a moment, then attacked. "You are speaking to Assistant Police Inspector Jacob Kaheru! And I'm telling you, if you cannot go to Peace Transition Home to pick up your child, I'm going to charge! I have the capacity to put you there! You would abandon your child in the home? What is that you are doing to your own child?" The Hammer shouted for a bit longer, as though he were alone in the room, until the person on the other end of the phone had evidently been ground into powder.

Jacob set his phone aside and returned to Gladys, not missing a beat. "I'm telling you, it is one hundred percent business. I am part of the team that visits children's homes in Uganda." As an inspector, he had visited dozens of homes, including Young Hearts. "Of course, I went as a born-again Christian." He clapped his hands and made a smile so wide it looked like the top of his head might fall off. "God bless!"

"Hallelujah!" Mike chimed in, tossing up his hands.

"Everyone was chatting, chatting," Jacob went on, still wearing the beatific expression, the versatility of his unremarkable features on full display. "I did not identify myself until they allowed me in. Then I pulled my card. 'I'm a police officer — can I have a visit around?'" His face abruptly contracted into a scowl. "Freddy has three big rooms where he keeps all those donated things from the sponsors, things that are supposed to be for the children. Brand-new, in boxes. And the kids are not having any of them."

Jacob was bellowing now, as if he were trying to halt a fleeing suspect. "Children were moving barefoot! In his school! All of them barefoot, and yet I saw boxes and boxes. Shoes and shoes. 'What is this?' I asked him. 'Why would you keep all this when the children are not even having slippers?'"

It was all falling painfully into place. The half-clothed babies, the indifferent matrons, perhaps even that toddler's swollen knee. Why were children doing the laundry in the yard while adults were standing around? Why was Pastor Fred taking a holiday in India while children went barefoot in his orphanage?

"Surely it stinks," said Gladys. "Mike, this is why Freddy didn't want us to look behind where the orphanage was."

Jacob puffed out his cheeks, gesturing at them with cupped hands. "You see this man is fat like this. How do you think he got like that?"

"Oh, good gracious me." Mike laughed.

The inspector listed other signs of misconduct. "I saw that the license was expired. There were no recommendations from the ministry. No one is supposed to have a children's home without an approval from the Ministry of Gender. No one!"

"Eh!" Gladys exclaimed. "The last comment Freddy made to me was, 'Gladys, you move with those people from the Ministry of Gender. Talk to them. They have not given us licenses. How do they expect us to help children?'"

"He must have a license. He must become responsible. Because if we find that you are not taking care of children in a good way, we charge you and we take you to court."

"What came out of the investigation?" asked Gladys.

Now it was Jacob's turn to deflate. His shoulders sank as he shook his head, his smile more rueful than bitter.

"Big people got in the way," Gladys concluded.

Mike smiled grimly. "Wow."

"So if these people have already gotten the legal guardianship order . . ." Jacob spread his hands. "As much as you want to protect these children, there's a point you reach where you say, 'God, take over.'"

But this case had not yet reached that point. If they could determine that any lies had been told in court, they had a chance of stopping an illegal action. Jacob's eyes narrowed as he asked the question that Gladys herself had posed in Pastor Fred's office: "What do the American couple want with the kids if they are already sponsoring a school here in Uganda? Why do they want the kids with them?"

Esther spoke up. "Mr. Jacob, we have another chance on Monday. We are supposed to meet with Freddy. To see the people who are taking the children."

The inspector's grin hardened into a thin line. "How sure are you that you are going to meet them?"

"Ah, no." Gladys shook off his skepticism. "We have made an appointment. Freddy will be coming to *New Vision*."

"Do you know that he can tell you, 'Oh, I have now a meeting, and I can't make it'? You may not find those people on Monday, and if you do see them, you may find that they are moving out that night."

Mike picked up the theme. "He might say, 'Oh, I'm sorry, can you believe it? They had to fly out already.'"

It was agreed that Adam would accompany Gladys to meet with

Freddy on Monday, as Jacob had other business scheduled. While Freddy was not likely to welcome the presence of a social worker, he would probably flee at the sight of the Hammer.

"He knows me *very* well!" Jacob snorted, one eyebrow raised. Recalling his visit to Freddy's home, he sounded almost wistful. "I photographed everything. Oh my God, I wish I had my laptop with me — I could show you. Boxes and boxes. Shoes and shoes. And children there are barefoot. And he still goes to the U.S. to ask, 'Would you adopt? Would you adopt?'"

Gladys pointed to the article on the table. "And I'm now helping Freddy by doing these things! Last Saturday we ran the success story: 'Orphans Find Care.'"

Mike laughed. "You are the conduit. You are the conduit!"

"Oh my God . . ."

"You are aiding and abetting!" Jacob chortled.

Esther jumped in mercilessly. "Next is Luzira Prison for two years."

Though she was as much a connoisseur of dark humor as anyone in the room, Gladys could only twist in her seat with misery. What if people did assume she was eating money? What if the authorities blamed her for not investigating the situation more thoroughly? "Okay, so we'll close the column. It is very easy to close the column. If it has such problems."

Jacob's response was immediate. "No. Continue. The column is very good."

"One thing to know," Adam said calmly. "The biggest thing you have, Gladys, is your big heart."

Gladys uttered a gasp of surprise, almost of disbelief.

"That heart is a very big asset to Ugandan children," Jacob agreed. He and Adam considered her with a sober, almost stern appreciation. "Let me tell you, did Mandela fear being put in prison to redeem the country of South Africa?"

"I have not heard of myself with Mandela!"

"He was put in prison for twenty-seven years. You have a heart for the children of Uganda. You are standing for them!"

• • •

IN THE CAR, Gladys slumped. She felt like the four hours of the meeting had drained the blood from her body, drop by drop. And yet it was not emptiness she felt, but a roiling dread. If her heart was big, as Adam and Jacob had said, then her skull was thick. How else had she come to trust Pastor Fred?

"What Jacob explained? That revelation made me so ... so ... so ..." She struggled for words. "It has disorganized me completely!"

Mike wore the expression of one who has just discovered maggots in his rice. "I had a very quiet life until this job. Now I'm meeting all these crooks like Freddy."

"By the way," Esther remarked, "they say someone who does not know something cannot get sick about it. That's why the educated get more sick than the uneducated."

"Ignorance is such bliss, you know?" Mike agreed. "If I had not found out anything about Freddy, I would've just thought of him as another guy."

"But then you get involved with Gladys," said Gladys.

Mike watched the traffic for an opening, his head swiveling like an owl's. Two children came up to the window, palms up, heads tilted in supplication. Mike gave a tiny shake in their direction and gunned his way into a gap between two *matatus*.

"There is a small story told about a sparrow," he announced with the authority of a speaker stepping up to a podium. "Once upon a time there was a very deadly winter coming. And all the birds began flying south. But the sparrow decided not to fly south. It flew north. As it flew north, its wings got covered in ice, and it fell down to the ground into a barnyard. It was lying in the barnyard thinking, 'Okay, I'm dead. I'm finished. My wings are frozen, I can't jump, I can't do anything.'

"Then a cow walked by. The cow stepped on the poor bird and pushed it into a heap of dung. Now in the heap, the heat of the dung warmed the sparrow's wings and the ice melted. The bird was so happy! It started chirping. A cat was walking by and heard the chirping sounds, so it quickly dug out the bird and ate it up!"

Despite themselves, Gladys and Esther giggled, the bigger woman's body convulsing as though shaken by an invisible giant.

"So the moral of the story is, if you are warm and happy in your pile of shit, keep your mouth shut." The women's squeals rose to shrieks, Mike's deep laughter swelling below, coals stoking the fire. "I was so warm and happy in my pile of shit, and now the cat Gladys walks by and I'm swallowed up in her issues!"

"Hee-hee-hee-hee-hee!"

"Your business is really getting under my skin!"

"Now the heart will get high blood pressure!" Esther chimed in.

"And everything has come because of this Gladys!" Gladys rocked back and forth and clapped, laughter hissing out of her like spray from a shaken soda can.

"You had been living as a happy man in Kampala. But now you are having a jigger in the head." Esther delivered the diagnosis soberly. "Very sorry."

"Oh my God . . ." Gladys sighed, wiping her eyes. "Now Mike hates me really. The other time he hated me so much because of George the First. And the other time at the garden, he couldn't believe what he was hearing from Zam and Robert. And this time it is Freddy. Ah! So I have really disorganized your sleep."

"I miss my pile of shit."

After a couple of long sighs and a few "Oh my God"s for good measure, they retreated again into an uneasy silence.

All the questions Gladys had started the day with still stood unresolved. Was the adoption final? Who were these Americans? Should Alex and his sisters go with them? Were any children safe with Freddy?

"But Gladys." Mike spoke suddenly, as though in answer to something she had said. "In every situation there is a lesson. If you look in with a magnifying glass, there is something you're learning. Adam had fantastic information for you."

"Yes," Gladys agreed.

Toward the meeting's end, Adam had counseled Gladys to find a way to generate income for her work with the children so she would not be so dependent on people like Pastor Fred. In fact, he and some of his colleagues had started digging in gardens to raise money for their outreach work. Even small harvests had helped fund their transportation. Gladys had listened with interest but declined to mention her Luwero project. Her big plans had not yet progressed enough to be shared.

"You could pull a leaf from Adam's book. Well, you are. You are getting things going."

Gladys appreciated the encouragement; her disappointments with Zam had pummeled her self-confidence. How had she been so blind to the dangers of relying on others? The answer, she knew, was desperation. The garden was vulnerable to thieves and cheats because she did not have the money to finish the building. Her children were vulnerable to abuse and neglect because there were too few places to put them. Like a hen seeking shelter in a storm, she may have led her brood to the butcher's kiosk.

"Trust Jesus! He is the only one! Trust Jesus!" A street preacher prowled around the traffic circle with a megaphone, roaring at the indifferent pedestrians. "You have been called to repent!"

ON MONDAY, as promised, Adam was waiting at the *New Vision* offices. In his perfectly pressed white shirt, gray tie, and polished black shoes, he looked like a billboard model of a young executive.

Gladys returned Adam's cordial greeting. Her white and black outfit—a dress and jacket topped by a ruffled collar—complimented his well, and the ringlets of her hairdo were as springy as ever. Nothing in her manner indicated that she had not eaten a meal since breakfast two days before. The new information about Freddy had erased her appetite, erased sleep, erased peace. But it was Monday now, and her unease would finally be exorcised. Once Freddy took her to meet the American couple, her questions would be answered, for better or worse.

Freddy was late, but delays were common for those entering Kampala in the morning. They waited at Mike's car, Gladys standing outside, scanning the street for the pastor, and Adam, Esther, and Mike sitting inside. Early that morning, Adam reported, he had contacted the probation officer handling the adoption case of Susan Nabugwere's children. The officer claimed that the department had conducted the proper investigations to look for existing family members.

"It's important to find out if a child is a total orphan or not," Adam said. "Because if a child has a relative, the child should be settled with that relative rather than be adopted."

Esther only half listened as she gazed through the open window, watching Gladys answer a call on her mobile phone.

"*Wangi,* Pastor," she heard Gladys say. "We are here at *New Vision.*"

After a moment Gladys dropped her arm as though the phone had suddenly become heavy.

"Do you know what?" Esther said, interrupting Adam's report. "I think what Jacob said would happen has happened."

"I told you," said Adam, "there was that possibility."

Gladys lowered her head to the window. "Freddy is not coming. He said he's still in Jinja." Her voice rose, untethered by disbelief. "Now he's telling me, 'Ah! I'm sorry. But you know, those Americans are not in Kampala today. They went north to check on the school they are sponsoring.'"

Mike and Esther exchanged a sour glance.

"He says even he can't come to meet us. He's very sorry—he lost a relative. He says he is at a funeral."

"The probation officer must have alerted him this morning that people were asking questions," Esther said, looking accusingly, if unfairly, at Adam. "And he changed his plan."

"He's assuring me that when the couple comes back from visiting the school, he will again arrange a meeting," said Gladys.

"He will not," said Adam.

"But he's telling me he will arrange another appointment for me!" Gladys insisted, the words sounding foolish even as she uttered them.

"Arrange it." Esther shrugged, this confirmation of Freddy's character giving her some sour satisfaction. "You will get the same results."

Adam spoke gently. "This is not a shock, Gladys. You remember what we discussed? We said don't be surprised."

"Let me not take it as a shock. But I am still surprised. I believed Freddy would meet me today! I believed it." She still could not accept it. Even when Jacob had warned her that Freddy might play tricks, Gladys had told herself, *No, no, no. I am meeting him. He will come.*

"I think he is buying time for those people to be able to go," Mike asserted. "For all I know, those kids could be halfway in the sky to the U.S."

They reflexively glanced up, as if the plane carrying Alex, Annet, and Mercy might be whisking by at just that moment. They saw only white clouds, solid as balloons, in a sky of born-again blue. A cheerful backdrop to Freddy's bit of theater.

Gladys took a last look around, as though she might spy the fat pastor peeking out from behind the *New Vision* building. There were security guards, the parking attendant, some skinny pedestrians. No Pastor Fred.

There was nothing to do. They sat in the parked car, stranded in their neat clothes like guests at a canceled wedding.

At this point only an actual relative could pursue the case, Adam explained. "The problem is that Gladys is just like a well-wisher here. She is out of the loop legally."

Gladys gazed out through the speckled windshield. "You know, what clicks in my mind is why Freddy is so much interested in children from these madwomen, or children who have been left in the latrine. If he has plans for those ones, no one will be following."

No one but Gladys, who could be brushed away like a mosquito.

Freddy had not even taken her seriously enough to inform her that he wasn't coming. Maybe he thought it was funny to have a carload of people in Kampala waiting to take him to a make-believe meeting!

Well, she would learn to laugh at Pastor Fred's jokes. She would just have to be more like Jacob. Expect frustration. Anticipate obstruction. Accept disappointment.

Could she truly accept it? It seemed inconceivable that she had come so far with Alex and his sisters, only to be denied the chance to learn their ultimate fate. But if Pastor Fred had pulled the curtain, that was it. The children were gone from her sight.

Her sigh had the finality of a last breath. "So we are at the end now."

Win Win

There were those days when a conspiracy of offenses, small and large, converged on Gladys from the moment she left her home. When the traffic stretched her morning commute beyond three hours. When the streets were lined with dead dogs, culled by city authorities with poisoned meat. When she reached for her phone, only to find it had been snatched. When one of her children tested positive for HIV. When her joints ached with the telltale pain of malaria. When her deadline loomed but her power was shut off. When the sun went down but the night was still hot.

It had started as one of those days. Still bruised from Freddy's games, Gladys had accompanied Adam thirty miles from Kampala to Nkokonjeru, a town in Buikwe District, where she interviewed the family of a five-year-old girl who had been raped by a local man. The girl's father had forcibly taken the rapist to the police, but when he tried to get the committal letter to send the case to high court, the bureaucrat in charge demanded a "fee" of 300,000 shillings. This was an astronomical sum for the father, a clothing vendor, who had spent everything he had on his daughter's medical costs. The letter was not produced, and the rapist returned to the village, yelling taunts at the girl's father. Soon the rapist was caught trying to attack another child, and a crowd beat him up. The family of the second child was afraid to go to the police, though, and the man remained free. It was said that he had even defiled a pig.

As Adam interviewed the parents, Gladys took out her camera.

The little girl grinned shyly, revealing a mouth full of baby teeth. Adam put his arm around her and gently turned her head toward his shoulder. They could not show her face in the newspaper.

BACK IN THE CAR, Adam expressed his commitment to pursuing the case. If he and Jacob had to open a new file, they would do it. "We will bring this case to high court," he vowed calmly.

Gladys nodded, assessing the damage. The family needed justice, and the community needed protection. The girl required continuing medical treatment. One man's depravity could cause such destruction. So easy to poison the well.

A jazzy ringtone interrupted her thoughts. Gladys glanced at her phone and blinked. It was Freddy.

"*Wangi,* Pastor."

The others listened in, tracking the occasional "hmm" and "okay" from Gladys's side. The conversation lasted less than a minute.

"Freddy is full of surprises," Gladys reported. "He is now telling a new story."

The pastor apologized for Monday's "miscommunication": the American couple had not left town after all. They were still in Kampala, but the man was flying back to the United States that night. If Freddy texted her the couple's number, would Gladys like to try to contact them? Perhaps she could still meet them and the children before they left.

"So that is the latest." A laugh rose from Gladys but did not take flight. The specificity of Freddy's offer gave her hope, which she now mistrusted. She was trying to learn from Jacob, after all. Would the Hammer allow himself be taken for a fool a second time?

As they waited for Freddy to text the Americans' number, the chorus of skepticism in the car grew louder.

"Two days ago he said they were out of town," said Mike. "And now he says they are flying home."

"The number will come when they are already in the air," Esther predicted.

"If he does send the number, don't be surprised if the phone is off," Adam warned.

Gladys chuckled darkly. "I'm now ready for whatever comes, because I'm no longer shocked by anything."

Three minutes went by, then five, then ten. How long did it take to text a phone number? The worm on Freddy's fishhook was looking dead.

"Do you know what he asked me?" Gladys snorted. "'Do you know how to read text messages?' What kind of question is that!"

"He must think you're really from a backward place," said Mike. "A national park!" Everyone laughed. And then Gladys's phone buzzed.

FLOWING SKIRT, bare shoulders, blond hair swept back in a loose ponytail, candy-colored paper beads circling pale neck and wrists: Michelle Griffen did not at first blush resemble a child trafficker.

"You found us," she called brightly, walking to meet them. With her pretty, unadorned features, she radiated the free-spirited air of a globe-trotting college student. It was only close up that one could see that she was close to forty, with a touch of wariness clouding her blue eyes.

Gladys, Esther, and Mike followed her through the yard of the rental complex where she and her husband were staying. A car tire wobbled across their path. Two small figures in bright pink shirts and brighter pink flip-flops danced behind it, as though they were starting a parade.

"Is that Annet? And is that Mercy?" Gladys's voice pitched an octave higher with each name. The two girls turned to throw their skinny arms around her. "It is good to see you!"

After a flurry of cooing and clucking, the party moved into the spacious apartment. Several bedrooms and a hallway branched off from the living room, which had church-high ceilings and a trio of brown fabric couches positioned around a flat-screen television.

A tall white man sat in one of the couches. In his gray T-shirt, khaki shorts, and bare feet, he looked more tourist than architect.

"I'm Phil." He stood up, hand extended. His long face was heavier at the bottom than the top, like a jackfruit. As with his wife, his smile did not quite reach his eyes.

"It's nice meeting you people. I'm Gladys Kalibbala, from *New Vision* newspaper."

A boy in a red shirt and loose blue shorts came skipping in, a ball tucked under one arm. It took a moment to register who this was. Gladys had never seen Alex skip before.

"He's going outside for football?"

"Yes," replied Phil. "He loves football."

Gladys was reluctant to disrupt the boy's play. "Okay, Alex," she sang to him. "You just come and say hello."

Alex bounded over, still clutching his ball, and gave her a one-armed hug.

Gladys pointed to Phil. "Okay, introduce him to me."

"That's my daddy," Alex said, a shy grin lifting his face even as he lowered his chin.

"Ah-hah!" Gladys exclaimed. "That sounds good. And what about your mother?"

Without turning to look, the boy pointed over his shoulder at Michelle. Gladys marveled at the casualness of the gesture. It was the way one might wave in the direction of one's home. "That's my mother," the boy said, then ran out the door with his ball.

"Shut the door, please!" Michelle called after him. Then, to her visitors, "They're learning how to shut doors. The first couple days, they would just run in and out. But they didn't have doors where they were living. In the orphanage, they just had cloth."

"And you can imagine what was happening before that, in the place that I got them," said Gladys. She lowered herself onto a couch, set down her purse, and looked up at the couple. "By the way, how did you get them?"

Phil looked up sharply, alert. "What do you mean?"

"How did you first find out about these ones?"

Michelle answered that she had heard about the siblings from a friend who had adopted a child from Freddy's home.

It seemed that the Griffens had indeed been led to the shortcut.

The process of acquiring the children was unfolding just as Jacob had said it would. A month ago the courts had granted them legal guardianship of the three children. The actual adoption would be finalized in the United States.

"We're just waiting for passports now," said Michelle. "Looks like this may be the week."

They made a bit of small talk, the three locals inquiring about New-braska and the Americans' interest in Uganda, the fair-haired couple expounding on their affection for the country even with its lamentable traffic. Despite the shared chuckles and knowing nods, a veil of tension as sticky as a spiderweb still divided hosts and visitors.

The Americans must have wondered why Pastor Fred had encouraged this meeting on the day Phil was to fly home. Indeed, the question had occurred to Gladys as well. Maybe Freddy calculated that if Gladys were to meet this well-to-do American couple, she would offer less resistance to future adoptions and send more children his way. Clearly her disillusionment with him had not registered; he did not consider her capable of throwing a wrench in the works.

Gladys had nothing to throw, nor did she know where to aim. What she sought here was not control but reassurance. This might be her only chance to get it.

Esther leafed through a book of photographs on the low table in front of her. Inside were pictures of the Griffen family, including grandparents and kids of all ages. All were potato-pale like Phil and Michelle. The kids posed in a swimming pool, in front of a Christmas tree, around picnic tables. Their lives seemed lit by birthday candles.

"How many children do you have?" Esther asked. It was hard to tell from the pictures.

"With these three? We now have seven," said Michelle.

Gladys gaped at her. "How many?"

"Seven."

"But from what I see, people in the U.S. don't want many children."

"Yeah, they're not big on big families," Michelle replied, wrinkling her nose. "But I always wanted a big family."

Annet and Mercy scampered back in from the yard, the slaps of their quick feet like applause on the smooth tile. They paused to nibble at a broken bar of chocolate on the table before flitting behind the couch to play with their new father's hair.

"Girls, what is that you are doing to your daddy?" Gladys asked, smiling.

For his part, Phil surrendered to the treatment, leaning his head back as the giggling girls ruffled and plucked at the fascinatingly straight strands. "They like to pretend that I've got bugs in my hair."

"They tease us," Michelle said, looking pleased.

"Back in the village where they were with the mother," Mike broke in, "you find there will be lice. In the hair and in the garments. And what they will do, they will pick the lice, and then break them with the teeth."

There was a half second of silence.

"Oh," said Michelle.

"So the younger ones have watched the older ones," Mike went on merrily. "If one has lice in her undergarments, for example, she will sit down one fine day and start picking them out, saying, 'This is my blood you're chewing.' She will start biting them with her teeth, to take back the blood that they have sucked from her. So that's what these ones are doing!" Mike's lone guffaw faded abruptly, like a sprinter's false start.

At that moment Alex bounded in with his ball under his arm, remembering to shut the glass door behind him. He plopped down on the couch, a pair of pink plastic sunglasses perched low on his nose.

Gladys looked down at the boy. "Alex, when your new dad and mom said that they wanted to take you into their family, what did you think?"

"I felt so happy." He drummed on the sunglass lenses, his feet kicking to the beat.

"If you had been taken alone and your two sisters had been left behind, would you still have been happy?"

Alex's squirming ceased. "No."

"It was always all or none," Michelle said after Mike had translated the Luganda. "We felt it would be hard for somebody here to adopt all three of these children and keep them as siblings."

But seven children? "Are you sure you are not from Uganda?" Esther quipped.

Michelle smiled and jerked a thumb at Phil. "He first thought I was crazy."

There was no reproach in his wife's voice, but Phil's long face contracted slightly. "I was coming back from a building mission. I was in the airport when Michelle told me about these three children. I'm sure I said, 'Are you crazy? We have four already!'"

"Eh-eh-eh-heh!" Gladys and Esther found this scenario singularly amusing. A woman pushing her husband for a bigger family? This man was lucky he had only one wife! It took a good minute for Gladys to compose herself.

"What made you change your mind?"

Phil sighed thoughtfully before answering. "If you own a business in America, you have resources. You have money, so you can do certain things. You can decide whether you want to have fancy cars, if you want to have homes elsewhere. What do you want to do with your money? And I felt, is there a better thing to do with your money than adopt children? We felt like these kids deserved a family who would love them, and a mother and father who would bring them back to Uganda to visit."

"You will be bringing them back."

"Yes. We need to keep bringing them back to see where they came from, to see their culture, to know their heritage. And to hopefully continue knowing some of the language."

"So we can expect to see you people once in a while when you return to Uganda?"

"Oh, definitely. When we come back, we'll visit the orphanage and maybe have a little party there," Phil said, brightening. "We'll make sure Freddy invites you guys."

Even the mention of the shifty pastor did not disturb the feeling of calm that descended on Gladys. The last two days had felt like a personal heatwave, and now it was as though a broken ceiling fan had miraculously kicked into life above her head.

These *mzungus* understood what Freddy had not: the need for these siblings to stay together and to stay connected with the land and culture that had raised generations of their ancestors. Life was hard in Uganda, but from that hardship sprouted strength and pride and an appreciation for small graces and everyday beauty. Alex and his sisters should not be cut off from that part of their heritage, especially as they were transplanted into the Griffens' bountiful new world, where every stare might remind them of their otherness and demand their gratitude.

With the veil lifted, hosts and visitors relaxed together. As Phil and Michelle chatted on about their affection for the children, they displayed that distinct American friendliness, an extravagance of nature afforded to people who could expect the world to treat them well. They exuded not so much a naiveté as a confidence. Problems could be fixed. There was always the Bright Side of Things. Something to Be Done. A Way Forward. It was Gladys-style optimism, but with a full fuel tank.

The kids wiggled in and out of their new parents' laps, climbing the sofa as if it were a play structure. Annet chattered into Phil's ear, eyes twinkling. *"Mzungu!"*

"Just wait," he teased, grabbing playfully at her hands. "Did you know that when you fly to America, when you land, your skin will turn my color? You will be a *mzungu* like me."

One had to marvel at the parents' openness. How easily Phil slung an arm around Alex's shoulder. How naturally Michelle and Mercy tilted their heads together.

Gladys addressed the kids in Luganda. "What kinds of pictures do you have in your mind about America? How do you feel about going there?"

"I feel great." Alex grinned, wriggling on the leather couch like an eel on a riverbank.

"When you get to America, will you be able to understand the *mzungus*?"

Alex tipped his head to the side, his mouth twisting.

"How are you going to respond to them?" Gladys persisted.

"If I don't understand them, I will just say yes."

"Ee-ee-eee!" Through hiccups of laughter, Gladys translated for the Griffens.

"It's true!" Michelle nodded vigorously. "I'll ask him something he doesn't understand, and he just nods and says yes."

"Alex, am I a cool dude?" Phil asked, looking at him through the pink sunglasses that Mercy had shoved onto his nose.

"Huh?"

"Is your dad really cool?"

The boy screwed up his face.

"You're supposed to nod and smile!" Phil protested, throwing up his hands. Alex smiled, basking in the novelty of naughtiness. The room erupted with more laughter.

"That smile," Mike remarked, as though to himself. "I can't get over it. When we saw him at Young Hearts, Alex couldn't smile."

"Alex?" Michelle exclaimed, eyes widening.

"He smiles all the time," said Phil. "More than any of them."

"He's a giggler," Michelle attested.

"The other day? He had me climbing the tree over there to bring a couple of guavas down." Phil pantomimed his struggle to shimmy up the trunk. "So here's this *mzungu*, I'm climbing the tree and getting the guavas, and he says, 'Okay, now you wash it and eat it.' So I said, 'I just bite it?' He says yeah, so I take a bite. It tasted like tree bark. I spit it out, and Alex goes, 'It's not ready yet! Hee-hee-hee-hee-hee!'"

"Hee-hee-hee-hee-hee!" giggled Alex.

Gladys reeled with delight. "Such jokes, from Alex?"

Phil raised his eyebrows, feigning indignation. "Now would a Ugandan child ever play a trick on their dad like that?"

The answer, unequivocally, was no. No son would dare to mock his father. The Ugandan notion of parental respect was highly traditional, certainly, but in so many of the families Gladys encountered there were other factors that inhibited playfulness. Poverty. Illness. It was hard to imagine that Susan Nabugwere and her three children had had many carefree moments together.

Mike could not stop staring at Alex. "I tell you, that boy could not smile. It made me feel really bad. Now he's all radiant and smiling and cracking jokes!" The tall man's voice, usually so clear, fogged up like a windshield during a warm-day downpour. "He touches me. He touches me."

THE CONVERSATION WENT on for a while, the pauses growing longer, in the way that cricket songs thinned in the cooling of an evening. The shadows now stretched from the glass doors to the far wall, and Gladys could sense Phil's concern about his journey to the airport.

"It's nice meeting you people," she said. What had been a perfunctory greeting was now a warm farewell. She chose her words deliberately, like steppingstones across a river. "I felt . . . that I needed to meet you. To see who are these parents who have come up to give assistance to my children? Because I always get many children like them."

She looked from Phil to Michelle, examining their attentive, earnest faces. These were caring people, she saw that. While no one could guarantee a good future for these children, these people exuded the fundamental kindness required to support the effort.

But.

Even as Gladys's heart swelled at the thought of these children having a family again, it ached for Susan Nabugwere. The children had loved their long-suffering mother, but they were young and excited to start a new life. With every day in America, with every haircut and birthday party and outgrown pair of shoes, it would become harder and harder to cling to her memory. Would they remember the hollow-eyed mother who had fled the hospital to spend her last days with them? Would the sound of her cough echo through their dreams? Would they even want to look back?

Gladys took one last opportunity to speak for Susan. "Before she died, what their mother told me was that she really wanted her children to get a good education. Because she couldn't provide it."

Michelle spoke up, her voice as soft as her eyes. "They will get it."

Gladys nodded. That promise would be fulfilled. But the children would get more than that, more than the material luxuries of school fees and new clothes and chocolate and flat-screen TVs. They would get the playing, the teasing, the tickling, the silly looks and the patient instruction, the pranks and the hugs and the fits of laughter.

"Look," Michelle said, holding up a cell phone. "We caught him dancing at the store."

On the shiny screen, there was Alex, merrily shaking his slender hips like a gourd rattle. Gone were the stiff shoulders, the folded arms, the frown carved from stone.

Not all wealthy families were kind, of course, nor were all poor families incapable. But in this case, no one sitting in this room could deny what money could buy: a chance at childhood. Something of which Alex had tasted very little. Now it lit his eyes. It swelled his cheeks. It unfurled his smile.

MICHELLE WALKED the visitors through the courtyard, everyone exchanging words of mutual gratitude and promises to stay in touch. Gladys took pictures with the three children, who were sweetly affectionate but eager to resume their games. Their farewell hugs lapped at her like a tide ebbing out to sea.

"All the shortcuts that Freddy does are for his own benefit," Mike concluded, scanning the driveway as he backed up the car. Nearby, Alex and his sisters were rolling out the big tire again, steadying it with a half-dozen small hands. "But in the process of cutting corners and making himself a buck, these kids are taken care of. It is what they call a win-win situation."

"Win-win," Gladys repeated thoughtfully.

Behind them the kids pushed the tire faster and faster, giggling at its wobbly progress. Mike waited for them to pass, then announced with more surprise than satisfaction, "This is a good day."

"Yes." Against all odds, it was.

Maybe there were no real losers in the case of Susan Nabugwere's children. Pastor Fred had not played fair, but it was of little use dwelling on fairness. One could complain that life was not fair, but what did that alter? In the end, being righteous mattered very little. At the moment it mattered not a bit.

All that mattered right now was a black rubber ring bouncing down a long brick path and the three children who chased it just to see how far it could go.

Yellow and Green

The streets were noisy places. It was not only the vehicles, the buzz of the boda bodas, the music pulsing out from every car and café, the amplified sermons from outdoor churches, the scratchy movie soundtracks leaking out of thin-walled *bibandas*, and the hollering of vendors and pedestrians and neighbors and children over it all. Even the signs seemed to shout at passersby. At every intersection there were road signs, business signs, warning signs, district signs, and billboards claiming a patch of real estate in Gladys's field of vision. *Look here!* the signs seemed to call out. *Turn here! Slow down! We can do the job for you! Hungry? Thirsty? Come this way! You are entering our town, take note! Feel lucky? Make a bet! How about a new hairstyle? Step in! We are savedee, shop with the Lord! Watch out! Get tested! This land is not for sale!*

In a country as densely populated as Uganda, it was hard to get noticed.

Even the calm highway to Luwero, with black-and-white cows nibbling at its green edge, was lined with business signs. Many were simple, displaying only a name: SUNNY RESTAURANT; PARADISE PHOTO STUDIO; NIMROD COUNTRY COTTAGES. Others contained too much information, with numbers and addresses crammed from edge to edge as tightly as the *matatus* in the Old Taxi Park. This visual chatter would normally command little attention, but Mike's passengers noted each passing rectangle of words.

Today Gladys would order her own sign. For the garden project.

"There should be some designs on it," Esther said from the front seat. "Some plants."

"Yes, plants. What kind of plants — fruits?"

"You can put vegetables."

Gladys considered the possibilities. "Like a cabbage. And an orange . . . even a mango."

"What about colors?"

"Maybe yellow. And green."

"Mmm."

"Green for a garden. For something growing. Yellow for the sun. Yellow is also for hope." Gladys spoke in the high, excited voice of a girl picking out a new dress. "Yellow for some hope somewhere!"

If yellow was hope, they needed this sign to glow like the yolk of an ostrich egg.

Given the series of setbacks Gladys's venture had suffered over the past couple of months, this sign would be less an advertisement than a sheet-metal flag staked in the ground — a declaration of the garden's permanence.

A casual observer might reasonably question that status. The garden had been sorely abused. It had suffered not only from pillaging and neglect but also from the drought. There had been a prolonged dry spell. Cattle farmers had begged the government for assistance. With no grass for grazing, no water for drinking, their animals were dying. On the TV news, Gladys saw images of emaciated cows, ribs as deeply corrugated as tin siding, wandering listlessly over expanses of dirt the color of ash. Her losses were less wrenching but nonetheless substantial. Out of the seventy coffee plants she had purchased, only one stubborn vine survived. The sun had burned all the rest.

Bad weather was tough, but it was impersonal. It was fair in its unfairness. Gladys did not toss in bed at night wondering how she could have handled the sun better to make it shine on her garden less harshly. Every farmer had to endure the destruction of drought and floods and locusts and the swarms of tiny queleas, birds that could ravage a millet crop as fast as wildfire with their tiny red beaks. These

natural difficulties Gladys could not control. As for the human cul-
prits, those sly, wingless queleas pecking away at her garden, she was
determined to shoo them away.

THE DAY AFTER the fateful visit in which Zam's "brother," Robert,
was revealed to be her husband, Zam departed for Kampala. She did
not plant the new trees Gladys had brought to the garden. She did
not even bother to water them. Accustomed to having her husband
do the work for pay that went into her own pocket, she was not about
to start working for pay that would go into her husband's pocket. Let
him tend to the trees and harvest the cassava. She would come and
go as she pleased.

Robert told Gladys that he had reminded his wife of her warn-
ings, but Zam had only shrugged, saying, "You know Gladys—she
can become very angry, but she is a simple lady. That one, I don't fear
her."

She did, however, fear Esther. That one looked at her with eyes
of chipped ice. So Zam cut her losses. At the end of the week she
returned to the gardens, accompanied by a man wearing a tie. They
packed up all the cassava and hauled it away.

Relating his wife's shameful behavior, Robert sat down and cried.
Zam had even stolen the beans and the maize flour that Gladys had
stored with them. There were not even enough beans to plant the
next crop. The only remaining "harvest" was the charcoal that Kiviri's man had burned. The felled trees had yielded ten bags. There
would not be much profit, as the charcoal was heavy and transport
was expensive, but the sale would bring the funds to send Robert his
monthly pay.

When Gladys went to the gardens, however, there was no charcoal to sell. Robert had absconded with all ten bags. Husband and
wife, well matched after all, had disappeared with the charcoal, the
baby, and anything else four greedy hands could carry.

At this, Esther lost patience. Her mild exterior provided thick
insulation for life's annoyances, but such transgressions pierced
through. The police should grab Robert and lock him up. Such
crimes must not go unpunished!

As hot and sick as Gladys felt, she could not arrest Robert. It would make life harder for Maria, and she would not punish a baby for a parent's crime. "No," she said. "Let the matter be."

Others might be irked by Gladys's decision, but plain revenge held no appeal for her. She salvaged a bit of solace in the knowledge that she was rid of the slippery couple. For all the trust she had placed in them, she had gotten nothing back save an expensive lesson in giving scoundrels second chances.

That, and a name for her beleaguered enterprise. The only name that seemed to say it all.

"PERSEVERANCE GARDENS."

"Perseverance?" The young man shot her a glance. Gladys gave him a firm nod, and he wrote it down on the order form. "Perseverance . . . Gardens."

The sign was for a farming concern, Gladys explained, and the colors and graphics should reflect its purpose. The eager shop proprietor quizzed her on the size, the material, the color scheme—green letters on yellow, or yellow letters on green?—and the selection of fruits and vegetables to draw the attention of passersby.

The proprietor went off to chat with the welder, leaving his customers to enjoy the shop's cheerful clamor of chatter and dancehall music, with the buzz of the circular saw hovering above it all like the whine of a mechanical bee. Gladys reviewed the invoice which he had started. Even with images of produce added to the design, its content seemed lacking. Uninspired.

She turned to Mike. "You know how when you go to an inn, the sign may say, 'For Better Meals and Rest.' Or a garden might have a line saying, 'For Better Fruits.' What small words can we use here?"

There was a long pause, in which Mike squinted toward the road as if he were trying to read the signs on the other side. "Let me say, for your kind of business it is different." Her motto, he believed, should speak to the nature of the whole enterprise, not just the selling of produce. "Like, 'Help for the Helpless.'"

"Eh!"

"You understand? Or maybe it's '*Hope* for the Helpless.' It becomes like your tagline."

Gladys's response was immediate. "Put it on the paper. 'Hope for the Helpless.' That one sounds good."

"They are not hopeless, but they are helpless," Mike went on, still pitching his idea. "All those kids, you're giving them hope. As they are helpless."

Gladys gave a nod. Her children deserved hope. Not those ones like Zam and Robert. That was help for the *hopeless*!

SEVERAL DAYS LATER, Gladys, Esther, and Mike headed back to the shop. The finished sign leaned prominently against the storefront. The frame was painted metal pipe six feet tall. Against a background of the same rich yellow as the national flag, green letters spelled out

PERSEVERANCE GARDENS
Nalongo Plot 115/116
P.O. Box 856 Entebbe
"Hope For The Helpless"

"But should we have put the word *welcome* on there?"

"No," said Mike. "It looks nice. Very nice. You don't need to say 'Welcome.'"

The shop proprietor came hustling over, slightly out of breath.

"Hello, son." Gladys greeted the young man coolly, sensing his nervous anticipation. Then she shook her head, sighing happily. "Woo-woo-woo."

He grinned. "Didn't I tell you? Tell me, how is it?"

"Fantastic." The single quiet word conveyed more appreciation than if she had leapt up and hugged him. Gladys unfurled a hand toward the sign, with its colorful images of cabbage, mango, and orange, as though she were presenting a painting in a museum. "The fruits have made it lively! Yes. It has come out properly. You look at it and you feel like eating a mango. Except we don't have mangoes in that place."

"You'll have mangoes," the young man assured her. "I'm sure you will have mangoes!"

They drove toward the garden in high spirits, leaving in their wake an intrepid boda man, who ferried the sign under his seat, the two long metal poles protruding from the back of his motorcycle like spears.

Ezra and Douglas met the Volvo in the driveway, their sunny faces sheened with sweat. It was school holidays, and the boys were helping with the garden. Despite the rustic conditions, they loved being there. They enjoyed their liberation from their desks, the chance to work the land and their muscles. They savored the fresh air and the peace of sleeping in the quiet country.

And there was another thing. At school, everyone lined up in a long queue for meals. A student might glance up hopefully from the little portion on his plate to the matron doling out the food, but he would not receive more. At the garden, though, the boys handled the food themselves. If they found a jackfruit, they could eat it. If they picked maize, they could roast it. They could eat as much as they could gather and cook. To a child who had viewed much of life from the back of the line, such freedom was intoxicating.

News of Perseverance Gardens had been relayed from student to student. Ezra's experience had attracted Douglas, which made Victor beg to be included, which made Jeremiah eager to join as well. When Gladys went to pick up the four boys, another one had looked on wistfully, asking, "Auntie Gladys, when is it my turn to go to the garden?"

At present, though, it was costing Gladys money to send a child to stay at the garden, and she could not take them all. If the garden became profitable, she could accommodate more boys, and eventually staff the place for girls to stay safely too.

A MAN FOLLOWED Ezra and Douglas down the driveway. He was her current hire to manage the gardens: her nephew Byron.

Gladys was a suspicious person now; at least, she was trying to be one. After Zam and Robert, she was determined to be more wary of outsiders. When she discussed the garden's losses with her son, Timothy, he encouraged her to look for employees within the family. "If you need someone, why don't you give Byron a chance?" he suggested. "He does not have steady work."

After his mother had passed away, this nephew had lived with Gladys for a time. Now in his thirties, he had been in occasional contact with Timothy.

Upon his first visit to the garden, Byron had pronounced his willingness to start immediately. Gladys breathed a sigh of relief. In the hands of a blood relative, the project would surely be safe.

It was only Byron's second full day at the garden, and he hung back on the unfinished veranda as Gladys handed Ezra and Douglas their sugar and soap, two mosquito nets, and a heavy stack of newspapers.

"I'm giving you these papers to look through," she told the boys, pointing to the "Harvest Money" pull-outs which she had been collecting every Tuesday for several months. "The ordinary papers, when you're finished with them, you can use for lighting fires. But not 'Harvest Money.' These sections here guide people in farming. They show how to cultivate, how to look after animals. Learn some tricks, get some ideas. I want you to be reading, not just looking at them."

This last comment was directed toward Ezra, whose English skills lagged far behind those of his younger classmate. It was imperative that Ezra commit himself to studying over the holidays; his last marks had been dismal. Quick-witted Douglas, on the other hand, was primed to advance to secondary school, if only the fees could be paid.

The boys began browsing through the newspapers, Douglas reading the articles while Ezra examined the images of chickens and papayas and grinning farmers. One cover photo showed a woman in a "Harvest Money" T-shirt cradling a plump white rabbit. Gladys read the headline out loud: "'How Rabbits Changed My Life.'"

She laughed heartily, hefting an invisible fruit the size of a melon. "You wait — within a few years I will be holding a big orange like this and telling you people how oranges have changed my life!"

Mike came over to inform her that the boda man had arrived,

and the boys ran to help unwrap the odd parcel on the back of the bike. Gladys, who enjoyed surprises, had not told them about this new addition to the enterprise.

The boys gaped at the imposing green-and-yellow sign, with its precise, professional lettering. Ezra beamed his asymmetrical smile, then, in a flash, produced a shovel and a hoe. He and Douglas began clearing a section of weeds and hacking away at the gravelly dirt beneath. As they dug, birds chirped madly in the trees, cheering the boys along.

When the posts had been set and braced with stones, the group gathered for photos, Gladys clucking like a hen that has just laid two eggs in one sitting. It was quite a view: the boys standing at proud attention on either side of the bright rectangle against the picturesque backdrop of the house, some fifty yards back from the road.

Sure, it was a little bit like putting a frame around an unfinished painting. The house still lacked a full roof, the walls had not yet been plastered, and the crops were struggling, none yielding enough surplus to sell. But the new sign mirrored Gladys's belief that toward the end of the project's rocky first year, it was turning a corner. Give the gardens a month or two of proper care and surely they would have something beautiful. Her nephew was ready to work, the boys loved the gardens, and the skies had finally blessed them with good rain.

The sun was once again a friend, not an enemy. The sun had turned the gardens green. Yellow and green, they looked good together.

Gladys spoke to the boys and Byron. "We need to bring life back into these gardens. Be practical. That is the Uganda we need."

"Yes, Mommy."

"Perseverance Gardens," Gladys said wonderingly, as though she were reading the sign for the first time. "That is what we have on the ground here."

"Perseverance, yes!" Mike chimed in. "Just keep pressing. That's the word: persevere!"

Lost Again

NO RELATIVES TWO YEARS LATER

Trevor Masembe was abandoned at Katalemwa Cheshire Home in March 2013 and taken to Kawempe Police Station.

A month later, the police failed to trace his family and handed him over to Good Samaritan Home in Matugga. The director of this place ran away after he had accumulated rent and disappeared with the children . . . The children were found stranded at a home in Rakai district and when the Police rescued them, Saturday Vision *identified Masembe. That is how he came to be admitted at Early Learning School in Entebbe.*

After a year at school, he developed suspected autism problems.

For a while the news of Trevor was good. Gladys's dentist friend had grown fond of the boy and bought him books and many other things to make him feel at home. "If it is a matter of footballs," he declared, "I will buy all the balls for him!"

This delighted Gladys, but she warned, "If he is chasing his ball outside, you must not take your eyes off him even for one second."

Trevor kicked his football around the corridors of the compound during the day, and every evening Dr. Kironde had someone escort him to a nearby field to play.

Dr. Kironde tried to strengthen Trevor's weak right hand by encouraging him to carry jerry cans. The boy still urinated in his sleep, so the doctor taught him to remove the soiled bedsheets from the bed and soak them in soapy water. The frequent wringing of the twisted cloth began to bring the limp fingers to life.

Sometimes the boy would wake up to discover that the sheets were dry. On those rare mornings he would run to the doctor's room. "Come see, Dad—I didn't pee on the bed today!" he would announce.

The boy began to speak more, and what he said surprised Dr. Kironde and Gladys: "I want to go to school again. The children at home, they are all in boarding school."

THEN TREVOR WENT missing.

Dr. Kironde's housemaid sent the boy to take a nap after lunch, but he slipped out of his room and disappeared. The neighborhood launched an all-out search. The dentist even paid for TV and radio announcements.

Three days later, Trevor showed up at the police station. When Dr. Kironde went to retrieve him, the officers grilled him about his relationship to the boy. Did he have official permission to take responsibility for the child? Why was the boy running away? An unnerved Dr. Kironde sat Trevor down and warned him that this must never, ever happen again.

It happened again, a few days later: another disappearance, another frantic search. Trevor returned late at night, just as the gate man was locking up. Almost casually the boy stated that he had been moving around Kampala. He had even met some friends who had bought him groundnuts.

The report rendered Gladys speechless. How could the boy deliver such a report and fail to understand the agitation he had caused? To a man who had shown him nothing but patience and kindness?

It happened a third time. Again Trevor appeared at the police station. Again the dentist had to explain why his ward kept running away.

Gladys knew it was high time she accepted the reality of the situation. No one could expect a busy housemaid and a full-time physician to look after such a child. He was too active, too slippery, too stubborn. Trevor did not want anyone telling him what he should do, what he could not do, or where he should be. She had to find a place that could provide both freedom and constant supervision.

With private facilities priced out of her reach, what were her options? L'Arche would not accept him. It was oriented toward older, more sedentary residents, not nine-year-old escape artists. It probably did not help that the sight of the community's more conspicuously disabled residents sent Trevor into wild giggling, as if he were watching a cartoon.

ONE SUNDAY, GLADYS called to check in with Dr. Kironde and found him at his wits' end. Trevor had taken a filthy wet mop and flung it at a Muslim cleric. The man's white tunic was stained all over with dirty water! It was only through Dr. Kironde's pleading that the cleric, a leader at the nearby mosque, had been dissuaded from going to the police. Meanwhile the boy hid among the flowerpots, laughing and laughing about what he had just done.

It would have been the last straw, but Trevor saved the dentist the trouble of putting him out by running away.

This time weeks passed with no sign of the child. Gladys called the police constantly. Through malaria and deadlines and crises at Perseverance Gardens and the needs of all her other children, she worried about this boy. The boy who would chase a ball through a traffic circle. The boy who would not talk. The boy who would follow any hand waving a hot chapati.

A year before, she had not been able to comprehend how a mother or a father could walk away from a child without looking back. She did not excuse Trevor's parents, but these days she often thought of them. What their lives must have been like before they got fed up and dumped their son. How they might have spent nights, as she did, wondering, *Where is he sleeping? How is he eating? Is he safe?*

"YOUR TREVOR is here!" Her colleagues at Old Kampala Police Station had called to report that the boy had been picked up along a nearby road.

When she arrived at the station, her relief curdled into dismay. It was as though she were suddenly transported two years back, to the church building in Rakai. A small, shabby apparition shambled toward her, preceded by the stench of sweat and urine. Clothes filthy, face wan, body streaked with grime.

Trevor. The sight broke her heart.

How was it that he had again sunk to such depths? It was not so very long ago that he had played in the courtyard of Early Learning School. What had happened to that boy? That boy was round-cheeked and healthy, with a football bouncing at his feet. This boy was blank-faced, shoeless, worn, like a discarded doll. He did not cry when he saw her. He was not eager to be rescued. Gladys sensed an inner contraction, a closing of some emotional aperture inside that thin chest.

Banange . . . This boy has gone through a lot, Gladys thought. *The time might come that he doesn't want to fight on.*

How much longer would Gladys herself want to fight on? This was undoubtedly the question on the minds of everyone around her. They were all fed up with this one, this stinky, disruptive, thieving child who would not even look someone in the eye.

No one would blame Gladys for putting him aside. Why keep washing a cracked cup?

IT WAS HARD not to contrast Trevor's fate with that of Alex and his sisters, who were now living with their new family in Nebraska. The Griffens had sent a photo of the siblings happily playing in a yard dotted with toys. There was no such happy option for Trevor, no well-to-do American family waiting to save the day. Gladys could not even get him admitted to a facility for the disabled. She had contacted a home in Jinja for kids with autism, but as it did not usually accept children from outside the district, there were endless bureaucratic delays.

As the weeks went by, Trevor made Old Kampala the base for his wanderings. Officer Rebecca did not like this. Whenever Gladys visited, the policewoman broached the same subject: "It's time to think about sending the boy to Naguru."

"No. Rebecca, no." Gladys would argue or plead, depending on the moment. "It will be very difficult for us to monitor him there. And I need to be able to monitor him to see whether he will be able to change as he grows up. He's young—maybe he fails to understand that people are helping. If he starts understanding, maybe we can continue helping him."

The doctors had told her that autism was not curable. But she detected in the boy some potential to engage. Sometimes he would tell her that he wanted to go back to Early Learning School. Other times, when she gave him a 500-shilling note for a chapati, he would flash her the old happy grin before running off.

One rainy day as she was leaving the station she heard him calling to her. She walked behind the building, but she couldn't see him at first. He was crouching inside one of the abandoned cars. His body odor stung the eyes, as he no longer bathed at all now. His clothes were ragged, the pants splitting at the seams like reused *kavera*. Gladys had stopped bringing him clothes from Dr. Kironde's place, as other children always stole them.

It hurt. After rescuing him repeatedly, putting him in schools, settling him in homes, and buying him clothes and shoes and supplies and food again and again, here he was, squatting in the rusty wrecks behind Old Kampala. What dreams did he have, sleeping in those cars that would never go anywhere?

AFTER TWO MONTHS, even the grudging hospitality of the police station came to an end. The traffic officers caught Trevor red-handed at their *piki-pikis*, siphoning gas from the bikes' tanks. Evidently he had learned to sell the fuel to street boys to earn money for chapatis. As Trevor met the spotlight of accusation with a sleepy smile, Officer Rebecca was shocked to catch the whiff of fuel underneath his he-goat smell. Like so many other street kids, Trevor was sniffing the toxic fumes to get high.

With this news, the police drew the line. Gladys could continue her search to find a better placement for the child, but in the meantime he must be confined.

What could Gladys do? She could not deny that freedom was a riptide dragging Trevor further and further into polluted waters.

And so the boy was sent to the place where boys like him were sent: Naguru.

Trevor was gone.

Seven Pieces of Cassava

KIBIRANGO IN SCHOOL

After Douglas Kibirango's story was published in Saturday Vision *a few weeks ago, explaining how he was stranded at Kawempe Police Station, Good Samaritans offered to help him.*

The management of Early Learning Primary School, Entebbe, took Kibirango on and he is now enrolled in the boarding section.

Kibirango left his parents' home in Katugo, Nakasongola, citing mistreatment by his father, Fred Bogere, and stepmother, Zaina Nambirige.

Two years ago Gladys had discovered Douglas, a skinny, feverish twelve-year-old with swollen legs and feet, at Kawempe Police Station. He had run away from home with only the clothes on his back and walked over seventy-five miles south from his village near Nakasongola to Kampala. The journey had taken him six days. Nearly a week of walking barefoot, scrounging for mangoes, and drinking from ponds. When she interviewed Douglas, he revealed the cause of his flight: an abusive stepmother. Wincing at the scars he showed her, Gladys took him under her wing.

Douglas's profile ran in "Lost and Abandoned" four times but generated no response. In the meantime the boy thrived at Early Learning. He was exceedingly capable and well-behaved. With his mild nature and easy smile, he made friends quickly. He achieved high marks in his classes, especially math and English. After two years he was a P7 candidate, preparing to sit for his Primary School Leaving Examinations — the first big step in his quest to become a mechanical engineer. He had never asked about the search for his family, and in the face of more pressing demands, it quietly slid down Gladys's list of priorities.

In recent months, though, the question of Douglas's family had resurfaced. The times he had stayed at Perseverance Gardens with Ezra, Victor, and Jeremiah, he had been no more than an hour's drive away from his village. In escaping his vicious stepmother, the child had left behind other relatives, and he had the right to see them. If the stepmother made any trouble, Gladys was ready to fight fire with fire.

ONE MORNING GLADYS and Mike went by Early Learning to pick up Douglas and Jeremiah. Mike was driving a van today, as the Volvo was in need of repair. As the boys stepped in through the sliding door, Gladys announced that in addition to visiting Ezra at Perseverance Gardens, they would be taking Douglas to his village. "After all," she asked him, "don't you think those people back home are now missing you? Don't you think they may have thought you died?"

To her surprise, the boy dropped his chin to his chest. "I'm sorry, Mommy."

"Sorry? For what?"

"I have been telling you a lot of lies."

Gladys gasped. These were words she had heard before. But she had never expected them from this mouth.

"I lied about why I ran away."

"What do you mean? It was not because your stepmother was mistreating you?"

"I was not even staying with a stepmom." Douglas was unable to meet her eyes. "I was staying at my grandmother's house."

What of the stories he had fed her of the stepmother's terrible beatings? He had spoken her name, he had displayed the scars. How

Gladys had wanted to squeeze that woman's neck! For so long this stepmother had lurked in Gladys's imagination, and now it appeared that that was the only place she existed.

"Why did you not tell us the truth before?"

Douglas turned toward the window. "I didn't want to go back home."

"Why?"

"My grandmother got more children to care for, and she said there would not be enough money for my school fees. I wanted to study. That's why I ran away."

Gladys's mind reeled in this new direction. Douglas had a grandmother? And he took such risks over a lack of school fees?

"Douglas, it has been over two years. For two years you have been lying to me?"

"I was going to tell you the truth after my Primary Leaving Examinations."

"Why wait?" Gladys asked, with a touch of pique. "What difference does two months make when you have lied for two years?"

"I feared I would be dismissed from school."

The severity of this logic gave her pause. The boy anticipated banishment. He must have reasoned that if he could maintain his deception through his exams, at least he could finish his primary education before being thrown back on the street.

Did he really think Gladys capable of such cruelty toward one of her children? What had he seen in her behavior to imagine that she would behave in such a petty way?

She considered this quiet, serious boy. He was wearing a yellow T-shirt with an image of a horse pulling a cart through a garden of flowers and the words AMISH COUNTRY printed above. In his hands he gripped a small blue Bible with DOUGLAS written in pen on the edge. There were spots on the shirt and the book where his tears had dripped from his lowered chin. It was pointless to scold him; nothing could make the child feel worse than he did now.

"Douglas, I don't want you to get scared. There's no need for you to be scared, okay?"

The chin trembled, shaking another drop onto the T-shirt.

"I'm not planning to go and dump you there," she reassured him. "No. Because after all the years I've spent on you, you are now a P Seven candidate. I can't just dump you. My concern is to get to know your people. And for them to get to know that you're still alive. I want them to know that you were not kidnapped and sacrificed. Or sold. Okay?"

AS THEY APPROACHED Nakasongola, driving down the very same road that Douglas escaped on two years before, the cloud cover darkened, producing a rain as sudden and steady as water from a tap. Mike flicked at the lever for the windshield wipers; the blades jerked across the glass like the arms of an impatient traffic cop. "I tell you," he called over his shoulder, "running away like that? This boy was two days from trouble."

"He was very lucky," Gladys agreed. If Douglas had spent even one more night on the streets, they would not have met at the police station. He might now be moving with those street kids who picked pockets, scavenged from dustbins, and sniffed gas fumes out of plastic bottles.

"What really is it under the sun that would drive a child from home to go sleep on the pavement of the town?"

"Without even a blanket!"

"No kid runs away from a good home. There is always a reason. A reason why they lie and lie and lie."

Gladys was all too familiar with these reasons: violence, poverty, alcoholism, sexual abuse, drugs, illness, or any combination of the above. "You'll find that there are a lot of bad behaviors at home," she said, "whereby a child would not want police to take them back. The reasoning is, *If I don't want to be taken back home, I have to make sure that I present my story so that it can't be traced,* you know? Some of them will tell you, 'I forgot the place,' 'I don't know the name of the road,' or 'I don't know where my family is.'"

"For me, that is very intelligent," Mike commented. "They make a dead-end story, and they stick to it."

"You are right." Gladys chuckled.

"Just lie yourself into the future."

At her side, the subject of their speculation sat huddled and motionless, lips moving above his open Bible, scouring the text for some magical phrase that would make him disappear.

She spoke to the boy. "Don't you think your family may have been looking for you?"

"Maybe. I'm not sure."

"Don't you miss them?"

"At first I missed them, but now I'm used to it."

"Who did you miss?"

Douglas's eyes instantly filled. Outside, heavy clouds clustered on the horizon.

"Are you afraid of taking us there now?"

He did not answer.

"Let's get this over with. Eh?" Gladys addressed him with a soothing matter-of-factness. "Whether your people are annoyed or what. Yes, of course they must be annoyed, but it's always good to get to that point where they can see you."

Still the boy did not speak. What made him freeze like a rabbit caught in an open field? What raptors circled overhead?

"Douglas," she said, "you should take me to where you feel comfortable."

"I will take you to where I ran away from."

"You know the place?"

"I was staying with my grandmother. Deborah Namusisi." Uttering the name, the boy was stricken anew. He breathed through his mouth and shut his eyes, as though preparing to submerge his head underwater.

Gladys let him be. A child with a secret could be like a snail retreating into its shell. No manner of shaking or prodding would dislodge it. But leave it alone and it would emerge when it felt safe.

DESPITE HIS ANXIETY, Douglas began to perk up as they turned down the road toward his home. From what Gladys could see through the gray wet, it was a typical rural village. As she quizzed him about the schools and churches and the horned cattle they passed, Douglas answered confidently, his excitement growing as the landmarks became more and more familiar. When the rain obscured the view out of the side windows, he peered through the windshield, thrusting his body between the front seats like the figurehead on a ship.

"That place there. That one is my grandmother's."

As Mike turned into the driveway, the sun burst through the clouds as abruptly as the yolk from a cracked egg.

"Ah! You can't believe. All of a sudden it is hot!" Gladys squinted skyward as she stepped out of the vehicle. In Uganda, it often felt like someone up there was playing with the switches.

In the bright light before them stood a house of medium size, with a kitchen on the right and a latrine in the back, all of red brick. Fruit trees bordered an orderly yard. Chickens stalked the periphery, on the hunt for grubs disturbed by the rain.

"It looks like a nice place," she remarked. "Whether it is sunny or rainy or what, it is a nice place. Look at it."

"There is even glass in the windows," Mike commented.

The door was locked. Douglas went around to the back of the house. He returned eating a green mango.

"Is your grandmother there?"

"No."

A couple of young boys came running up. They were neighbors, not relatives, but they greeted Douglas with excited smiles. Soon they were chattering away in Ruuli, the local language.

"Why would you run away from a good home like this one?" Gladys asked rhetorically.

"I expected a very poor place," Mike said.

It did not add up. She had braced for squalor and disrepair. Perhaps a leaky mud hut. A place like that of George the First—or George the Second—where there was so much poverty that a boy might think it was futile to stay. But this was a sturdy, finished house. There was nothing to indicate a distressed situation.

"Eh, today is what? Sunday. The family is probably at church." The neighbor kids nodded, confirming Gladys's hunch. "Let us go and look for them."

As they drove, Gladys struggled to fit the odd pieces into the puzzle. "Help me to understand," she entreated Douglas. "What got you so annoyed with this home that you ran away?"

"The long distances to school," he muttered.

"Eh?"

The boy claimed that he did not like to walk two hours to school and two hours back. Gladys frowned. It was a long way, but in rural places like this, such distances were common.

"What is so special about you that you can't endure that?"

Douglas gave no answer.

"It's not making sense," she said, sighing. The story kept changing. Hadn't he stated that he had run away because his grandmother could not pay his school fees? Would a boy who balked at walking two hours to school walk six days to Kampala in search of school fees?

Approaching the church, Mike drove through an area of intersecting paths dotted here and there with clusters of people exchanging Sunday greetings. Two middle-aged women stood at the side of the road, one holding a bicycle.

Douglas whipped around. "That one is my grandmother."

Mike hit the brakes, sending a tremor of excitement through the van. The women on the road turned as the door slid open. The one with the bike wore a silky sleeveless black-and-orange blouse over a fitted skirt; she had a blue leather tote tucked under one arm, braided hair swept back in a voluminous bun. There was a dignity to her bearing, a natural poise.

When she saw Douglas emerge, everything dropped: her jaw, her bike, her composure. She rushed to the boy, then hesitated, as though he might be an apparition. Gingerly her fingers touched his cheek. Douglas began to cry.

Gladys studied the grandmother, this Deborah Namusisi. The tightened lip, the rising brow—signs of what? Anger? Worry? Relief? Yes, relief. But also hurt.

"What made you leave this place?" Deborah asked.

Douglas sniffled loudly, too overcome to speak. She caressed his brow with her palm, but the boy ducked away. In a smooth motion she pulled him to her, cradling his head in her arms. It was a brief moment, but its significance registered. No woman could offer such tender comfort to a child she did not care for.

Abruptly Deborah grabbed for Douglas's left hand and pulled it to her. Missing a fingernail, his pinkie ended bluntly, like the top of a carrot.

Gladys laughed. "Are you sure now? That it is really him?"

The grandmother did not answer. She saw no one but the boy. "I've dreamed so much about you. I've dreamed and I've dreamed till I was tired of dreaming. What did I do? I didn't scold you or anything, but you just left." Douglas only wept harder, his hand wilting in her grip. "What happened? What did I do to you? Why did you go?"

The question echoed in Gladys's head. Why had this child run away from this gentle-looking woman? What was he trying to escape?

A sizable crowd had collected, the way it always did. Once a few neighbors stepped closer to hear the conversation, a dozen quick-footed kids appeared, drawn to any gathering with the potential for drama. Stragglers filtered in, their steady encroachment belying their indifferent expressions. A couple of toddlers waddled up last, led by their bellies.

"Don't cry," the grandmother pleaded, unsettled by Douglas's distress. "Why are you crying? Are you happy? Are you annoyed?"

"Maybe he has forgotten the language," a neighbor speculated.

"It's just that he's crying, he can't speak," said another.

Gladys sensed a public forum gathering around them. "I suggest that we go to your home and talk there," she said to Deborah in a low voice. "I will explain everything."

WHEN THEY RETURNED to the house, Gladys proposed that they convene on the veranda. A pinched nerve in her back was acting up, and she was eager to sit.

The rain began to fall again, hastening the assembly process. A dozen bodies squeezed onto the rectangle of cement, the visitors on chairs and the family on the floor, circled by local kids who ran over to find shelter under the lip of the roof. The veranda felt like an overloaded lifeboat.

Gladys asked Deborah if she had heard of *New Vision* newspaper.

"I have heard of it. I've heard it is big."

"Yes, we are big!" Gladys replied. Sensing the turmoil of emotions on the veranda, she spoke with casual cheer, as though they were sitting down for Sunday tea. "We give you the news from all over the country. We even give you the news from here."

She explained her newspaper column, the repeated listing of Douglas's story, his placement at Early Learning School, and everything leading up to today's arrival at the village. Perhaps it was the challenge of listening through the rain, but across the crowded veranda there was no fidgeting, sniffling, coughing, or absent-minded scratching, even from the children. Deborah concentrated on Gladys with the alert stillness of a fisherman holding a finger to a taut line.

"Up until this very morning, I believed Douglas had run away from this stepmother who beat him. For two years I have been wishing to find this horrible stepmother so I could blast her!" Gladys gritted her teeth and shook her fists in the air, her pantomime of vengeance drawing a flicker of a smile from Deborah. She let her hands drop. "But the child lied to me."

Douglas, who was seated on the floor near his grandmother, could not look up. He appeared to be staring at his tiny Bible, although his eyes were so puffy it was unlikely he could see much of anything.

"If there is a genuine reason as to why this boy ran away, I have not seen it." Gladys paused. On cue, a tremendous thunderclap blasted over the house, its lingering rumble a drum roll announcing cascading rain. Big fat drops boiled up the red soil, infusing the veranda with the rich, clean smell of wet earth. Chickens scurried for cover, as ungainly as ladies crossing a busy street in high heels. A yellow dog, its fur already damp, shambled with resignation through the yard.

"So now, Deborah Namusisi, what is your side of the story?

When the boy disappeared, did you strip yourself naked and scream? Did you fall down and roll on the ground? What happened?"

The woman cleared her throat. She seemed a soft-spoken sort, and it required some effort on her part to speak louder than the rain. "This boy was given to me at the age of five years," she began. Although she called herself his grandmother, technically she was Douglas's great-aunt. Douglas's father, a fisherman, was her nephew. When Douglas was dumped by his mother, no one showed up to take him. He was passed around to several relatives before landing on Deborah's doorstep.

"Has he ever lived with his father?"

"The boy doesn't know his father. He has only seen him once."

Deborah took Douglas into her home. She placed him in the village school, but over the years it became apparent that the standards were too low for the boy's high potential. In particular, he displayed an affinity for electronics.

"He used to tinker with broken phones and torches and stuff like that," she explained. "At school and at home. He would open them up, fiddle with them, and they would work. People would even bring their radios to him and he would fix them."

Gladys had heard similar reports of Douglas's skills at Early Learning. "Where did he learn how to repair such things?"

"The boy learned it by himself. I don't know how he did it." Deborah shrugged, but there was pride in her voice. Douglas could build things too, she asserted. From the spare parts of his repair jobs he had cobbled together his own working receiver. Set within an old jerry can, it was his rudimentary version of a portable radio. "I thought that eventually he could go to a college and train properly to repair those machines. So for P Five I wanted to take him to a private school."

Gladys glanced from Deborah to Douglas. This was a direct contradiction of his claim that his grandmother intended to stop his education.

"I loved the boy," Deborah said emphatically, following the reporter's gaze. "Whatever I ate, he could eat. He was such a humble boy, a fine boy."

"So all along his behavior has been good?"

"The boy was so well-behaved!" Deborah's voice rose defensively. "If you told him to do something, he would do it. The whole village loved him!"

Several heads nodded. Douglas pressed his lips together and stared at the floor.

"I had to find a way to earn money for his private-school fees. So I would make chapatis and samosas to sell at the market. Douglas would deliver them to a shop in the morning, then bring back the money in the evening. But after some time, no money came back. He reported that the chapatis didn't sell. I didn't sense any trouble, because the boy was always so good and obedient.

"Then I started to lose money. I had fifty thousand shillings stored in the house that disappeared. I didn't think the child would steal money from me, but something was going on. Maybe the wind blew it away. Maybe it was taken. I spoke to him directly: 'Douglas, if you took the money, maybe you have eaten some of it. But if there is any balance left over, please bring the rest back to me.' He denied the theft totally.

"The day he disappeared, it was a Saturday. I asked him to deliver the buckets of chapatis and samosas to the shop, and I went to cultivate. At the end of the day I waited for him to come to the garden, but he didn't show up. I went home, but Douglas was not there either. He was nowhere to be found. I searched the entire village for him."

"Did you ask about him at the trading center?"

"Yes." Deborah nodded. "People said they had seen him passing through at about nine o'clock in the morning."

"Did they say anything else?"

"They said he was carrying a new radio."

No one spoke for a moment. Sheets of water strafed the tin roof. On the ground circling the veranda, puddles formed at time-lapse speed. Old corncobs listed, canoelike, in the overflowing trenches.

"Now I want to hear in his own words why he ran away," Gladys said, gesturing from Deborah to Douglas. "Ask him. But not in Ruuli, because I won't know what you're saying."

The woman turned to the boy. "Can you tell me what it was that made you run away?"

Douglas looked up at the trees, which were momentarily backlit by lightning. A rolling boom followed, so low that it was felt as much as heard.

"Tell me, is it the truth, what she has said?" Gladys pressed. "Or is your grandmother lying? Did you take that fifty thousand?"

The boy did not answer.

"Eh?" Gladys prompted.

His lips moved, but no sound came.

"Yes or no?"

"Yes!" Douglas had to shout over the storm, the very heavens compounding his humiliation.

"You took money out of her pocket?"

"I took it."

"So now your pocket was healthy. Now what did you do with that money?"

"I bought a radio."

DEBORAH HAD FOUND it hard to accept that her grandson had run away. The boy's clothes were still at home, and no food was missing. But she could not find him in the village or the trading center, so she walked to the next trading center. She waited until nightfall, checking the bars to see if he was hiding somewhere. No Douglas. She returned the next day, and the next.

"I thought maybe he had hopped onto a ferry, or maybe he had drowned. Maybe he had been kidnapped and sacrificed. I went to the local chairman and the police. They took my report, but they only said that if we found the boy to come back and tell them."

She continued looking, the scope of her search widening like a torch beam. She traveled to other villages, Ninga and Kapundo. She wandered up and down the lakeside. She interrogated children who claimed they had seen him looking after some cows. She tracked down the cattle herders. Still no Douglas.

He had moved with some hunters, someone told her. Deborah

traced those areas but found no clues. She went to funerals, making announcements at burial sites about her missing grandson, but no one ever reported seeing him.

The boy had simply disappeared.

Months passed, then years. *He was twelve,* she would have to tell people, *but he would be thirteen now. No, now he would be fourteen.* If he was still alive.

"I was feeling so much pain in my heart. I kept searching for the boy, but after all that time, I could only pray that God was looking after him."

Douglas pulled the neck of his yellow T-shirt up over his face and wiped his eyes.

All of this torment, Gladys thought, for one cheap radio. "What happened to that radio, Douglas?" she asked. "I never saw you with it. Where did it go?"

"I gave it away," he mumbled.

"Come again?"

"I gave it away."

"Am I hearing correctly? Oh my God. What friend did you give it to?"

"It was not a friend. A guy said he would give me food if I gave him the radio. So we traded."

"Food for how long?"

"One meal."

"Eh! Today I'm just getting shock after shock after shock!" She might expect such irrational behavior from Trevor or Rose, but Douglas? Steady, sensible Douglas? "So with all that damage behind you, you traded that radio for a meal. How much food was it?"

"Seven pieces of cassava."

The bounty for his betrayal. His thirty pieces of silver.

The boy blinked at the yard, not bothering to wipe his eyes. He could as readily stop the rain. Around the house, the puddles had swelled and connected into a moat. It was three feet wide and growing; no one could leave the veranda now without stepping in the muddy water.

"Douglas. Stop crying. Right now I need the truth." Gladys softened her voice as much as she could, given the surrounding din. "Let me take you back a bit. Why did you want to buy a radio?"

No answer.

Gladys shifted forward in her seat. "We don't have much time. We need to get back to Entebbe, to get you back to school. So please answer me directly. Why did you want that radio?"

Douglas knew his auntie was not going to let anyone off this veranda until everything had been laid bare. After a trembling exhalation, he began.

THERE WAS A blind boy in the village. His name was Ibra. Ibra owned a portable radio that he would carry around the trading center. How cool he looked, strutting around in a fog of music, like the star of a movie. Douglas, who loved both music and radios, would follow the blind boy for hours. But it was Ibra's radio and he chose what they would hear.

One day Ibra told him, "You must buy a radio like mine. That way we can move together, and each listen to what we like." From that day forward, Douglas became obsessed with securing his own radio. Not one made from rusty parts stuck in an old jerry can, but a slick new one, with chrome knobs and an antenna that pierced the air like a blade.

"What backward behavior," Gladys interjected, unable to contain her disapproval. "Douglas, did you think that was really swag, to have a radio on the street? Eh? Is that swag? Such swag that you stole money for it?"

Now she could imagine how it had played out. Douglas had been twelve years old at the time. As clever as he was, he was young. His blind friend's treasure blinded him; he did not see that he was making a mistake he could not repair.

Once he held the new radio in his hands, the realization must have hit him: there was no way he could get away with such a theft. How could he play his new radio without explaining where it came from? Everyone would know that this "fine boy" was no better than a common thief. No, an uncommon thief—one low enough to steal from his own grandmother.

Such a crime could never be forgiven. He had to run away.

By nightfall he would have reached Nakasongola. Hungry, tired, and alone, he must have cursed the useless radio. He could never hold it up to his ear without hearing the echo of his betrayal. So for a few bites of food he gave it up. And he kept walking.

"Douglas, if I had heard all this when I found you at the police station, I would have whipped your bottom and sent you back home," Gladys admitted. "But despite your lies, God was merciful to you. You were given a great chance in life. You still have that chance. But don't think you should go forward and lie to people ever again." She gave this warning its requisite weight, although it seemed unlikely that Douglas would need reminding.

"And now what you need to do is apologize to your grandmother. With a voice that everyone can hear. Whether she forgives you or doesn't forgive you, I don't care. Me, I'm not of your clan. That is her business. Stop crying and face her."

There was precious little room to maneuver on the veranda; Douglas's shuffling efforts to navigate around the tangle of legs were reminiscent of Mike's parallel-parking struggles at Old Kampala Police Station. At length he was able to kneel before his grandmother. "I beg you to forgive me for all the wrong I have done to you," he said. "Please forgive me for what I did."

Gladys urged him on. "You must claim what you did. What are you asking her to forgive you for?"

"For the money I took. And for running away."

"Grandmother, what do you say?"

Gazing at the kneeling boy, Deborah did not need to search for words. "I forgave him a long time ago." She pressed a handkerchief to her eyes. "He has always been in my heart. All I prayed for was for him to come back to me."

"So you have forgiveness. Give yourselves a hug."

At this, the two stood. The woman reached out with both arms, and the boy leaned against her, gulping with relief, as though she had just pulled him from the sea.

"I forgave you a long time ago." The grandmother spoke softly, the way one would soothe a much younger child. "Now you know I forgive you. Whatever you did, I still love you."

Douglas took a shuddering breath. His day of reckoning had arrived. He had feared it as the day when he would be forced to start walking again. Instead, two long years later, he could finally rest.

COULD GLADYS FAULT herself for failing to detect Douglas's secret? No. The boy had been set on exacting his own penance. The self-containment he displayed had been a kind of imprisonment. Was there anything more isolating than shame?

Of course, the unprincipled were immune to shame, but a single dose could paralyze the decent. Douglas had almost given up his life to pay for one callow action.

Clasping the hand with the flawed pinkie, Deborah looked at Gladys. "Thank you so much for bringing this boy back to us. I am so grateful."

"And Grandmother, I must thank you for having such a big heart. A heart that can forgive. Because children can make mistakes."

The two discussed Douglas's education. Deborah agreed that Douglas should remain at Early Learning, assuring Gladys that he would be welcome in her home for school holidays or any time he wanted to visit.

The rain had tapered to a drizzle. Throughout the meeting, the storm had punctuated the unfolding drama with uncanny synchronicity, and now, on cue, the clouds lifted. The moat around the veranda began to recede. A hen stepped daintily on the outlines of damp ground appearing between puddles. A pig snuffled through shiny grass.

Deborah turned back to Douglas and cocked her head at the yard. "Help me catch a rooster to give to your auntie."

The boy followed his grandmother to the edge of the veranda, and together they stepped off.

Hope for the Helpless

It wasn't supposed to happen again. But it had. The familiar nightmare with a different bogeyman. Zam. Robert. And now Byron.

Gladys's nephew's arrival should have signaled a turning point for Perseverance Gardens. The rains had come; the crooks had gone. At the end of the driveway, the beautiful sign stood tall.

Gladys should have been able to trust Byron. He was from her family. And he seemed earnest about his new job, telling her that he needed 1.5 million shillings to buy additional equipment and pesticide for the tomatoes. But after she gave him the money, it soon became evident that he had spent it all on himself.

Once again there was no harvest at Perseverance Gardens.

When confronted about his cheating, Byron didn't run away. He did not hang his head in shame. In fact, he made rude remarks as Gladys stood in the doorway of the room, watching him pack up his things.

She locked the metal doors to the house, satisfied that he had not taken anything that belonged to the garden. But Byron must have been watching. After she left, he apparently climbed up the side of the house, squeezed into the gap between the wall and the unfinished roof, dropped into the room, and took everything inside. He stole the pump, the rubber boots, the panga, the hoes, the jerry cans, even the plates.

The brazenness of the robbery stunned Gladys. How could this be her own nephew? Her son, Timothy, was incensed. He had been the one to recommend Byron to his mother, and now he wanted his cousin arrested. Jail would teach him a lesson!

Once again, though, Gladys could not do it. This man was a relative. In the African way of thinking, it would be very hard to set the police on him even though he had done these bad things. Other people, especially relatives, might not understand. *This was flesh and blood,* they would say. *Gladys must have mistreated him in some way.* To be sure, his story would be very different from hers.

Anyway, Zam and Robert had been just as bad, or worse. And she had not thrown either of them behind bars. So how could she send the police after her own kin?

WITH THE GARDEN again unsupervised, Gladys wrestled once more with the problem of finding a trustworthy replacement. Eager to help, Ezra sent a message back home to his village, asking a friend to take the job. "He is a born-again Christian, Mommy," the boy said, vouching for him. "And I know his father."

The young man arrived with nothing, and as he was Ezra's friend, Gladys allowed him to reside in the house and use the mattresses and bedsheets. But then two more young men arrived from Ezra's village to work in the adjacent gardens. When the two newcomers moved in, Gladys felt there was no way she could refuse them the same hospitality. It made no sense to have them sleep outside on the ground when a room with mattress and sheets was standing right there. So the three men stayed in the house together.

The gardens were not producing much, and the trio complained of not having enough beans to eat. Whenever Gladys visited she would bring them food, soap, sugar, paraffin—whatever she could spare at the time. When one man fell off the bicycle, she paid his medical bills. She felt that she was building a good relationship with the new workers, but others did not share her charitable view.

Kiviri said, "When we bring in laborers, they sleep on mats. Why do you give them mattresses and bedsheets? After all, they are earning salary."

Timothy said, "Two of them aren't even working for you. Why are you providing housing for all three?"

Even Ezra sent urgent, disjointed texts: *But mommy what I beg you don't send money up to anyhow for them . . . Bye mommy, don't spoil our money to him. Be careful.*

"You know what," Gladys responded, "there are times where you need to help such people, because they are from a different area. You never know, one time you may also need them."

The ending of this chapter was predictable to everyone but Gladys. Shortly after receiving their monthly pay, the three men ran away, taking everything with them—all the supplies she had replaced from the last theft. Even the bedsheets.

This time her people seemed angrier with her than with the three thieves.

Timothy fumed to Esther, "The bad thing about Mommy is that she can't adapt. She lets people get away with everything."

Kiviri, who knew a thing or two about cons, expressed dismay. "Madam, I really don't know. Everyone here is wondering about the way you treated these people. Giving them even blankets and even bedsheets and even mattresses? And whenever you come you bring them bread and you bring them sugar and you bring them soap?"

Didn't she know that deprivation provided motivation, that fear ensured discipline? Everyone in the neighborhood had witnessed how she had let the crimes of Zam, Robert, and Byron go unpunished. What would keep the three new scoundrels from following in the footsteps of the old ones?

Gladys's brothers even questioned her birthright. "You are too soft," they said. "You need to become more Ugandan."

In spite of everything, Gladys laughed—a long, sputtering laugh that evaporated into a sigh. "It is too late for me. I fear it is too late for me to learn."

WAS GLADYS REALLY so soft? She had never thought of herself as a soft woman, and those she encountered in her professional life certainly would not characterize her as such. She had no trouble being tough when it came to threats against her children. She would ride on a boda for hours, in the rain, feverish from malaria, to the middle of cannibal country. She would face down an angry spouse, a hostile family, even a police officer. There was a clarity that came with fighting for a child's welfare. The garden project, though, was for her own welfare as well. And that, perhaps, is what muddied the waters. She was not as tough on her own behalf as she was on the children's.

Late at night her mind drifted and pitched, a boat unmoored on a roiling sea of doubt. She thought about the three young men from Ezra's village. They had been given jobs, a place to stay, and provisions. What had caused them to toss it all away?

She pictured Ezra's village. Although the building at Perseverance Gardens was still unfinished, it was a grand structure compared to the small mud huts there. Those men may not ever have slept with blankets and bedsheets. They may not ever have received so much money, 150,000 shillings a month. Free accommodation, food, *and* salary? They may have gotten so excited that they thought they had already won the lottery.

For many who had had little in life, you did not invest in good luck, you cashed in. If you caught a chicken, you didn't wait for it to lay eggs. Better to cook it and eat it before it ran away. Maybe these men did not trust that the kindness she had shown them would last, so they had traded it in for a quick payoff.

She had never had such an occasion to question the pros and cons of kindness. Her actions sprouted not from a conscious desire to be virtuous but from instinct. It was the way she was made, the way she had been raised by her grandparents: to help, to share, to empathize. Following that instinct had brought her much satisfaction, even joy.

Of course she did not expect the universe to kneel to her every time she extended a hand; she had come across many, many people who met goodwill with indifference. But this series of hostilities, this threat of ruin — this was new.

It was her fault. And her fate.

Even if she could go back in time, she could not have thrown Zam, Robert, and Byron in jail. She could not have refused to pay baby Maria's medical bills. She could not have locked up the building and told the three young men from Ezra's village to sleep on the ground. She could not have become vengeful or miserly or cold-hearted. She was who she was, and if the project's success depended on her ability to change, then Perseverance Gardens would fail.

KIVIRI CALLED GLADYS to notify her that someone was attempting to steal the doors from the house. She rushed to the gardens, her heart plummeting into her stomach.

The lower hinges of all three doors had been pried away. One door hung by only a single bolt; someone must have been working at it all night, knowing that the building was unoccupied.

The sight of those bent hinges broke something within her. People had stolen her crops, taken the bedding, run off with her tools and plates and charcoal and jerry cans. But the doors? Her beautiful red wrought-iron doors? It was like yanking the shoes off an accident victim.

Or a corpse. Wasn't the place already dead? There was nothing left to protect. The house was empty. There was no one staying there, no one working there, no supplies, no tools.

Perseverance Gardens. Persecution Gardens was more like it.

For the first time, Gladys thought about walking away.

"No!" Esther slapped the notion away. "We have a goal, we have integrity, we will not give up."

Gladys acquiesced to her friend's exhortation, but the sense of defeat remained. She had tried again and again to plant trees for her children, but it seemed they would never have shade.

THERE WAS ONE person who possibly felt worse than Gladys. At the start of the school holidays, Ezra returned to the gardens.

The place was in wretched condition. It had been raining daily since the three men from his village had run off. Untended, the bush had returned in force, erasing crop rows and tangling plants. What little produce was coming up could not even be harvested because of the undergrowth.

The choked fields, the looted rooms, the broken doors: each dealt a blow. But what hit Ezra the hardest was the sign. It was not so very long ago that they had posed proudly beside the new marker for Perseverance Gardens. Now the bush had grown so tall around it, one could no longer see the fruits or read "Hope for the Helpless."

The first thing Ezra did was clear the sign. He hacked with the panga and pulled with his hands, not pausing until every weed had been ripped away. When he returned to his village, he vowed, he would go looking for each of those three men.

OVER THE SCHOOL holidays, Ezra, Douglas, and Jeremiah, the quiet boy to whom Mike had given the yellow shirt, trimmed the overgrowth from the entire plot. The place began to resemble a proper farm. When Gladys praised their progress, the boys raised their chests like cockerels.

They had become quite an organized team, these three, maintaining their own schedule of prayers, chores, work, meals, and relaxation. And how neatly they kept the place! Gladys knew boys in Uganda to be very untidy. They would not know where their socks were; they would throw their shirts around like candy wrappers. But on Ezra's watch? *Banange!* Their room was as neat as a teacher's desk.

Admittedly, the boys had few possessions to manage. There was no bedding to arrange; Gladys was too broke to replace it. So resilient, these ones: six weeks with no blankets! They claimed not to notice the nighttime cold.

In the beginning they had asked for sugar. "You people," Gladys would say with a sigh. "Not everyone who stays in rural areas takes sugar! As long as you have porridge to eat. And when the porridge runs out, get some cassava in the garden there. If you get tired of boiled cassava, you can fry it!"

Unlike the adults she had recently dealt with, the boys respected the precarious nature of the enterprise. Jeremiah lacked slippers, but he uttered no complaint. Douglas sought help only after someone stole his laundry: *Mummy, I have wrote this letter in a humble heart . . . as you see me here I have only one clothing which I came with, and this is a secrete that even the inside body wear I have only one but it is gone. I tried to work for money in Nalongo but I felt the bush in our dear land was too much.* These boys knew that Perseverance Gardens belonged to them. To them, its upkeep was more important than slippers or underwear!

But Gladys did not believe that frugality should come at the expense of every small pleasure. When she had been a girl in her grandmother's garden, a morning of digging had sometimes ended with a treat. Handing the boys money for supplies, she slipped in an extra 2,000 shillings. "Go buy a couple of sugarcane stems, such that you can plant them around the house."

On her next visit, Douglas proudly pointed out the slender green stalks next to the house. Soon the boys would get more stems from these two, and in no time at all they would have enough to harvest.

"Eh-ehhh!" Gladys chortled. After working in the gardens, there would be no better reward than sitting in the shade with a crisp, fat stalk, having earned every last every bit of sweetness one could gnaw out of it.

AFTER A FEW days Ezra made an announcement. Rather than returning to school, he intended to stay and manage the gardens.

The declaration caught Gladys and Esther off guard. Although no one held him responsible, this was clearly Ezra's effort to atone for the thieves from his village. A noble gesture, but a reckless one. How could one student, a primary school student at that, maintain three acres?

Instinctively the women tempered their responses, offering thoughtful nods and neutral *hmm*s. They did not want to make the young man feel small. Soon reason would dampen emotion, and he would see that his place was back in the classroom.

As the days went on, though, it became apparent that Ezra's plan to stay at Perseverance Gardens was less a daydream than a decision. He insisted that he could live in the unfinished house and transfer from Early Learning to a local school in Luwero.

Gladys was alarmed. Academic standards were very low in rural areas. With his Primary Leaving Examinations just months away, surely this plan made no sense.

"Will you be able to pass? Which school can you join? Is it very far away?"

Ezra responded calmly. His worry was not over school or exams but "our home." If their home was not protected, what future would they have?

If Ezra's future did lie with the garden, was there anything wrong with that? "Harvest Money" had run several recent stories about university-educated people who had turned to farming. A couple of Mike's nephews had quit their city jobs to manage land.

At sixteen Ezra had knelt at her feet, seeking her help in returning to school. But he had struggled in the classroom. Eight years of missed schooling had created an unbridgeable gap, and his stunted progress left him discouraged. It was hard to be the biggest bird in the nest yet still unable to fly.

When it came to farming, though, Ezra showed a renewed focus. He made valiant attempts to read "Harvest Money," his eyes moving as slowly over the page as though he were tracking an ant.

From the gardens, he would send her texts. Sometimes they carried advice: *Mumy we must spray this trees. The leaves growing funy they dont look fine.* Sometimes they were just messages of comfort: *Dont worry mummy everything is fine. dont mind mummy.* Even if the news—and the punctuation—was bad, Gladys was delighted. This was a boy who had not been able to tell her the letters from A to Z. And now, to see him using English! All of those school fees had not gone to waste.

ON ONE OF her visits to the garden, Ezra invited Gladys to sit down on the veranda. He served her tea and roasted some maize. Then he announced that he wanted to build a structure for raising pigs. Pointing to an area he had cleared, he described the layout and showed her a drawing of the structure he imagined.

Gladys was astonished. First, Ezra had been raised a Muslim! When he started working at the gardens, she had bid farewell to her dream of a bustling piggery. Second, how did he know how to do such a thing? Smiling shyly, Ezra produced a book in which he had studied the plans for a successful pig farm.

"Ah, okay, we will be thinking of this," she said, marveling over his neat drawing. At the moment they had no money for piglets or materials to build a sty, but what a plan!

Grand schemes aside, Ezra knew that the gardens needed hands to pull the weeds and sweep the grounds. He was still angry about all the damage that the place had suffered. "Now that I'm here," he vowed, "nothing else bad will happen to this place. I will restore this place to its feet."

And so Ezra began to take care of the gardens. As he attended class during the day and studied over the weekend, it was a struggle. He would run back from school to be able to dig a little bit before the sun went down. The gardens lacked the daily labor they needed to thrive and to keep the daytime thieves at bay, but at least the house did not suffer further nighttime break-ins.

Out of the last batch of trees Gladys had purchased back when Zam was still around, only about a dozen out of the forty-five were still alive. A loss of over thirty trees was nothing to be proud of, but the survivors were doing nicely under Ezra's care. He attended to the sickly ones and kept their trunks clear of weeds.

Even though he was the compound's lone occupant, Ezra always kept the front of the house well swept, cleared of bush. With all the negligent adults who had come and gone, Gladys had never seen the place look so good.

How balanced life's ironies could be. From the day she and Ezra met, he had been the one who needed help. And now this boy whose hand she had held in the operating room was trying to rescue her, as she had rescued him. If she had ever doubted her instinct toward kindness, Ezra had erased that doubt. The Zams and Roberts and Byrons of the world were mere weeds in the land her goodwill had watered. Ezra was the tree.

Naguru

I t was the same set of buildings, the vacant playground featuring a single slide, the perimeter wall spiked with glass shards. But to Gladys it was an unexpectedly welcome sight. Naguru Reception Centre.

For four months she had made countless phone calls and endured sleepless nights trying to find her way inside this gate. For four months she had not seen Trevor. She could not even obtain official confirmation that he was still at Naguru.

Her pushing and pleading enervated those around her. After the boy's misbehavior, his rudeness, his wandering, his stubbornness? Their enthusiasm for the cause, more of a flicker than a flame to begin with, had all but fizzled out. These days when she approached her colleagues for help, some refused, some sighed, some stopped returning her calls. They misplaced their phones, they were out of the office, their batteries died. But Gladys persisted. "Everybody needs someone," she would say. "That is my argument."

That's all fine and good, everyone seemed to think. *As long as that "someone" is someone else.*

She had tracked down the name of the probation officer who had referred Trevor's case to Naguru, one Peter Lwanga Mayanja. "But this man does not know me," she fretted to Officer Carol. "Even if I call him, he will not allow me to visit Trevor. I know they are strict."

Then, late that evening, a miracle. The probation officer answered her call. He listened as Gladys explained her desperate need to visit the reception center to see if the lost child was still there. To her absolute shock, he replied, "Come by my office. I can escort you."

So easy? Just like that? The call ignited hope in Gladys's heart, followed by fresh spasms of anxiety.

At 3 a.m. she was still trying to email her column to her editor. Cursing the slow Internet, then praying, *Please God, help me! I will not have time to go to the office.* After two hours of fitful sleep, she stood in the bathroom pouring cold water over herself. *Someone at Naguru could still refuse to let me in. Oh God, just help me.* Even as she walked out the door into the gray-blue morning: *God, help me to see my boy.*

NATURALLY MIKE RECOGNIZED the probation officer. He and Peter Lwanga had met on a film shoot a couple of years back. In addition to working for Kampala Capital City Authority, Peter had starred in television shows like the soap opera *Mountains and Valleys.* As the two sometime actors clapped shoulders and swapped memories, Gladys marveled over the way life could surprise the persistent. The gate to Naguru had been locked to her for so long. And then suddenly the universe had delivered the key in the form of a sympathetic probation officer who happened to be a handsome TV star. *God is really great!*

Climbing the veranda steps, they could see that the facility had undergone some much-needed renovation. The brown fence had been replaced by rainbow-painted railings, and the floor was tiled. The cheerier atmosphere only penetrated so far, however. Outside the classroom they were met by a sullen, seated matron. She eyed their approach with the impotent hostility of a guard dog who knows too well the length of her chain.

"Do you know if Trevor Masembe is here?" Gladys asked, her voice low and pleasant.

"Masembe is around," the matron answered flatly.

"How is he? Has he been very naughty?"

The matron shrugged. "He refuses to tell anyone what concerns him. He just cries."

"Ah-*hahhh*," Gladys agreed heartily, as though they were swapping stories about a favorite nephew. "One never knows what concerns Trevor."

Stepping over, Peter Lwanga glanced around the veranda, then back at the matron, planted in her lone plastic chair like a sit-down striker. "Are you going to give us a seat somewhere? Or is there nowhere to sit?"

If the woman journalist had made such a request, she might be standing there until Museveni was no longer president. But at the dashing probation officer's request, chairs appeared within seconds.

"By the way, he is as good-looking as we always see him on TV, eh?" Gladys quipped as Peter sat down. The matron said nothing, but the corner of her mouth dimpled just perceptibly.

As they waited several long minutes for Trevor to arrive, anticipation frayed Gladys's composure. Her mind could not settle until she had laid her eyes on the child.

Of course they could not fail to produce Trevor now. Or could they? What about that time they sent me the deaf-and-mute girl to interview?

To distract herself, she asked the matron a half-dozen questions about the kids packed in the adjacent classroom. What were they all doing lying on the floor? Were they able to study with no chairs or desks? How was their writing? She greeted each of the matron's monosyllabic responses as a gem of insight, forcefully infusing the exchange with collegiality.

Two figures crossed through the dark classroom to the veranda. The first was another matron, and behind her a skinny, familiar figure. Trevor's expression was sulky, his feet bare, and his limp more pronounced than usual. He was still small for whatever age he was; the oversized yellow T-shirt he wore made him appear no more than eight years old.

Gladys's face lit up. "Trevor Masembe, come greet me!"

The boy stopped, still a few paces from the group. Left eyebrow arched, he glanced past them, a celebrity ignoring his fans. He began to pick his nose.

"Who do you know?" Peter spoke to the boy in a cheerful, coaxing voice. "Eh? Who do you know here?"

Trevor gave no answer, not even a blink of acknowledgment. He continued to pluck at his nose with the concentration of a concert violinist. Peter and Mike glanced at Gladys. The reunion was not the stuff of which movies were made.

Gladys chuckled. In the boy's mind, he had been forgotten in this place, and he was publicly declaring his displeasure.

"He is such a crybaby," she said affectionately. "Everybody says he fights. I don't know if he's a fighter, but he is a crybaby. Trevor —come over here."

The boy shuffled incrementally in her direction. Gladys laughed merrily, as though she were watching a baby take its first steps.

"Trevor. Trevor Masembe! How are you?" Impatiently she reeled him in with an arm, her hug so forceful it popped the finger out of his nostril. "What happened to your leg?"

He looked beyond her, casting his thousand-yard frown.

"Come on, tell me! Don't make a bad face here." She asked again, softly, "What happened to your leg?"

"I knocked it," he mumbled.

"Were you playing football?"

"We don't allow football here," the matron interjected. "Because the kids break the windows. No football."

Poor Trevor! He probably had not smiled for four months. In this crowded holding pen, a child like him would receive no attention, no protection from the older boys, no sugar for his porridge. All that he could survive. But no football? Football was his sun.

With her arm looped around the boy like a safety belt, she recounted Trevor's troubled case history to her audience. Trevor still would not look at her, but he did not move away.

Peter proved a thoughtful listener, his unblinking attentiveness no mere actor's habit. When Gladys got to the part about Trevor flinging the dirty mop at the cleric, Mike let out a giggle. But the probation officer merely steepled his fingers and touched them to his lips.

When Gladys finished, he looked away for a beat, as though deciding something. In the distance, children shrieked like fighting cats.

"So do you want to take the child somewhere, or do you want to leave the child here? That is what I need to know."

The directness of the question startled Gladys. She had never imagined that she would be offered such a choice, if it was indeed an offer. After a long pause, she admitted, "I don't know where to take him." She had exhausted her contacts with schools and doctors and homes. "Even the police are fed up with Trevor, because every time he runs away it puts them under a lot of pressure. They told me, 'Gladys, don't bring that boy back to us. We don't want him anywhere near police!'"

There was still no place to put Trevor, the journalist and the probation officer concluded. They would have to keep looking.

As the conversation slowed, the matron grew restless. Eventually she stood and disappeared in the direction of the office, leaving the visitors alone.

Gladys wheeled around. "Oh my God. Eeeee!" she squealed. "This is an achievement, you know? We have seen Trevor. Hee-hee-hee! We have achieved greatly! Because of Peter. Thank you so muuuuch!"

The probation officer looked pleased, if a tad surprised. "The good thing is that we know where he is," he said. "And from here we will see the way forward."

"Ah-*hahhh*," Gladys agreed, noting his generous use of the second person plural. "All of us know where he is."

Holding Trevor at arm's length, she inspected the boy a final time. He was too thin, but he did not smell of fuel or garbage. His shirt looked clean. Seeing him here, alive, felt like the first rain after a long dry season.

She pressed her lips into a satisfied smile, then gave a nod. "We've seen our boy. Yes."

AFTER THEY HAD signed the visitors' ledger, snapped a round of pictures, and exchanged phone numbers, they headed for the car.

"Don't fight with the other kids, okay?" Gladys told Trevor, trying to catch his eye. "I want you to behave well."

The boy recognized a goodbye when he heard it. His lower lip protruded like a baby's. The protest was scrawled across his wounded brow: *After all this waiting, I'm again left behind?* Without a word, he turned and shambled off.

She watched him as he approached the stairs. One foot on the bottom step, chin lowered to his chest, as though he were ascending the gallows. A few steps across the veranda and through the door, and the sea of kids would again swallow him up.

She could hear the doubting voices. *Three hundred kids. Why care for this one, who does not even bother to say goodbye?*

For nearly three years this boy had disorganized everyone who tried to help him, Gladys most of all.

Even if the boy survives childhood, what will become of him? What kind of life can he possibly have?

Gladys could not say. No one could. But it was the child's life, and he had a right to it.

"Trevor," she called after him. "Come to say goodbye."

His bare foot halted on the second step. Then he turned and rushed back, as though he had only been waiting for her word. His small face crumpled as he reached her. She sheltered him like an ancient tree, enfolding him in thick branches.

"Don't leave me here."

Didn't he know?

"Trevor, Trevor." She bent her head to his and spoke the words a child needed to hear. "I'll always come back for you."

Epilogue

To Ezra, the gardens looked most beautiful at daybreak. As he rose each morning before dawn, he witnessed the light returning to the land, touching down on the earth and the plants and the roof of the house. The honeyed hue of that first light was so lovely it even had its own name — *akalenge.*

Each day he faced was full of activity. There were rooms to be tidied, grounds to be swept, fields to be tended, chickens to be fed. But Ezra liked to start with the pigs.

The piggery had been occupied for almost a month now, by one fine sow in one stall and two weaned piglets in another. He tended to hover over the sow, who would soon give birth. It gave him satisfaction to watch her snuffle at her feed, and at the greens he gathered for her in the afternoons.

Although he had not done it for long, caring for the pigs made Ezra feel that he was capable of anything. The penciled sketch that he had presented to his mother Gladys a year ago had become a reality. Here the structure stood, rendered in timber and concrete and pink bodies and twitching ears and contented grunts. Soon all five stalls would be filled with pigs, generating income, biogas, and fertilizer.

Since Ezra had begun living at Perseverance Gardens, there had been many developments. For one thing, the thefts that had plagued the garden had ceased altogether. During the day neighbors could see the young man working in the fields; in the evening they could see the smoke from his cooking fire. No longer could anyone stroll onto the grounds and simply take food, tools, materials, what-what. The place had someone.

Through study and trial and error, Ezra had learned many things: how to inspect leaves for diseases and pests; how to root out the *lumbugo* and other weeds that could choke his crops; how to time his plantings so that harvesting could take place before the rains; how to keep tabs on the going rates for produce in the local markets. As occasional workers were hired on for various projects, he had grown comfortable with delegating responsibility.

There were still challenges, of course. The current drought had sucked the life out of most of the recent crops, the soil was tired, and his new fieldhand sometimes indulged in drink. The gardens' yields were modest, but there was some surplus to sell.

Most of the sales were small, made to locals strolling up the path with a few shillings for cassava or *matoke* for their family's needs. But there had been a few large transactions too, to wholesalers coming by with small trucks. Those ones would buy an entire harvest to take to the town markets.

Large or small, any sale excited Ezra. It charged him up to think that this seed he had planted in the ground had grown into something that others wanted to buy, that his own sweat had produced a tangible financial result. *Just imagine,* he would marvel. *These are just the few small crops we've got now. If we can expand, the sky is the limit for us.*

LONELINESS HAD PLAGUED him in his first months at the garden, but these days the place was lively. Construction workers had begun digging a well. Victor and Jeremiah stayed for a month of school break. And over Christmas there was a big celebration. Gladys invited several family members, including her own children, Timothy and Sarah; Esther brought her son and nephew. Every room was filled with chatter and laughter. And how well they ate! Chicken, rice, *matoke,* cassava, squash, watermelon, pineapple, mango, and a thick round cake with white frosting.

Among those sharing the cake were two new faces: a young mother, Monica, and her five-year-old daughter. From what Gladys had told him, Ezra understood that this little girl had been born with a terrible defect: she had emerged from the womb with her insides outside of her body. Certain that the newborn would die in a day or two, the delivery nurse declined to waste a vaccination on her. But Monica wrapped her baby in cloth, held her, fed her, and gave her a name: Kudhura. Year by year, she managed to keep her daughter alive.

When Gladys met Kudhura, the three-year-old was delicate but stable, the membrane of her abdominal sac having thickened over time. Gladys ran several articles that sparked the interest of surgeons from Turkey, Germany, and the Netherlands, who offered free services to the indigent family. After two years it appeared that Kudhura would finally be given her chance. But after months of examinations and hospital visits, all the doctors concluded that it was too late to operate — the surgery should have been done before the child reached her first birthday.

Monica was a strong young woman, but the stress of raised and dashed hopes had worn her down. Gladys had some ideas about how to support the family and keep Kudhura healthy, but in the meantime she invited mother and daughter to stay at Perseverance Gardens for a couple of months. Monica, Ezra was told, should be expected only to rest.

But when Monica saw the gardens, she did not want to rest. The aborted surgery plans had left her feeling helpless, and idleness only deepened her mood. She proposed planting a sweet potato patch, and Ezra agreed. Kudhura loved to tag along as the adults worked, making everyone laugh with her questions and funny remarks.

Ezra doted on Kudhura, although his affection was tinged with sorrow. When he first laid eyes on the pretty child with the shocking protuberance pushing out the front of her dress, he immediately flashed back to his own past, to his thirteen years of suffering with his swollen face. Ezra returned every one of Kudhura's smiles, but in private he shed tears. How cruel it was, to have help arrive too late.

For Ezra, help had arrived just in time. With the chance he had been given, he would someday help others like Kudhura. *Whatever time I have on earth,* he told himself, *I must use it well.*

IT WAS THOUGHTS like these that prompted Ezra not to pursue his secondary education. He could not claim to have excelled in his primary leaving exams, but he had done his best, and that was enough schooling for him. He braced himself for Gladys's reaction, but she did not protest. It was his choice, she said, as he was a man now.

In truth, at Perseverance Gardens, Ezra did feel like a man. He was making decisions that would shape the future not just for himself but for many others like him.

"Hey! This boy is really a powerful boy, here!" Gladys would crow when he showed her some new project, like the recycled-water-bottle drip system he had set up for the eggplant patch. "He is getting to be so powerful."

In the afternoon, at rest between duties, Ezra would meditate on where he had started and where he was now. His mother never failed to thank him for what he was doing. But he knew: *It is really me who should drop to my knees and thank her.*

One day, he vowed, this project would be far bigger than his mother had ever imagined. The trees would be tall and the fields dense and green, the pigs and chickens would be joined by goats and cows, and Gladys's children would share a large compound as one family. In the evenings they would gather to discuss important issues, like behavior and money and faith and goals. No one would want for anything, least of all a home.

He was not abashed by his idyllic vision, though it was drawn in bolder outlines and more glowing colors than the stained glass in a church. After all the miracles that had come his way, how could he succumb to doubt?

AS MUCH AS he loved planning the future, Ezra could not keep his thoughts from imagining what his life would have been if Gladys had not entered it. The exercise fascinated him, because every route without his mother led to an empty space. Without her, there was no existence at all. His health, his sustenance, his education, his community—everything was blank.

Ezra could never repay her. It was out of the question. Gladys was truly his mother, and how would one pay back a mother? He could only honor her by continuing down the path she had begun to clear.

Every morning, when he opened the door and saw the golden light unfolding, he was flooded with a sense of peace. The rooster from Douglas's grandma always crowed, in loud appreciation of finding himself ruler of the roost rather than fodder for the pot. And as the sun warmed the earth, it lit up Ezra's heart.

Life contained such difficulty, such possibility. You just had to give all to what you were given.

And so he faced the morning with fire and hope. *I will give everything,* he would tell himself. *Let me go and meet the* akalenge.

Author's Note

While the stories in this book are rooted in my observations and Gladys's shared insights, their order reflects a few shifts in chronology. Given the sensitivity of circumstances surrounding a few of the children's cases, characters in some stories have been given pseudonyms and some identifying details have been changed, like the invented name Young Hearts Orphanage. Additionally, Byron is a pseudonym for Gladys's relative.

The chapter epigraphs are from Gladys's "Lost and Abandoned" column in *Saturday Vision*, published by Vision Group. In one instance, names and details in the column text were altered.

The events in the book span the nearly four years I spent following Gladys and her work, during which I returned to Uganda usually twice a year for a couple of weeks at a time. In the interest of transparency: I did not give Gladys any direct financial support during this period, but I supplied transportation and minor provisions as needed. Also, on a couple of occasions I acted as the go-between for donations made to her by individuals. There was no attempt to solicit such support by either Gladys or me.

Acknowledgments

This book owes its existence to the early encouragement of my irreplaceable friend Greg Critser.

I first met Gladys Kalibbala in March 2013, while working on a documentary on population issues called *Misconception*. I'd like to acknowledge Participant Media for having provided that opportunity, and my friend and producer Elise Pearlstein for her moral support.

I must also express my deep gratitude to:

· The indispensable Michael Wawuyo, for his good humor, invaluable insights, and fortitude on our many long journeys throughout Uganda with Gladys.

· Esther Bwekembe, Ezra Muzamiru, and all the children and families in the stories.

· Gladys's colleagues, who welcomed (or tolerated) my presence, including her coworkers at New Vision Media and all the hardworking police officers, social workers, probation officers, and children's home staff members who make up an essential part of her support structure.

· My editor, Deanne Urmy, and my agent, Jin Auh, for their warm and wise counsel, for taking a chance on an untested writer, and for embracing Gladys's story so fully and immediately.

· Timothy Farrell, my English teacher at Gunn High School, for teaching me to appreciate the beauty of a well-constructed sentence.

· My mother, Connie Young Yu, for her idealistic spirit, and my father, John Yu, for being the only Chinese American parent I know of ever to deter a daughter from going to law school.

· My dear husband, Mark Salzman, for his unflagging support and for cheerfully holding the fort during my frequent sojourns to Uganda, and my daughters, Ava and Esme, whose curiosity about the world and compassion for its inhabitants provided me with the motivation to pursue this book.

· And finally, Gladys, for throwing open the doors to her world and letting me enter so freely. Such rare trust is a gift and a responsibility. Like so many others I've met over the past four years, I am forever thankful for her kindness and generosity.